Grand Vistas

200 Homes with a View

HOME PLANNERS, LLC

Published by Home Planners, LLC
Wholly owned by Hanley-Wood, LLC
3275 West Ina Road, Suite 110
Tucson, Arizona 85741

Distribution Center:
29333 Lorie Lane
Wixom, Michigan 48393

Jan Prideaux — Editor In Chief
Marian E. Haggard — Editor
Nick Nieskes — Plans Editor
Jay C. Walsh — Graphic Designer
Teralyn Morris — Graphic Production Artist

Photo Credits
Front Cover: Laurence Taylor
Back Cover: Living Concepts Home Planning

10 9 8 7 6 5 4 3 2 1

Library of Congress Catalog Card Number: 2001089600

ISBN softcover: 1-881955-92-3

On the front cover: In our collection you will find many home plans offering covered patios, balconies and terraces—perfect for wide open views.

On the back cover: Designed to take full advantage of any view you choose, Design HPT250003 by Living Concepts Home Planning, offers plenty of livability. See page 18 for more information.

TABLE OF CONTENTS

Which Window For You?

Let the sun shine in through a multitude of windows that bring light and beauty to your life. Choosing the right windows for your new home brings not only grace and balance to its design, but also ensures comfort and increasing value. Because windows are a structural component of your home and affect both interior and exterior design, they deserve a closer look.

A decade ago, a large expanse of glass would not have been practical—windows were not as well insulated, and lots of sunlight often meant an increase in cooling costs. Today's advanced technologies, however, work to reduce heating and cooling costs. Consider choosing windows with Low-E (low-emissivity) glass; this transparent metallic coating will reduce heat gain in warm weather and combat heat loss in cold weather. Low-E glass also filters the type of sunlight that fades carpets and furniture. Some manufacturers offer double-paned windows with a layer of argon glass between the panes; this tightly sealed glass also increases insulative power.

Optimally, for the sake of light and ventilation, at least forty percent of living-space walls should be devoted to windows. Some of the questions you should focus on when building your new home and planning your windows are:

• *Where do you want to direct light?*

• *What views do you want to frame?*

• *What design and function options would you like—such as specialty grilles or pre-painted finishes?*

To answer the first question, you need to look carefully at the benefits that a window could bring to the room. A myriad of sizes, shapes and styles of windows provides virtually unlimited possibilities in putting a room together. Floor-to-ceiling windows can change the appearance of your home, both inside and out. They make the most of a beautiful view and allow light to flow deep into the heart of a home. Skylights and venting roof windows can transform a potentially dingy attic into the sunniest room in the house.

Next, the type of window you choose will also be the frame around the view you have available on your property. How you take advantage of that view depends on the size and function of the window you choose. If you'd like to have an unimpeded view, the window wall is the best option. This can combine with both moveable and unmovable portions, offering access as well as beautiful views. If you don't have the option for that much openness, then a series of smaller window combinations might be just what the architect ordered. Decorative windows, such as arches, circles and triangles, placed near the ceiling can let in a good deal of light while still preserving your privacy.

Finally, consider the design and function of the window—do you want one that can open, or is a fixed window best for your situation? Essentially, a window consists of a glass pane or panes and a frame. Together, these elements form a sash. There are seven basic window styles with many variations, offering good looks as well as convenience.

Double-hung or tilt windows—These have two sashes that move up and down, one behind the other. Half the window area can be opened—the top, the bottom or a little of both. Some window designs tilt the sash toward you, so you can clean both sides of it from inside the house.

Single-hung windows—These are the same as double-hung units except the top sash doesn't move.

Casement windows—Hinged on one side, these are operated by a crank. Look for multi-point locking, especially on tall windows, both for safety as well as to create a tight seal.

Sliding windows—These have two or more panels that cross each other when they are open, like a double-hung window set on its side. They are unobtrusive and easy to open, close and clean.

Awning windows—These are like casements, only sideways. They're hinged at the top and the crank turns the bottom out—allowing air in, but keeping rain out.

Fixed windows (also known as direct sets)— These don't open at all. For instance, often the center part of a bay is fixed. These win-

dows offer wonderful flexibility for those enchanting views you'd like to capture, coming in all shapes and sizes—perfect for a window wall.

Bay and bow windows—This is a combination of three or more windows that angle out from the house. the center unit is parallel to the house, while the side units sit at an angle. Bow windows are multiple windows that curve gradually rather than forming angles. If the bay is formed with right angles, it's called a box bay.

EXTERIOR CHOICES:

Wood—Traditional and durable, these windows can come pre-finished or primed and ready for your special color.

Vinyl—Most economical in many cases. This material offers low maintenance and easy operation, comes in a wide variety of colors and is paintable.

Hybrid—Some building environments call for specialty products. The seacoast is a perfect example— homes built near the ocean take a beating from the saline-filled environment. Thus, constructs of vinyl exteriors for durability and wood interiors for charm is the perfect choice.

GRILLES:

One of the most important options for windows is the grille selection. Grilles are the dividers on or within the window, giving the window depth and design personality. Grilles can add beauty to any interior while accentuating the exterior of the home.

Classic, contemporary or Craftsman, sleek Southwestern or elegant French, expansive windows allow the rich beauty of nature indoors to brighten our lives—now with greater efficiency, economy and ease than ever before. Don't just take our word for it— open your home to the great outdoors and see for yourself. After all, nobody ever drove by a home and said, "That house has a really attractive subfloor."

During the summer, heat invades homes. Winter months bring the problem of heat loss. Many homeowners don't understand that up to 25 percent of their average summer and winter utility bills is due to heat pouring in and out of windows. This heat gain/loss puts such a load on air conditioners and furnaces that the units keep running and electric meters keep spinning. As energy rates soar, everyone needs an affordable way to beat the heat.

Have Your View And Save Energy Too!

The Biggest Problems in the Home are the Windows

The best place to start cutting home energy costs is at the windows. Up to forty percent of a house's heat loss/gain is due to its window space—making up approximately twenty-five percent of a utility bill. For people out West, sun coming in means a lot of cash going out. But you've just built a beautiful home and specifically chosen the site and windows to take full advantage of the fantastic views. You don't want to block all that out with drapes or blinds! What's the alternative?

One Solution = Window Film

Window film is one very good solution to block heat, fading and possible snow-glare. The summer/winter films, offered by such companies as 3M or MSC Specialty Films Inc., save energy year-round, reduce glare and really help cut down on faded furniture. These films are designed to block UV rays and reduce the amount of solar heat transmitted through window glass. They help prevent sun damage to upholstered furniture, art and antiques, and reduce energy costs, all while not impeding your view. These days, companies offer extra-wide film to cover almost anything, even if your view is through a large picture window.

Potential Savings are Significant

The most energy efficient insulating films reflect up to seventy percent (and some claim they block up to ninety-nine percent of UV rays) of the sun's energy outside. They significantly reduce heat gain/loss, improve comfort and reduce air conditioning and heating bills. On an average 2,000 sq. ft. home, a heat control window film applied to all the windows can reduce utility bills up to fifteen percent in most parts of the country. In Northern states like Wisconsin and Michigan, this can mean nice, low winter bills, while in Western states like California, Arizona and Nevada, savings during summer months can be even more. Actual benefits depend upon window age, type, exposure and climate. The difference is immediate, the payback can be less than a year, and these films work up to ten years. After that, replacement is quick and cheap and the savings begin again.

Window films improve the situation in at least six different ways. They reduce utility bills and improve comfort. They don't block the view like "standard" window coverings. They are readily available at home centers like Home Depot and Lowe's. They cost less than a dollar per square foot. They improve existing windows. They are designed for relatively easy do-it-yourself application, and the job is a perfect weekend project for two. Just in case, major brands have hotlines, Web sites and satisfaction policies if someone forgets to read (or follow) the instructions.

Shade Only

Traditional efforts to stop summer heat invasion or winter heat loss include two major options: hanging something in front of or behind the window or replacing the window completely with a new, much more expensive window. Among the many popular "hanging" options are shutters, shades, screens, awnings and even trees. These offer shade when fully closed, which turns a room into a cave, not to mention blocking any sort of view. But they can't stop the heat boiling in or out through windows because none of these products are applied directly to the glass. The glass is the point of entry for heat that pours from the hot side to the cool side, whether summer or winter. Unlike more efficient insulating materials (like metal, brick or wood), glass alone can't stop heat transfer. Even hiding behind curtains, which also block the mountain, lake

(Left) An elegant sun room waits to welcome you, encouraging you to relax and savor your meal. Rather than pull the drapes, using window film makes it possible to have your cake AND enjoy the view!

(Below) A beautiful window wall graces this elegant staircase. Imagine how dark it would be if shutters or drapes were the only answer to blocking out the damaging power of the sun?

The new Panorama designer window film package by MSC Specialty Films Inc. is almost undetectable once installed. All Panorama films block 99% of damaging ultraviolet to help reduce fading of carpets, walls and other furnishings. These films also reject up to 68% of total solar energy which reduces annoying glare and energy costs.

or golf course view you once treasured, the heat is there to stay once it gets inside your home. Only a sun-control film applied directly onto the glass will help keep the heat where it belongs.

New Windows, Another Option

Full window replacement from single-pane to insulated windows is another choice for people who can afford to spend the money. Unfortunately, many new homeowners cannot afford this choice when faced with all the other construction costs piling up. For them, a major advantage of sun-control window films is that they "add on" to existing windows only what is needed to improve comfort immediately. No waiting period. No bank loan needed. No contractors required.

Naturally, the perfect solution to sultry summer heat gain or dreaded winter heat loss is to apply a heat-control film, install outside sun screens, hang black out thermal curtains, turn out all the lights and plant an evergreen tree. However, if the budget is tight and patience is wearing thin, applying heat-control window films makes good sense.

Help The Utility Companies, Too

During the 1980s, utility companies in Florida, Texas, Arizona and other states offered rebate programs for certain sun-control films that reflected at least fifty-five percent of the heat and were professionally installed. With deregulation, many of these programs have disappeared, but the energy-saving value of heat-control films on hot "peak load" afternoons can be significant for utility companies in the sweltering sunny days of the sunbelt.

Shop Around

Many leading do-it-yourself brands feature heat control, glare control and privacy films for homes. Heat-control ratings usually appear as numbers or icons on the packaging. Some films are virtually invisible. Some are darker to block glare. Others are mirrored or frosted for greater privacy and personal protection. Most films are sold in pre-cut rolls near other window treatments or insulation products. The sizes are varied, with the recent addition of extra-wide film for today's trend of window walls. Each manufacturer's application instructions may vary from product to product, but patience and teamwork can make short work of a perfect weekend project that will pay for itself this summer and for years to come.

This home, as shown in the photographs, may differ from the actual blueprints. For more detailed information, please check the floor plans carefully.

Photos courtesy of Exposures Unlimited, Ron and Donna Kolb

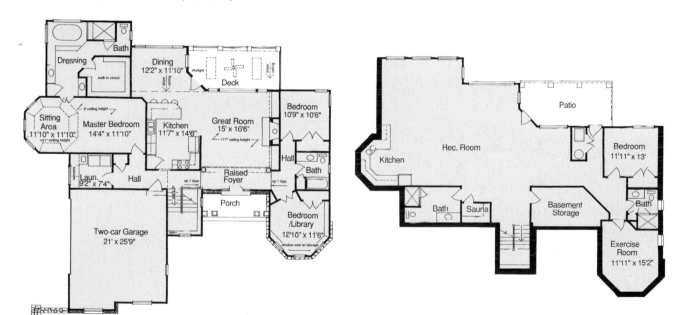

First floor plan labels:

Bath
Dressing
Dining 12'2" x 11'10"
Deck
skylight
Sitting Area 11'10" x 11'10" 10'1" ceiling height
Master Bedroom 14'4" x 11'10"
9' ceiling height
walk-in closet
Kitchen 11'7" x 14'6"
Great Room 15 x 16'6" 11'7" ceiling height
Bedroom 10'9" x 10'6"
Hall
Bath
Laun. 9'2" x 7'4"
Hall
up 1 riser
Raised Foyer
up 1 riser
Two-car Garage 21' x 25'9"
Porch
Bedroom /Library 12'10" x 11'6"
window seat w/ storage

Basement floor plan labels:

Patio
Kitchen
Rec. Room
Bedroom 11'11" x 13'
Bath
Sauna
Basement Storage
Bath
Exercise Room 11'11" x 15'2"

DESIGN

Total Square Footage: 2,041

Basement: 2,041 Square Feet

Bedrooms: 3

Bathrooms: 2

Width: 67'-6"

Depth: 63'-6"

HPT250006

Attention to detail and a touch of luxury create a home that showcases the owners excellent taste while providing an efficient floor plan. From the raised foyer, a striking view is offered through the great room to the elegantly styled windows and beyond to the covered deck. The spacious kitchen offers an abundance of counter space and cabinets and easy access to the dining area and rear yard. Split bedrooms provide privacy to the master suite, where a sitting area is topped by an exciting ceiling treatment. A full walkout basement is available with this plan, offering additional living space and an extra-large recreation area.

This home, as shown in the photographs, may differ from the actual blueprints. For more detailed information, please check the floor plans carefully.

Photos by Laurence Taylor

Talk about a plan with adaptability! Due to the challenge of a golf path running right past the rear of the property, Pat Stokes of Wyman Stokes Builder in Florida chose to build plan HPT250002, designed by The Sater Design Collection. Instead of all the outdoor entertaining focused at the back of the home, this plan wraps itself around a spacious courtyard—the perfect place for luxurious plantings and a custom pool. "This made the decision easy," Pat said. "We placed the pool in the courtyard, which gave it plenty of privacy." But that wasn't the only selling point of this fine design. "Each room has a view," said Pat, "including the guest house." From the covered lanai of the guest house, there is a direct view of both the pool and gardens. The main house is also full of gorgeous views. When you stand at the kitchen sink, you "have a view of the courtyard, the golf course and a lake," said Pat. The octagonal study is even more special with the way "the pool comes right up to the windows," she added. The home features a lavish master suite—complete with His and Hers walk-in closets and vanities and a TV niche in the bathroom—designed to pamper the homeowner. For the rest of the family, two bedrooms—each with a private observation deck—are tucked away upstairs and share a full bath. The octagonal grand salon features a beamed ceiling and views of the golf course.

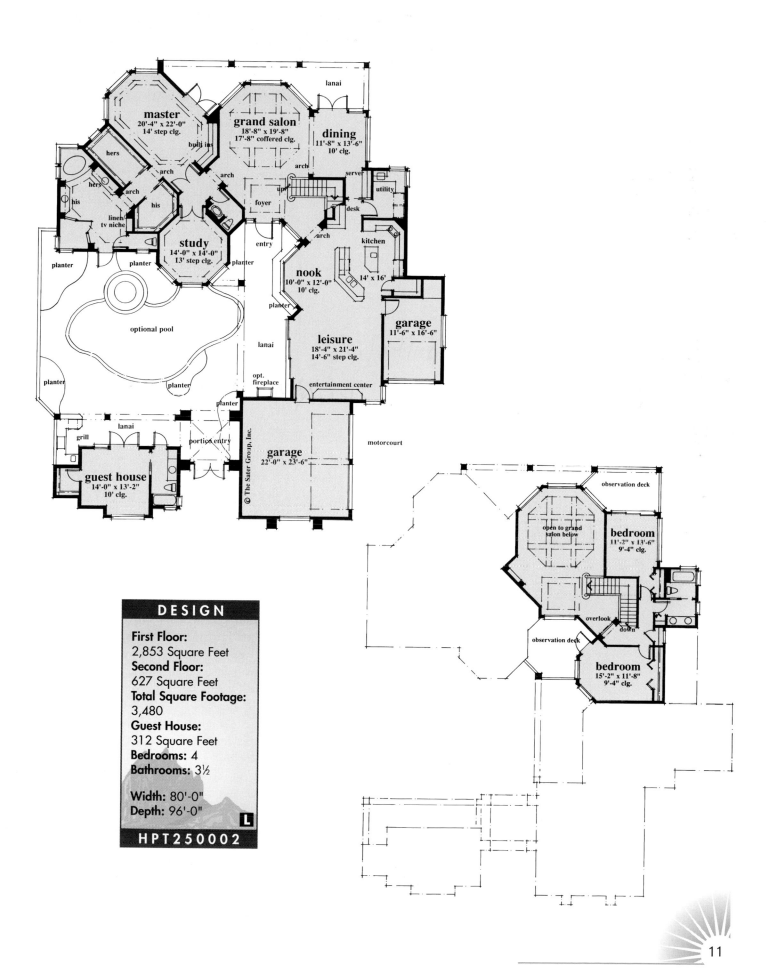

master
20'-4" x 22'-0"
14' step clg.

hers

hers

his

his

arch

arch

arch

linen/
tv niche

planter

planter

planter

study
14'-0" x 14'-0"
13' step clg.

foyer

entry

planter

optional pool

planter

planter

planter

lanai

grill

lanai

guest house
14'-0" x 13'-2"
10' clg.

portico entry

grand salon
18'-8" x 19'-8"
17'-8" coffered clg.

dining
11'-8" x 13'-6"
10' clg.

lanai

up

dn

arch

server

desk

arch

utility

kitchen
14' x 16'

nook
10'-0" x 12'-0"
10' clg.

planter

leisure
18'-4" x 21'-4"
14'-6" step clg.

garage
11'-6" x 16'-6"

opt.
fireplace

entertainment center

garage
22'-0" x 23'-6"

motorcourt

© The Sater Group, Inc.

observation deck

open to grand salon below

bedroom
11'-2" x 13'-6"
9'-4" clg.

overlook

down

observation deck

bedroom
15'-2" x 11'-8"
9'-4" clg.

DESIGN

First Floor:
2,853 Square Feet
Second Floor:
627 Square Feet
Total Square Footage:
3,480
Guest House:
312 Square Feet
Bedrooms: 4
Bathrooms: 3½

Width: 80'-0"
Depth: 96'-0"

L

HPT250002

An open bay window makes an attractive sitting area in this well-furnished bedroom.

You can enjoy views of the pool from many of the rooms via both floor-to-ceiling windows as well as sliding glass walls.

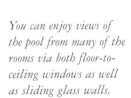

DESIGN

First Floor:
2,612 Square Feet
Second Floor:
1,300 Square Feet
Total Square Footage:
3,912
Bonus Room:
320 Square Feet
Bedrooms: 4
Bathrooms: 3½ + ½

Width: 95'-6"
Depth: 64'-0"

HPT250012

This home, as shown in the photographs, may differ from the actual blueprints. For more detailed information, please check the floor plans carefully.

Photos by Kerr Photography—Ron Kerr

Lovely stucco columns and a copper standing-seam roof highlight this stone-and-brick facade. An elegant New World interior starts with a sensational winding staircase, a carved handrail and honey-hued hardwood floor. An open, two-story formal dining room enjoys front-property views and leads to the gourmet kitchen through the butler's pantry, announced by an archway. Beyond the foyer, tall windows brighten the two-story family room and bring in a sense of the outdoors, while a fireplace makes the space cozy and warm. The center food-prep island counter overlooks a breakfast niche that offers wide views through walls of windows and access to the rear porch.

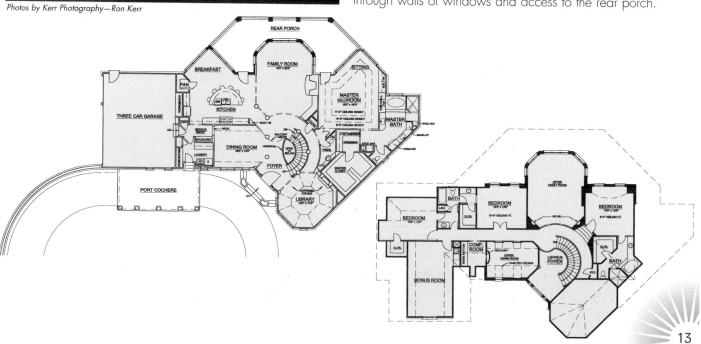

This home, as shown in the photographs, may differ from the actual blueprints. For more detailed information, please check the floor plans carefully.

Photos by Chris A. Little of Atlanta and courtesy of Chatham Home Planning, Inc.

Perfect as a seaside abode, this pier-foundation home has an abundance of amenities to offer, not the least being the loft lookout. Here, with a 360-degree view, one can watch the storms come in over the water or gaze with wonder on the colors of the sea. An elegant staircase leads up to the welcoming covered porch. Inside the home, just off the porch and through lovely French doors, the living room is complete with a corner fireplace. The spacious kitchen features a cooktop island, an adjacent breakfast nook and easy access to the dining room. From this room, a set of French doors leads out to a small deck—perfect for dining alfresco. Upstairs, the sleeping zone consists of two family bedrooms sharing a full hall bath and the deluxe master suite. Amenities here include two walk-in closets and a private bath.

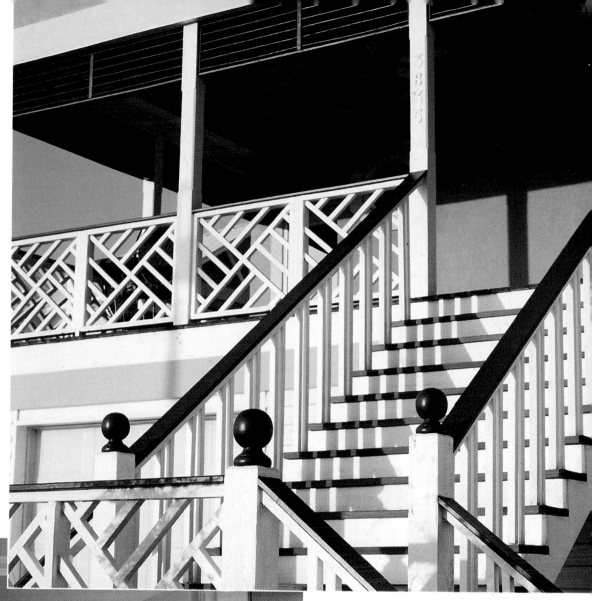

Sunlight and special framing create graceful and symmetrical patterns on the front stairs.

Attractive French doors open into the comfortably casual living room where hardwood floors and a hodgepodge of furniture create a very welcoming atmosphere.

15

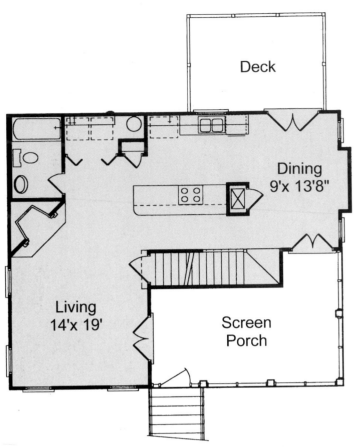

Deck

Dining
9'x 13'8"

Living
14'x 19'

Screen
Porch

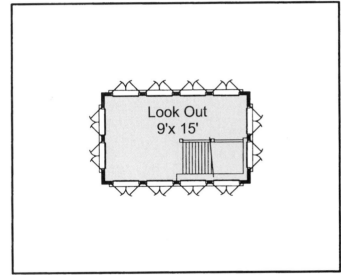

Look Out
9'x 15'

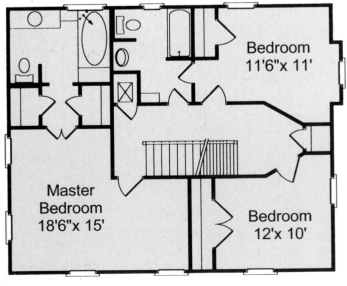

Bedroom
11'6"x 11'

Master
Bedroom
18'6"x 15'

Bedroom
12'x 10'

This home, as shown in the photographs, may differ from the actual blueprints. For more detailed information, please check the floor plans carefully.

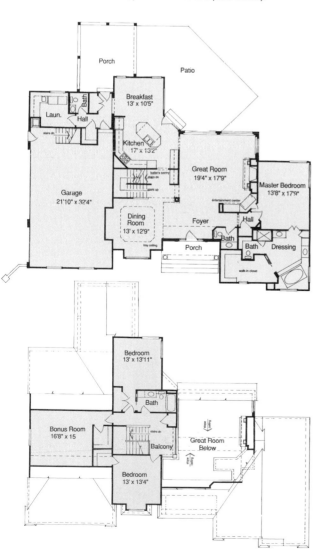

Porch

Patio

Breakfast
13' x 10'5"

Laun. | Bath | Hall

Kitchen
17' x 13'2"

Great Room
19'4" x 17'9"

Master Bedroom
13'8" x 17'9"

Garage
21'10" x 32'4"

Dining Room
13' x 12'9"

Foyer

Hall

Bath

Porch

Bath | Dressing

walk-in closet

Bedroom
13' x 13'11"

Bath

Bonus Room
16'8" x 15

Balcony

Great Room Below

Bedroom
13' x 13'4"

Multiple gables, a box window and keystone lintels combine to create a dramatic appearance on this two-story European classic home. The great room offers a wall of windows, a sloped ceiling and a built-in entertainment cabinet. The kitchen offers an angled island that parallels the French doors and enhances the large breakfast room. The dining room features a furniture alcove for extra roominess. The luxury and convenience of the first-floor master suite is highlighted by His and Hers vanities, a shower and a whirlpool tub. The second floor provides a private retreat for a guest suite, another bedroom and a bonus room.

DESIGN

First Floor:
2,192 Square Feet
Second Floor:
654 Square Feet
Total Square Footage:
2,846
Bonus Room:
325 Square Feet
Bedrooms: 3
Bathrooms: 2½ +½

Width: 75'-0"
Depth: 70'-0"

HPT250005

This home, as shown in the photographs, may differ from the actual blueprints. For more detailed information, please check the floor plans carefully.

Here's an upscale, multi-level plan with expansive rear views. The first floor provides an open living and dining area, defined by decorative columns and enhanced by natural light from tall windows. A breakfast area with a lovely triple window opens to a sun room, which allows light to pour into the gourmet kitchen. The master wing features a tray ceiling in the bedroom, two walk-in closets and an elegant private vestibule leading to a lavish bath. The upper level is complete with a reading loft that overlooks the great room and leads to a sleeping area with two suites. A lavish lower level offers a recreation room with a corner fireplace, an office with a window wall, an exercise room and a sumptuous guest suite with a separate sitting room. A covered patio finishes this level with grace.

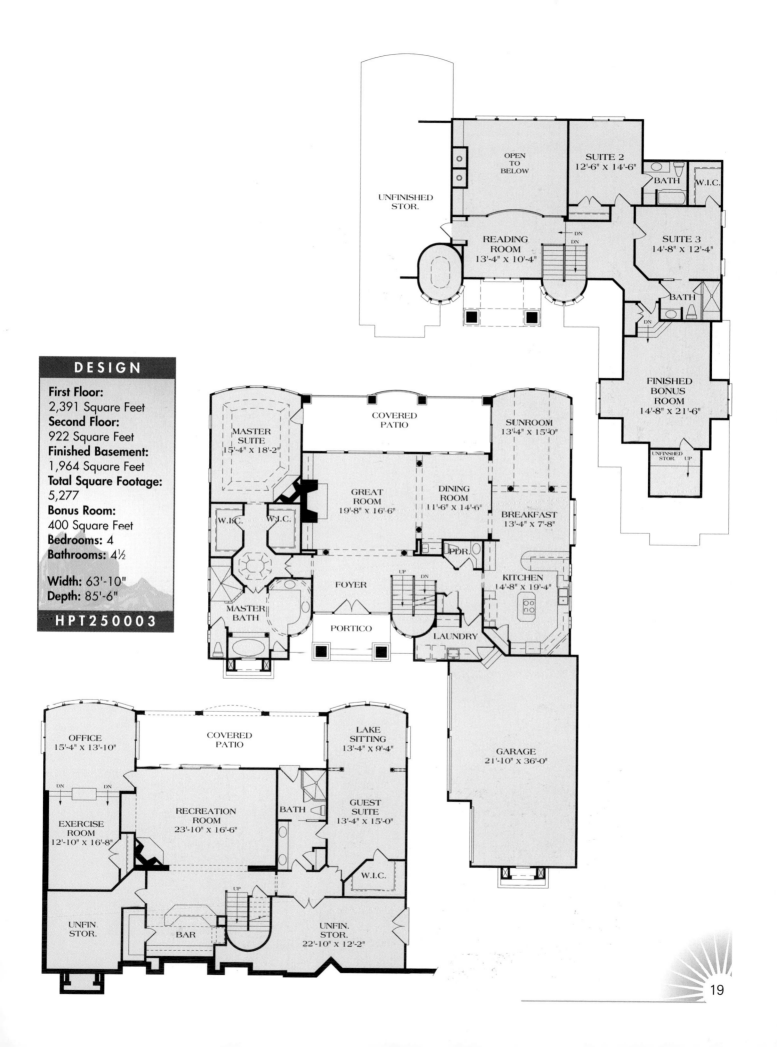

UNFINISHED
STOR.

OPEN
TO
BELOW

SUITE 2
12'-6" x 14'-6"

BATH

W.I.C.

READING
ROOM
13'-4" x 10'-4"

DN

DN

SUITE 3
14'-8" x 12'-4"

BATH

DN

FINISHED
BONUS
ROOM
14'-8" x 21'-6"

UNFINISHED
STOR.

UP

DESIGN

First Floor:
2,391 Square Feet
Second Floor:
922 Square Feet
Finished Basement:
1,964 Square Feet
Total Square Footage:
5,277
Bonus Room:
400 Square Feet
Bedrooms: 4
Bathrooms: 4½

Width: 63'-10"
Depth: 85'-6"

HPT250003

MASTER
SUITE
15'-4" x 18'-2"

COVERED
PATIO

SUNROOM
13'-4" x 15'-0"

W.I.C.

W.I.C.

GREAT
ROOM
19'-8" x 16'-6"

DINING
ROOM
11'-6" x 14'-6"

BREAKFAST
13'-4" x 7'-8"

MASTER
BATH

FOYER

PDR.

KITCHEN
14'-8" x 19'-4"

UP

DN

PORTICO

LAUNDRY

OFFICE
15'-4" x 13'-10"

COVERED
PATIO

LAKE
SITTING
13'-4" x 9'-4"

GARAGE
21'-10" x 36'-0"

DN

DN

EXERCISE
ROOM
12'-10" x 16'-8"

RECREATION
ROOM
23'-10" x 16'-6"

BATH

GUEST
SUITE
13'-4" x 15'-0"

W.I.C.

UP

UNFIN.
STOR.

BAR

UNFIN.
STOR.
22'-10" x 12'-2"

This home, as shown in the photographs, may differ from the actual blueprints. For more detailed information, please check the floor plans carefully.

Photos by Oscar Thompson

DESIGN

First Floor:
2,066 Square Feet
Second Floor:
810 Square Feet
Total Square Footage:
2,876
Bonus Space:
1,260 Square Feet
Bedrooms: 3
Bathrooms: 3½

Width: 64'-0"
Depth: 45'-0"

L

HPT250004

When you own a home near the seashore, you're sure to have visitors. If you plan to entertain, this is the plan for you—complete with an open layout and many amenities.

A large, open floor plan offers soaring, sparkling space for planned gatherings. The foyer leads to the grand room, highlighted by a glass fireplace, a wet bar and wide views of the outdoors. Both the grand room and the formal dining room open to a screened veranda for outside enjoyment.

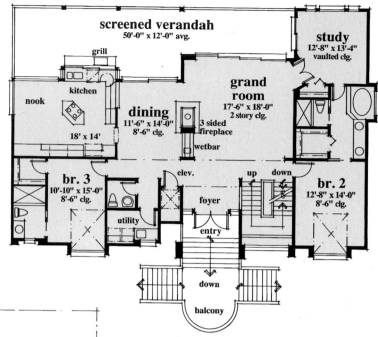

The kitchen is large enough to hold a cook-top island and an informal breakfast nook. A pass-through from the kitchen to the grill just outside is a boon for outdoor entertaining. The first floor includes two spacious family bedrooms and a secluded study which opens from the grand room.

The second-floor master suite offers sumptuous amenities, including a private deck and spa, a three-sided fireplace, a sizable walk-in closet and a gallery hall with an overlook to the grand room.

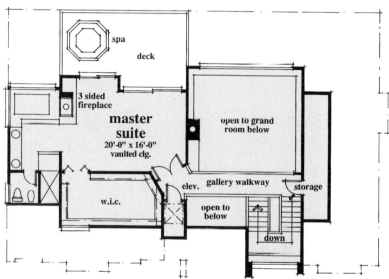

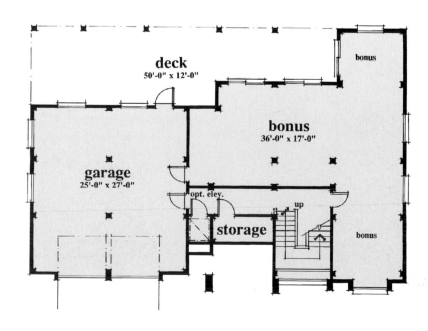

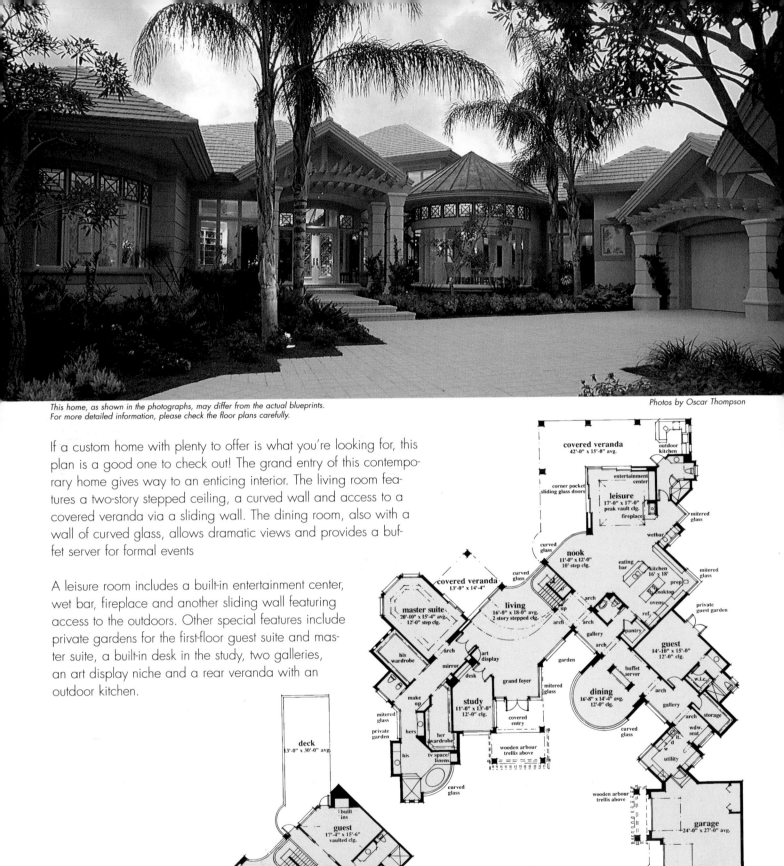

This home, as shown in the photographs, may differ from the actual blueprints.
For more detailed information, please check the floor plans carefully.

Photos by Oscar Thompson

If a custom home with plenty to offer is what you're looking for, this plan is a good one to check out! The grand entry of this contemporary home gives way to an enticing interior. The living room features a two-story stepped ceiling, a curved wall and access to a covered veranda via a sliding wall. The dining room, also with a wall of curved glass, allows dramatic views and provides a buffet server for formal events

A leisure room includes a built-in entertainment center, wet bar, fireplace and another sliding wall featuring access to the outdoors. Other special features include private gardens for the first-floor guest suite and master suite, a built-in desk in the study, two galleries, an art display niche and a rear veranda with an outdoor kitchen.

This home, as shown in the photographs, may differ from the actual blueprints. For more detailed information, please check the floor plans carefully.

Photos by Oscar Thompson

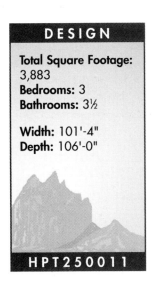

The Spanish-tile roof and striking stucco exterior of this rambling single-story home introduce an interior that revisits the past in glorious style and sets a new standard for comfort and luxury. Double doors with sidelights brighten the foyer, which leads directly into the formal living room. To the left of the foyer, the formal dining room features a bay window, an octagonal tray ceiling and an arched alcove. The well-planned kitchen provides a walk-in pantry, an island counter, a snack bar and plenty of counter space and is easily accessed by the nook and leisure room. Don't miss the outdoor kitchen on the veranda.

DESIGN

Total Square Footage:
3,883
Bedrooms: 3
Bathrooms: 3½

Width: 101'-4"
Depth: 106'-0"

HPT250011

Veranda

Outdoor Kitchen

Veranda

Leisure Room
20'-0" x 17'-0"

Nook
10'-0" x 10'-0"

Master Suite
21'-6" x 14'-9"

Guest Suite 2
13'-4" x 14'-4"

Living Room
16'-0" x 14'-0"

w.i.c.

Pwdr Bath

Kitchen
16'-0" x 16'-0"

Guest Bath 2

Master Bath

Guest Bath 1

Pantry

Foyer

w.i.c.

Dining
14'-6" x 14'-6"

Entry

Study
14'-0" x 15'-0"

w.i.c.

Guest Suite 1
14'-4" x 14'-4"

Utility

3 Car Garage
22'-0" x 36'-6"

This home, as shown in the photographs, may differ from the actual blueprints. For more detailed information, please check the floor plans carefully.

Photos by Bri Mar Photography

This unusual stucco-and-siding design opens with a grand portico to a foyer that extends to the living room with a fireplace. Proceed up a few steps to the dining room with its coffered ceiling and butler's pantry, which connects to the gourmet kitchen. The attached hearth room has the requisite fireplace and three sets of French doors to the covered porch. The family room sports a coffered ceiling and a fireplace flanked by French doors. The second floor boasts four bedrooms, including a master suite with a tray ceiling, covered deck and lavish bath. Two full baths serve the family bedrooms and a bonus room that might be used as an additional bedroom or hobby space.

three-car garage
34' x 27' & 23'

study
12' x 12'2

ldr

K

hearth rm
10'6 x 13'6

WET BAR

ART NICHE

FOYER

din
13'2 x 17'2

COFFERED CEILING

fam
15' x 19'10

liv
18' x 15'

bonus rm 18'4 & 22'4 X 15'

WHIRLPOOL

SKYLIGHT

ELEV.

DECK

br4
12'2 x 9'

OPEN TO FOYER BELOW

W.L CLOSET

ART NICHE

SKYLIGHT

HIGH CEILING OVER LIV. RM.

mbr
18'6 x 20'10

DECK

br3
8'8 & 18' x 15'6

DECK

br2
12' x 15'6

This home, as shown in the photographs, may differ from the actual blueprints. For more detailed information, please check the floor plans carefully.

Photos by Bob Greenspan

Perfect for a hillside, this fine four-bedroom home has plenty to offer. Spacious rooms of unusual shape are the theme inside, including the sunken great room which features a corner fireplace, built-ins and deck access. The formal dining room offers floor-to-ceiling windows, creating an amazing ambiance. The huge kitchen also provides wonderful views out to the deck. Designed to pamper, the master suite is complete with a corner media center, a large walk-in closet, a sumptuous bath, deck access and big picture windows. The lower level also provides outdoor access, as well as three bedrooms, three baths and a sunken game room with a corner fireplace.

DESIGN

Main Floor:
2,792 Square Feet
Finished Basement:
2,016 Square Feet
Total Square Footage:
4,808
Bedrooms: 4
Bathrooms: 4½

Width: 81'-0"
Depth: 66'-0"

HPT250008

This home, as shown in the photographs, may differ from the actual blueprints.
For more detailed information, please check the floor plans carefully.

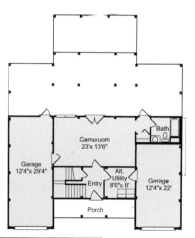

Garage
12'4"x 29'4"

Gameroom
23'x 13'6"

Bath

Entry

Alt.
Utility
8'6"x 8'

Garage
12'4"x 22'

Porch

Deck
24'7"x 8'

Porch
24'7"x 8'

Bedroom
10'4"x 14'

Living
24'3"x 17'

Master
Bedroom
12'4"x 14'

Dining
13'x 13'

Bedroom
12'4"x 13'

Porch
23'x 5'

Bedroom
12'4"x 14'

Open To
Below

Bedroom
17'5"x 19'

DESIGN

Main Level:
2,061 Square Feet
Upper Level:
464 Square Feet
Finished Basement:
452 Square Feet
Total Square Footage:
2,977
Bedrooms: 5
Bathrooms: 4

Width: 50'-0"
Depth: 63'-0"

HPT250015

This waterfront home offers classic seaboard
details with louvered shutters, covered porches
and an open floor plan. The lower level is com-
prised of two single-car garages, a game room
with an accompanying full bath and a utility
room. The U-shaped staircase leads to the main,
living areas where the island kitchen is open to
the dining room. The living room offers a wall of
windows with access to the rear porch and deck.
Two bedrooms lie to the left and share a full bath.
On the right are the master suite and a fourth bedroom—each with a private bath. Upstairs, a fifth
bedroom with a bath completes the plan.

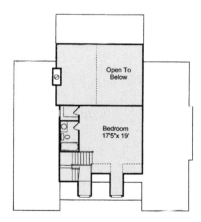

This home, as shown in the photograph, may differ from the actual blueprints.
For more detailed information, please check the floor plans carefully.

DESIGN

First Floor:
1,113 Square Feet
Second Floor:
543 Square Feet
Total Square Footage:
1,656
Bedrooms: 3
Bathrooms: 2

Width: 44'-0"
Depth: 32'-0"

D

HPT250010

QUOTE ONE®
Cost to build? See page 214
to order a complete cost estimate
to build this house in your area!

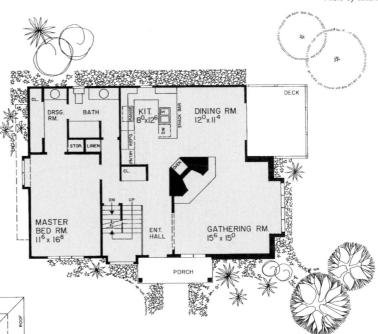

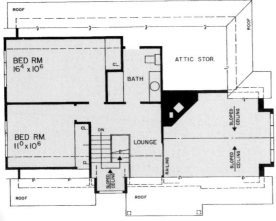

For a lakeside retreat or as a retirement haven, this charming design offers the best in livability. The gathering room with a corner fireplace, a U-shaped kitchen with an attached dining room, and the lovely deck make a complete and comfortable living space. The first-floor master bedroom boasts His and Hers sinks, a walk-in closet and extra storage space. Upstairs, two bedrooms with a full bath and a balcony lounge complete the design and provide sleeping accommodations for family and guests.

This home, as shown in the photographs, may differ from the actual blueprints.
For more detailed information, please check the floor plans carefully.

DESIGN

First Floor:
1,387 Square Feet
Second Floor:
929 Square Feet
Total Square Footage:
2,316
Bedrooms: 4
Bathrooms: 3

Width: 30'-0"
Depth: 51'-8"

HPT250007

QUOTE ONE®

Cost to build? See page 214
to order a complete cost estimate
to build this house in your area!

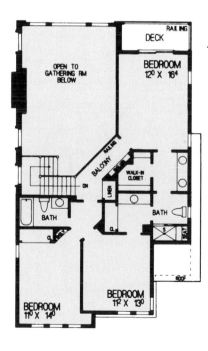

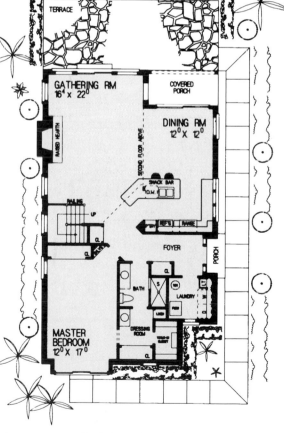

Perfect for a narrow lot, this shingle-and-stone Nantucket Cape home caters to the casual lifestyle. The side entrance gives direct access to the wonderfully open living areas: the gathering room with a fireplace and an abundance of windows; the island kitchen with an angled, pass-through snack bar; and the dining area with sliding glass doors to a covered eating area. Note also the large deck that further extends the living potential. Also on this floor is the large master suite with a compartmented bath, private dressing room and walk-in closet. Upstairs you'll find the three family bedrooms.

This home, as shown in the photographs, may differ from the actual blueprints. For more detailed information, please check the floor plans carefully.

Photos by Design Basics, Inc.

Fam. rm. 16⁰ x 19⁴

Bfst. 12⁰ x 12⁰

Kit. 12⁰ x 17⁰

Gar. 24⁰ x 21³

Gar. 24⁰ x 21⁰

Liv. rm. 20⁰ x 17⁴
10'-0" CEILING

Mbr. 19⁸ x 15⁰
10'-0" CEILING

Din. 14⁰ x 15⁶

Sit. 10⁴ x 13⁰

Den 12⁰ x 13⁸
11'-0" CEILING

WHIRLPOOL
DRESSING
COVERED
SERVERY
PANT.
WET BAR
BOOKS
HUTCH
DESK
SNACK BAR
LIN.
TRANS.
STOOP
COVERED STOOP
TRANS.

Br. 2 13⁰ x 17⁴
10'-0" CLG.

Br. 4 12⁰ x 15⁶
10'-0" CEILING

Br. 3 14⁰ x 15⁶

SEAT
DN
OPEN TO BELOW
LINEN
BOOKS
TRANSOMS

The stone facade of this traditional design evokes images of a quieter life, a life of harmony and comfortable luxury. An elegant floor plan allows you to carry that feeling inside. The tiled foyer offers entry to any room you choose, whether it be the secluded den with its built-in bookshelves, the formal dining room, the formal living room with its fireplace, wet bar and wall of windows, or the spacious rear family and kitchen area with its sunny breakfast nook. The master suite offers privacy on the first floor and features a sitting room with bookshelves, two walk-in closets and a private bath with a corner whirlpool tub. Three family bedrooms, each with a walk-in closet, and two baths make up the second floor.

DESIGN

First Floor: 2,813 Square Feet
Second Floor: 1,091 Square Feet
Total Square Footage: 3,904
Bedrooms: 4
Bathrooms: 3½

Width: 85'-5"
Depth: 74'-8"

HPT250018

This home, as shown in the photographs, may differ from the actual blueprints. For more detailed information, please check the floor plans carefully.

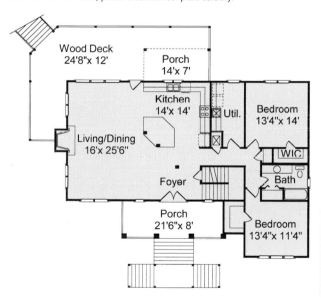

Wood Deck
24'8"x 12'

Porch
14'x 7'

Kitchen
14'x 14'

Util.

Bedroom
13'4"x 14'

Living/Dining
16'x 25'6"

WIC

Foyer

Bath

Porch
21'6"x 8'

Bedroom
13'4"x 11'4"

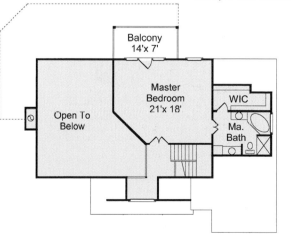

Photos by Chris A. Little of Atlanta, courtesy of Chatham Home Planning, Inc.

Balcony
14'x 7'

Master Bedroom
21'x 18'

Open To Below

WIC

Ma. Bath

DESIGN

First Floor:
1,552 Square Feet
Second Floor:
653 Square Feet
Total Square Footage:
2,205
Bedrooms: 3
Bathrooms: 2

Width: 60'-0"
Depth: 50'-0"

HPT250016

A split staircase adds flair to this European-styled coastal home where a fireplace brings warmth on chilly evenings. The foyer opens to the expansive living/dining area and the island kitchen. A multitude of windows fills the interior with sunlight and ocean breezes. The wraparound rear deck finds access near the kitchen. The utility room is conveniently tucked between the kitchen and the two first-floor bedrooms. The second-floor master suite offers a private deck and a luxurious bath with a garden tub, shower and walk-in closet.

This home, as shown in the photographs, may differ from the actual blueprints. For more detailed information, please check the floor plans carefully.

Photos by Laszlo Regos

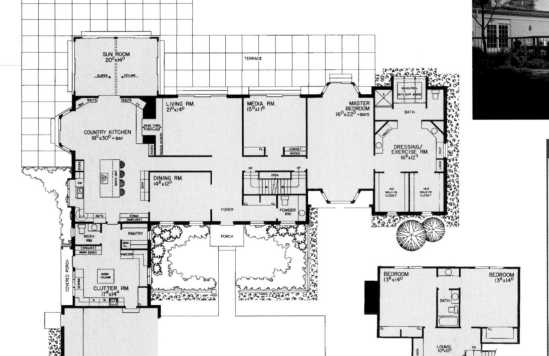

DESIGN

First Floor:
3,215 Square Feet
Second Floor:
711 Square Feet
Total Square Footage:
3,926
Sun Room:
296 Square Feet
Bedrooms: 3
Bathrooms: 2½ +½

Width: 97'-8"
Depth: 101'-4"

L D

HPT250014

Organized zoning makes this traditional design a comfortable home for living. A central foyer facilitates flexible traffic patterns. Quiet areas of the house include a media room and luxurious master suite with a fitness area, spacious closet space and bath, as well as a lounge or writing area. Informal living areas of the house include a sun room, large country kitchen and an efficient food-preparation area with an island. Formal areas include a living room and formal dining room. The second floor holds two bedrooms and a lounge. Service areas include a room just off the garage for laundry, sewing or hobbies.

Tee Time
Homes designed for golf course living

No other game combines the wonder of nature with the discipline of sport in such carefully planned ways. A great golf course both frees and challenges a golfer's mind.

— Tom Watson

This traditional Western ranch home offers impressive living space and captivating character. Upon entering, notice the ten-foot ceiling and built-in cabinets in the foyer. The dining room will entertain with its ten-foot ceiling and windows that overlook the front of the home. The study amazes with its cathedral ceiling and impressive views. The master suite features a massive walk-in closet, generous private bath and unusual cathedral ceiling. Downstairs, three family bedrooms and a recreation room finish the design.

DESIGN

Main Level:
1,800 Square Feet
Lower Level:
1,325 Square Feet
Total Square Footage:
3,125
Bedrooms: 4
Bathrooms: 2

Width: 74'-8"
Depth: 65'-8"

HPT250019

This amazing home is detailed with sloped roofs, a stone facade and muntin windows. Enjoy the stone fireplace whether relaxing in the great room or sipping a drink at the bar extended from the kitchen. Adjacent to the kitchen, a dining area includes sliding glass doors leading to a covered patio. A private patio area is available to the master bedroom, as well as a spacious private bath, which includes a double-bowl sink and a vast walk-in closet. Two family bedrooms each have double-door closets and share a full bath. A three-car garage resides to the far right of the plan, with an entryway opening to the utility room.

DESIGN

Total Square Footage: 2,061
Bedrooms: 3
Bathrooms: 2½

Width: 88'-0"
Depth: 40'-9"

HPT250020

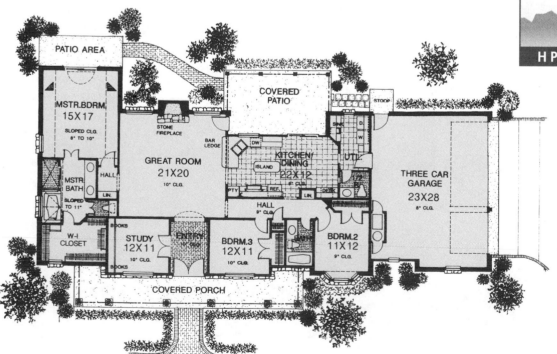

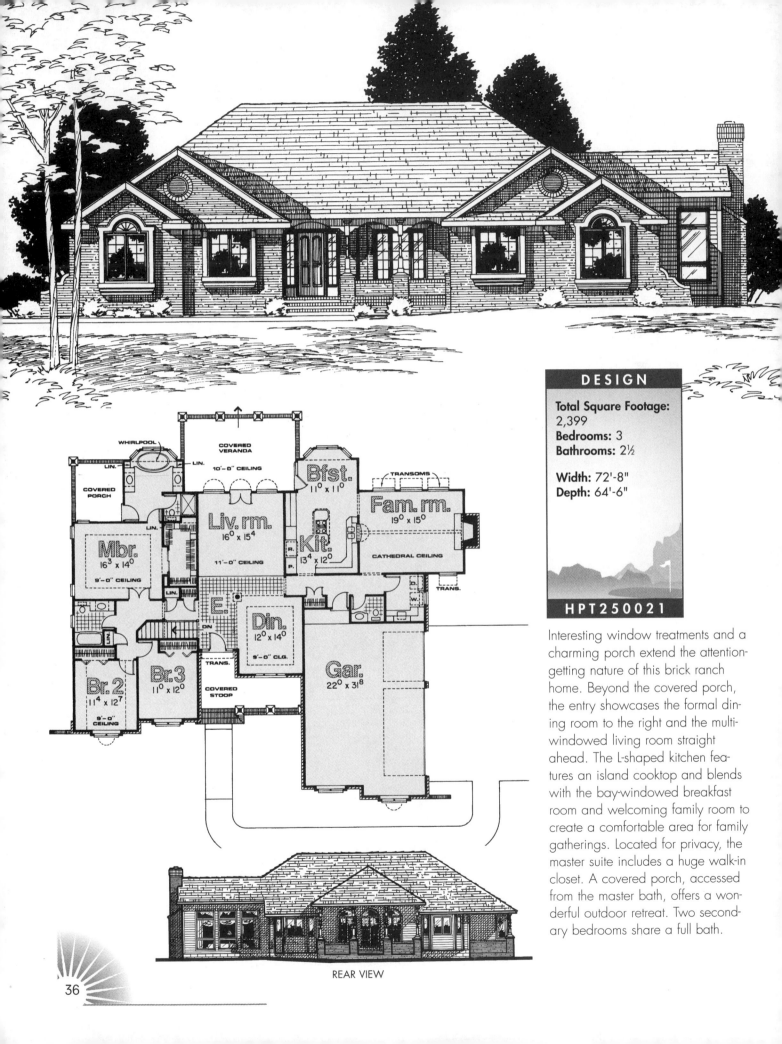

DESIGN

Total Square Footage: 2,399
Bedrooms: 3
Bathrooms: 2½

Width: 72'-8"
Depth: 64'-6"

HPT250021

Interesting window treatments and a charming porch extend the attention-getting nature of this brick ranch home. Beyond the covered porch, the entry showcases the formal dining room to the right and the multi-windowed living room straight ahead. The L-shaped kitchen features an island cooktop and blends with the bay-windowed breakfast room and welcoming family room to create a comfortable area for family gatherings. Located for privacy, the master suite includes a huge walk-in closet. A covered porch, accessed from the master bath, offers a wonderful outdoor retreat. Two secondary bedrooms share a full bath.

Floor plan labels:
WHIRLPOOL
COVERED VERANDA 10'-0" CEILING
Bfst. 11⁰ x 11⁰
TRANSOMS
Fam. rm. 19⁰ x 15⁰
COVERED PORCH
LIN.
Liv. rm. 16⁰ x 15⁴
11'-0" CEILING
Kit. 13⁴ x 12⁰
CATHEDRAL CEILING
Mbr. 16³ x 14⁰
9'-0" CEILING
LIN.
E.
Din. 12⁰ x 14⁰
9'-0" CLG.
Gar. 22⁰ x 31⁸
TRANS.
W.
Br. 2 11⁴ x 12⁷
9'-0" CEILING
Br. 3 11⁰ x 12⁰
TRANS.
COVERED STOOP

REAR VIEW

36

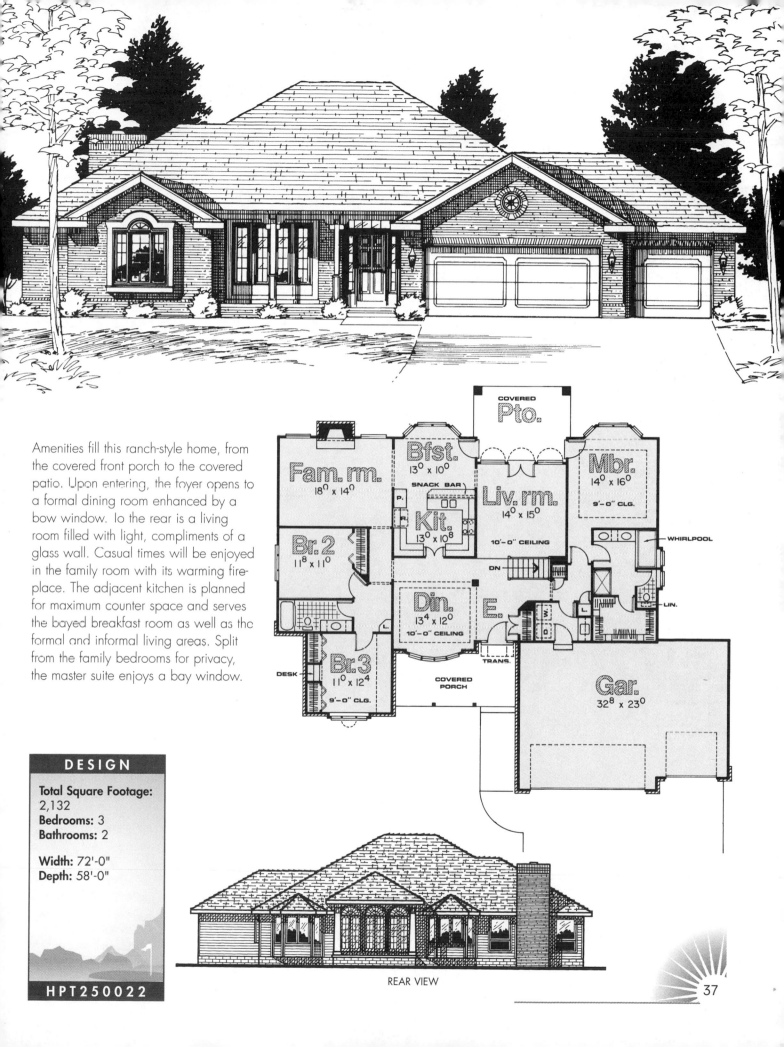

Amenities fill this ranch-style home, from the covered front porch to the covered patio. Upon entering, the foyer opens to a formal dining room enhanced by a bow window. To the rear is a living room filled with light, compliments of a glass wall. Casual times will be enjoyed in the family room with its warming fireplace. The adjacent kitchen is planned for maximum counter space and serves the bayed breakfast room as well as the formal and informal living areas. Split from the family bedrooms for privacy, the master suite enjoys a bay window.

COVERED Pto.

Fam. rm. 18⁰ x 14⁰

Bfst. 13⁰ x 10⁰

SNACK BAR

Mbr. 14⁰ x 16⁰

9'–0" CLG.

Br. 2 11⁸ x 11⁰

P.

R

Kit. 13⁰ x 10⁸

Liv. rm. 14⁰ x 15⁰

10'–0" CEILING

WHIRLPOOL

DN

Din. 13⁴ x 12⁰

10'–0" CEILING

F.

LIN.

L

DESK

Br. 3 11⁰ x 12⁴

9'–0" CLG.

COVERED PORCH

TRANS.

W
D

L

Gar. 32⁸ x 23⁰

DESIGN

Total Square Footage: 2,132

Bedrooms: 3
Bathrooms: 2

Width: 72'-0"
Depth: 58'-0"

HPT250022

REAR VIEW

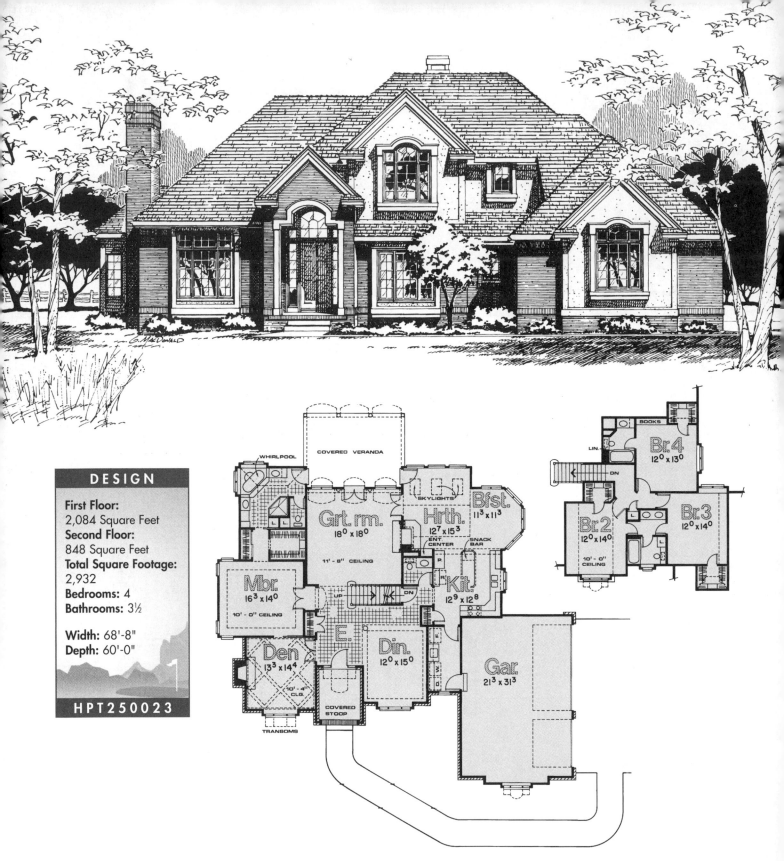

DESIGN

First Floor:
2,084 Square Feet
Second Floor:
848 Square Feet
Total Square Footage:
2,932
Bedrooms: 4
Bathrooms: 3½

Width: 68'-8"
Depth: 60'-0"

HPT250023

COVERED VERANDA

WHIRLPOOL

Grt. rm.
18⁰ x 18⁰

11'-8" CEILING

Hrth.
12⁷ x 15³

SKYLIGHTS

ENT. CENTER

SNACK BAR

Bfst.
11³ x 11³

Mbr.
16³ x 14⁰

10'-0" CEILING

Kit.
12⁹ x 12⁸

UP   DN

Den
13³ x 14⁴

10'-4" CLG.

E.

Din.
12⁰ x 15⁰

Gar.
21³ x 31³

COVERED STOOP

TRANSOMS

BOOKS

Br.4
12⁰ x 13⁰

LIN.

DN

Br.2
12⁰ x 14⁰

10'-0" CEILING

Br.3
12⁰ x 14⁰

The combination of brick, stucco and elegant detail provides this home with instant curb appeal. The entry is flanked by the formal dining room and the den, with a fireplace and an intriguing ceiling pattern. The great room offers a through-fireplace to the hearth room and French doors to a covered veranda. A sunny breakfast room and kitchen feature an island with snack bar, wrapping counters and a pantry. The first-floor master suite affords luxury accommodations with two closets, a whirlpool tub, His and Hers vanities and access to the covered veranda. Three secondary bedrooms on the second floor offer walk-in closets and access to bathroom space.

SIDE VIEW

DESIGN

Main Level:
2,464 Square Feet
Lower Level:
1,887 Square Feet
Total Square Footage:
4,351
Bedrooms: 4
Bathrooms: 3½

Width: 59'-0"
Depth: 81'-0"

HPT250024

This gorgeous hillside design offers an unassuming front perspective, but behold the side view with its elegant deck flanked by the great room and master bedroom, each with an enormous arch-top window. Inside, the dining room, island kitchen, nook and great room enjoy an open plan with decorative columns and tray ceilings defining the dining and great rooms. The master suite finds privacy to the right with a luxurious bath. The staircase near the kitchen leads to the lower level where three additional bedrooms are found. The game room offers a built-in media center with a wetbar and wine cellar close at hand.

Floor Plan Labels

First Floor:
- LOWER TERRACE
- BRKFST 10'-6" x 8'-0"
- GATHERING ROOM 16'-0" x 21'-0"
- KITCHEN 14'-0" x 13'-0"
- LIVING ROOM 14'-10" x 16'-6"
- MASTER SUITE 14'-0" x 16'-10"
- DINING ROOM 12'-6" x 16'-0"
- FOYER
- W.I.C.
- W.I.C.
- PDR.
- LAUN.
- MASTER BATH
- 2-CAR GARAGE 23'-0" x 23'-0"
- 1-CAR GARAGE 21'-0" x 13'-10"

Second Floor:
- SUITE 3 14'-8" x 13'-6"
- PLAY ROOM 15'-0" x 16'-8"
- OPEN TO BELOW
- BATH
- SUITE 2 12'-6" x 12'-6"
- OPEN TO BELOW
- BATH
- BALCONY
- SUITE 4 11'-0" x 12'-0"

REAR VIEW

DESIGN

First Floor:
2,430 Square Feet
Second Floor:
1,624 Square Feet
Total Square Footage:
4,054
Bedrooms: 4
Bathrooms: 3½

Width: 70'-4"
Depth: 95'-9"

HPT250025

This charming home combines hipped rooflines, shingles and brickwork to create a design with European elements. Enter through the foyer, and to the left is a vaulted dining room. The gathering room—complete with a fireplace—and living room flank the kitchen. A bayed breakfast nook looks out to the lower terrace. The first-floor master suite on the right side of the plan includes such amenities as a tray ceiling, His and Hers walk-in closets, a full bath, garden tub and separate shower. Suites 2 and 4 share a full bath, and each boasts balconies. Suite 3 enjoys a private bath and a walk-in closet.

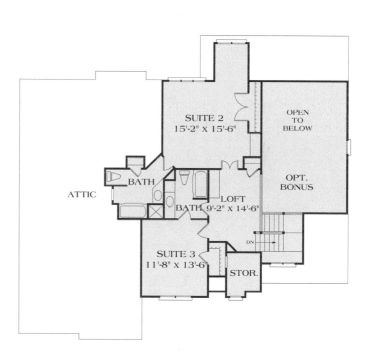

Stone and siding lend a rustic nature to this traditional home. A covered stoop is enhanced by a graceful arch and a glass-paneled entry. A formal dining room is served by a gourmet kitchen through a butler's pantry with a wet bar. The great room provides a fireplace and a French door to a golf porch. An angled tub and an oversized shower highlight the master bath, while a box-bay window and a tray ceiling enhance the master bedroom. Each of the second-floor suites has a generous bath. The loft overlooks the great room.

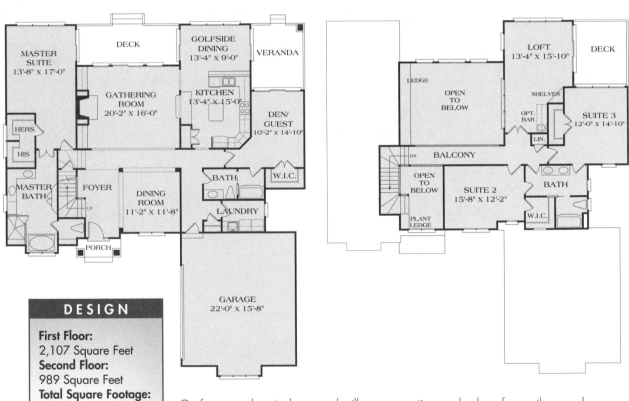

MASTER
SUITE
13'-8" x 17'-0"

DECK

GOLFSIDE
DINING
13'-4" x 9'-0"

VERANDA

GATHERING
ROOM
20'-2" x 16'-0"

KITCHEN
13'-4" x 15'-0"

HERS

HIS

DEN/
GUEST
10'-2" x 14'-10"

MASTER
BATH

FOYER

DINING
ROOM
11'-2" x 11'-8"

BATH

W.I.C.

LAUNDRY

PORCH

GARAGE
22'-0" x 15'-8"

LOFT
13'-4" x 15'-10"

DECK

LEDGE

OPEN
TO
BELOW

SHELVES

OPT.
BAR

SUITE 3
12'-0" x 14'-10"

LIN.

DN

BALCONY

OPEN
TO
BELOW

SUITE 2
15'-8" x 12'-2"

BATH

PLANT
LEDGE

W.I.C.

DESIGN

First Floor:
2,107 Square Feet
Second Floor:
989 Square Feet
Total Square Footage:
3,096
Bedrooms: 3/4
Bathrooms: 3

Width: 59'-0"
Depth: 69'-5"

HPT250027

Craftsman-style windows and pillars supporting a shed roof over the porch combine to give this home plenty of curb appeal. The two-story foyer leads to a formal dining room on the right and a spacious gathering room directly ahead, where a fireplace is flanked by built-ins and adds warmth and cheer to the room. The second-floor balcony divides the foyer from the gathering room while offering beautiful views out the back windows to the rear deck. The master suite is designed to pamper, with two walk-in closets, a separate tub and shower and a dual-bowl vanity. A den/guest room features a walk-in closet and access to a full bath.

Photo by Living Concepts Home Planning

This home, as shown in the photograph, may differ from the actual blueprints. For more detailed information, please check the floor plans carefully.

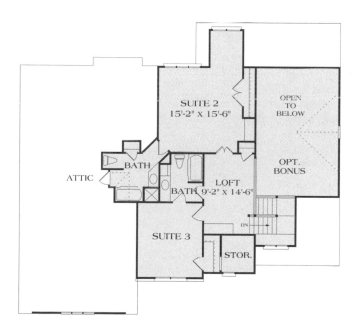

MASTER SUITE
14'-6" x 15'-6"

MASTER BATH

W.I.C.   LAUNDRY

GARAGE
21'-6" x 22'-8"

PDR.

BAR

DINING ROOM
11'-8" x 13'-6"

FOYER

STOOP

BREAKFAST
10'-6" x 8'-0"

GOLF PORCH

KITCHEN
15'-2" x 15'-6"

GREAT ROOM
15'-0" x 23'-4"

UP

PORCH

SUITE 2
15'-2" x 15'-6"

OPEN TO BELOW

ATTIC

BATH

BATH

LOFT
9'-2" x 14'-6"

OPT. BONUS

SUITE 3

STOR.

DN

DESIGN

First Floor:
1,824 Square Feet
Second Floor:
842 Square Feet
Total Square Footage:
2,666
Bedrooms: 3
Bathrooms: 3½

Width: 59'-0"
Depth: 53'-6"

HPT250028

Horizontal siding, double-hung windows and European gables lend a special charm to this contemporary home. The formal dining room opens from the foyer and offers a servery and a box-bay window. The great room features a fireplace and opens to a golf porch as well as a charming side porch. A well-lit kitchen contains a cooktop island counter and two pantries. The first-floor master suite provides a tray ceiling, a box-bay window and a deluxe bath with a garden tub and an angled shower. A convenient powder room maintains privacy for the master suite. Each of the upper-level bedrooms privately accesses a full bath. Suite 2 has a dormer window and leads to sizable attic space.

The symmetrical front of this home conceals an imaginatively asymmetrical floor plan beyond. A keeping room, a sitting area in the master bedroom and a second bedroom all jut out from this home, forming interesting angles and providing extra window space. Two fireplaces, a game room, a study and His and Hers bathrooms in the master suite are interesting elements in this home. The bayed kitchen, with a walk-in pantry and a center island with room for seating, is sure to lure guests and family alike. The open floor plan and two-story ceilings in the family room add a contemporary touch.

DESIGN

First Floor:
1,537 Square Feet
Second Floor:
812 Square Feet
Total Square Footage:
2,349
Bedrooms: 3
Bathrooms: 2½

Width: 45'-4"
Depth: 50'-0"

HPT250030

Dramatic rooflines complement a striking arched-pediment entry and a variety of windows on this refined facade. A fireplace warms the great room, which sports a tray ceiling and opens to the rear porch through lovely French doors. The gourmet kitchen serves a stunning formal dining room, which offers wide views through a wall of windows. The private master suite enjoys a coffered ceiling, walk-in closet and private access to one of the rear porches.

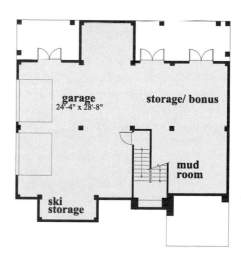

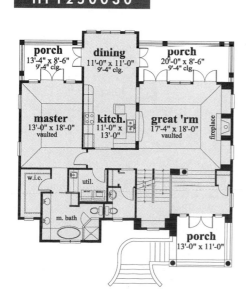

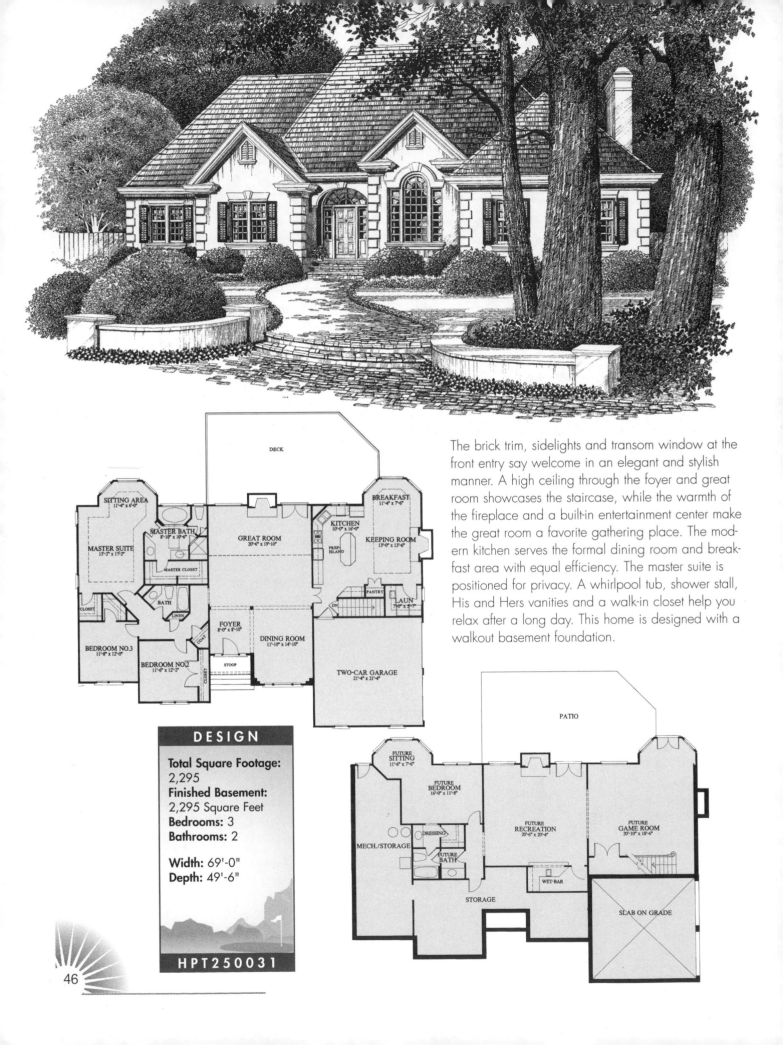

The brick trim, sidelights and transom window at the front entry say welcome in an elegant and stylish manner. A high ceiling through the foyer and great room showcases the staircase, while the warmth of the fireplace and a built-in entertainment center make the great room a favorite gathering place. The modern kitchen serves the formal dining room and breakfast area with equal efficiency. The master suite is positioned for privacy. A whirlpool tub, shower stall, His and Hers vanities and a walk-in closet help you relax after a long day. This home is designed with a walkout basement foundation.

Floor plan labels (main level):

- DECK
- SITTING AREA 11'-4" x 6'-0"
- MASTER BATH 8'-10" x 10'-6"
- MASTER SUITE 13'-2" x 17'-2"
- MASTER CLOSET
- BATH
- LINEN
- CLOSET
- BEDROOM NO.3 11'-8" x 12'-0"
- BEDROOM NO.2 11'-6" x 12'-2"
- COAT
- CLOSET
- STOOP
- GREAT ROOM 20'-6" x 19'-10"
- KITCHEN 10'-0" x 16'-0"
- PREP ISLAND
- BREAKFAST 11'-4" x 7'-6"
- KEEPING ROOM 13'-3" x 13'-6"
- PANTRY
- DN
- LAUN 7'-0" x 5'-7"
- FOYER 8'-0" x 8'-10"
- DINING ROOM 11'-10" x 14'-10"
- TWO-CAR GARAGE 21'-4" x 21'-4"

Floor plan labels (basement level):

- PATIO
- FUTURE SITTING 11'-6" x 7'-6"
- FUTURE BEDROOM 16'-0" x 11'-8"
- MECH./STORAGE
- DRESSING
- FUTURE BATH
- FUTURE RECREATION 20'-6" x 20'-4"
- FUTURE GAME ROOM 20'-10" x 18'-6"
- WET-BAR
- STORAGE
- SLAB ON GRADE

DESIGN

Total Square Footage: 2,295

Finished Basement: 2,295 Square Feet

Bedrooms: 3

Bathrooms: 2

Width: 69'-0"

Depth: 49'-6"

HPT250031

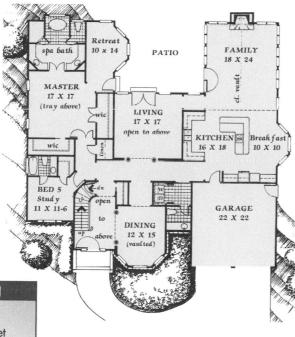

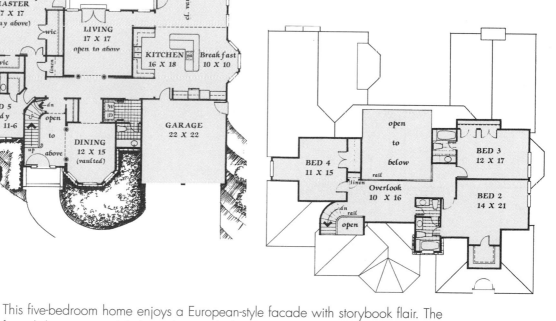

This five-bedroom home enjoys a European-style facade with storybook flair. The formal dining room delights with a vaulted ceiling. The family room is found beyond the adjoining island kitchen and bayed breakfast area. Here, three walls of windows lend an air of open space and elegance. On the opposite side of the plan, the master suite offers a private retreat that features a bay window. Three family bedrooms reside on the second floor along with two and a half baths. Back on the first floor, Bedroom 5 converts easily into a guest suite with a private bath.

With a touch of tradition, the brick facade of this home makes an elegant first impression. The floor plan boasts a two-story family room with a fireplace, which overlooks a rear veranda. Double doors open to a quiet study. The master suite is secluded on the first floor for privacy and includes a whirlpool bath and two walk-in closets. Three additional family bedrooms reside upstairs, along with an optional attic. Please specify basement or slab foundation when ordering.

DESIGN

First Floor:
1,844 Square Feet
Second Floor:
794 Square Feet
Total Square Footage:
2,638
Attic:
324 Square Feet
Bedrooms: 4
Bathrooms: 3½

Width: 65'-6"
Depth: 56'-10"

HPT250033

This home, as shown in the photograph, may differ from the actual blueprints.
For more detailed information, please check the floor plans carefully.

DESIGN

First Floor:
1,862 Square Feet
Second Floor:
1,044 Square Feet
Total Square Footage:
2,906
Bedrooms: 3
Bathrooms: 3½

Width: 60'-0"
Depth: 60'-0"

HPT250034

A gently sloping, high-pitched roof complements keystones, arch-top windows and a delicate balcony balustrade and calls up a sense of cozy elegance. The foyer opens to a grand room with a focal-point fireplace and access to a screened room that leads to the veranda. The gourmet kitchen offers a walk-in pantry, acres of counter space and a morning room with outdoor flow. An island wardrobe highlights the master suite, which boasts a secluded lounge with a door to a private area of the veranda. Upstairs, two secondary bedrooms enjoy a balcony overlook to the foyer, and each room has its own access to an outdoor deck.

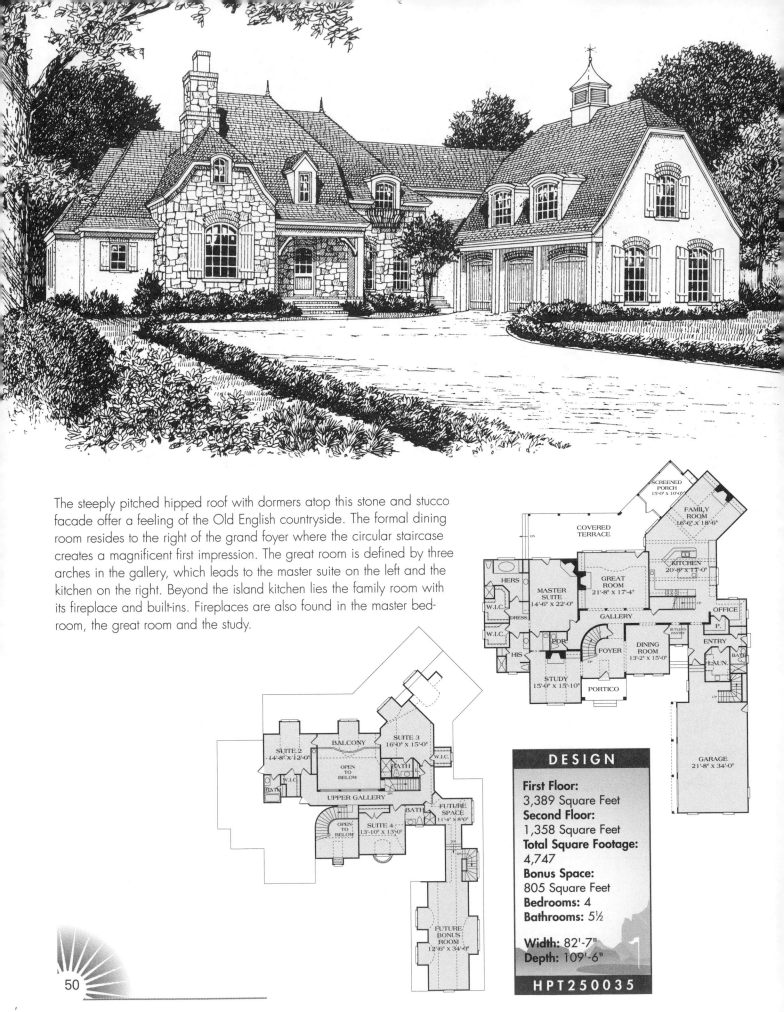

The steeply pitched hipped roof with dormers atop this stone and stucco facade offer a feeling of the Old English countryside. The formal dining room resides to the right of the grand foyer where the circular staircase creates a magnificent first impression. The great room is defined by three arches in the gallery, which leads to the master suite on the left and the kitchen on the right. Beyond the island kitchen lies the family room with its fireplace and built-ins. Fireplaces are also found in the master bedroom, the great room and the study.

DESIGN

First Floor:
3,389 Square Feet
Second Floor:
1,358 Square Feet
Total Square Footage:
4,747
Bonus Space:
805 Square Feet
Bedrooms: 4
Bathrooms: 5½

Width: 82'-7"
Depth: 109'-6"

HPT250035

The side-loading garage on this four-bedroom home keeps the front exterior clean and fresh. A sweeping staircase highlights the grand foyer that opens to the living room and dining room. The gallery leads to the family room where the fireplace shares a hearth with the entertainment center. The luxurious master suite enjoys a lavish bath, an enormous walk-in closet and a built-in entertainment center. A see-through fireplace is shared by the master bedroom and the study.

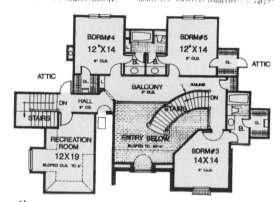

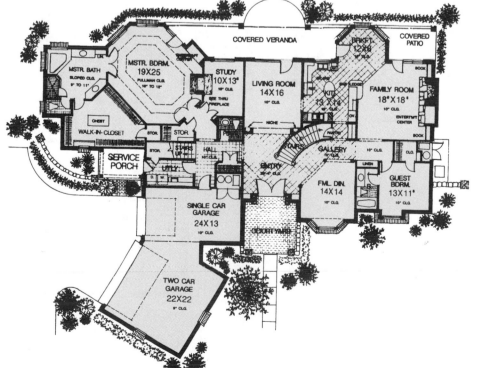

DESIGN

First Floor:
3,145 Square Feet
Second Floor:
1,306 Square Feet
Total Square Footage:
4,451
Bedrooms: 4
Bathrooms: 3½

Width: 96'-0"
Depth: 79'-8"

HPT250036

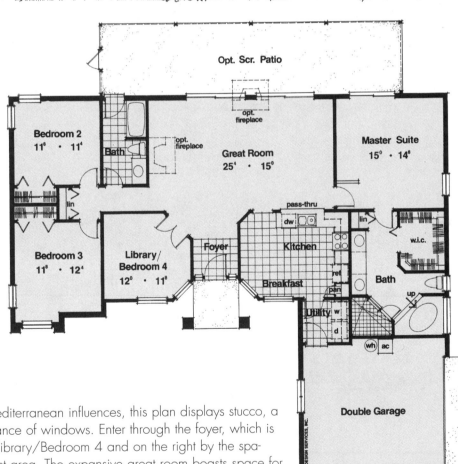

DESIGN

Total Square Footage:
1,771
Bedrooms: 3/4
Bathrooms: 2

Width: 60'-0"
Depth: 54'-4"

HPT250037

A home reminiscent of Mediterranean influences, this plan displays stucco, a high entry and an abundance of windows. Enter through the foyer, which is flanked on the left by the library/Bedroom 4 and on the right by the spacious kitchen and breakfast area. The expansive great room boasts space for two optional fireplaces. The master suite resides on the right side of the plan for increased privacy and boasts sliding glass doors to the patio, a garden tub, separate shower and spacious walk-in closet. The left side of the plan holds the two family bedrooms, which share a full bath.

© 91 HOME DESIGN SERVICES, INC.

I.N. HANSEN P.T.L.

Bedroom 4
13⁰ · 11⁰

Family Room
18⁸ · 14⁰

fireplace

Covered Patio

Bath

Breakfast

lin

lin

Kitchen

dw

Living Room
16⁰ · 14⁰

Master
Bedroom
18⁰ · 15⁰

Bedroom 3
13⁰ · 11⁰

ref

pantry

Utility

Pdr.

w.i.c.

w.i.c.

w

lin

ac

wh

d

Dining
12⁸ · 10⁸

Foyer

Bath

up

Double Garage

Entry

Den/
Bedroom 2
12⁰ · 11⁰

lin

DESIGN

Total Square Footage:
2,287
Bedrooms: 3/4
Bathrooms: 2

Width: 63'-4"
Depth: 62'-4"

HPT250038

Low-pitched roofs and a grand, columned entry introduce a floor plan designed for the 21st Century. Ceramic tiles lead from the foyer to the breakfast area and roomy kitchen, which offers an angled wrapping counter and overlooks the family room. French doors open off the foyer to a secluded den or guest suite, which complements the nearby master suite. A gallery hall off the breakfast nook leads to family sleeping quarters, which share a full bath.

Family Room
volume ceiling
17⁰ • 16⁰

fireplace

m   m

Breakfast
opt. summer kitchen
volume ceiling
dw

Bedroom 2
volume ceiling
12⁰ • 11⁴

n

Bath
lin

Covered Patio
volume ceiling

Kitchen
pan
ref

Bath

Master Bedroom
volume ceiling
13⁸ • 17⁸

Living Room
volume ceiling
14⁸ • 17⁰

lin

Bedroom 3
volume ceiling
12⁰ • 11⁴

Utility
w
d

ac   wh

Dining
volume ceiling
11⁰ • 14⁰

Foyer

Bedroom 4
Den/Study
volume ceiling
10⁰ • 11⁰

w.i.c.   w.i.c.

Bath

up

Entry

Double Garage

DESIGN

Total Square Footage:
2,362
Bedrooms: 3/4
Bathrooms: 3

Width: 65'-8"
Depth: 73'-4"

HPT250039

The grand entrance is only the beginning in this well-balanced home. The foyer opens to the centered formal living room, with a wall of glass through which to view the outdoor living space. Traffic areas, tiled in marble, add graciousness and practicality as you walk through the home. The master wing begins with a convenient and versatile den/guest room/library adjacent to the master suite and pool bath. The perfectly balanced master bath has a beautiful bay window framing the soaking tub, with matching spaces for the shower and toilet chamber, matching vanities and two walk-in closets.

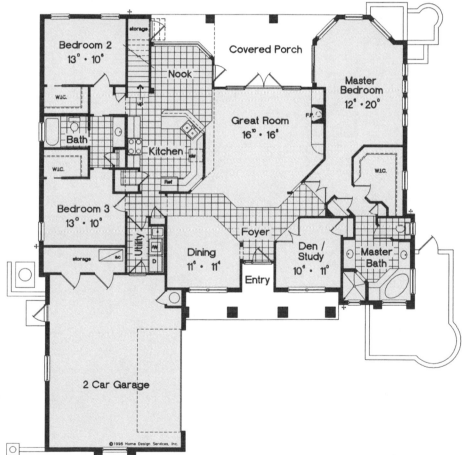

Bedroom 2
13⁰ · 10⁰

storage

Nook

Covered Porch

Master Bedroom
12⁶ · 20⁰

W.I.C.

Bath

Great Room
16¹⁰ · 16⁸

F.P.

up

Kitchen

W.I.C.

Bedroom 3
13⁰ · 10⁰

Ref

Foyer

Utility

Dining
11⁰ · 11⁴

Den / Study
10⁶ · 11⁰

Master Bath

storage

ac

Entry

2 Car Garage

©1998 Home Design Services, Inc.

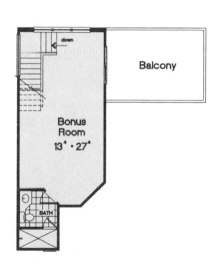

down

Balcony

Bonus Room
13⁴ · 27⁴

BATH

DESIGN

Total Square Footage:
2,237
Bonus Room:
397 Square Feet
Bedrooms: 3
Bathrooms: 3

Width: 60'-0"
Depth: 70'-0"

HPT250040

The elegance and grace of this plan are apparent at first sight. Impressive arches lead into the foyer, with the wide-open great room beyond, opening to a covered porch through French doors. Enter both the master suite and the adjacent den/study through French doors. From the nook and near two good-sized bedrooms with a shared bathroom, stairs go up to a bonus room, which includes a large balcony to take advantage of your lot with a view.

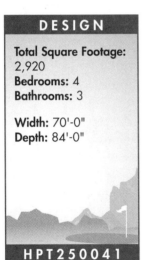

Artfully designed, this Floridian-style one-story home welcomes visitors with a grand entryway. Inside, the rooms are spacious and inviting: formal living and dining rooms and a casual family room surround the kitchen and breakfast nook. A den or study is tucked away to the left of the foyer, near a master suite with a grand bath. Two family bedrooms share a full bath on the right side of the plan. A utility area with washer and dryer space leads to the three-car garage. Note the covered patio at the rear, accessed via the master bedroom, the pool bath, the living room and the breakfast nook.

Columns add the finishing touches to this dazzling plan. Two elevations provide the homeowner with exemplary options for a magnificent home. The double-door entry opens to the foyer, which leads to the vaulted living room, with sliding glass doors to the covered patio. The kitchen is open to both the living room and the bayed nook. A bow window and a fireplace define the family room. The master suite features access to the covered patio and provides dual walk-in closets and a spa tub. Two additional bedrooms share a full bath that has a box-bay window.

ALTERNATIVE ELEVATION

DESIGN

Total Square Footage:
2,258
Bedrooms: 4
Bathrooms: 3

Width: 66'-0"
Depth: 73'-4"

HPT250042

This home, as shown in the photograph, may differ from the actual blueprints.
For more detailed information, please check the floor plans carefully.

Photo by Living Concepts Home Planning

This charming European-style home, with its elaborate exterior of bayed windows and an intricately designed hipped roof, is perfectly suited for the elegance and beauty of a golf course lot. Graceful columns define the dining room, which features an oval tray ceiling and bay window, and the entrance to the gathering room. The gathering room includes a fireplace and access to the covered veranda. An island kitchen is open to a five-sided breakfast nook with windows facing the veranda. Glass-block windows enclose the master bath and shower, while the master bedroom features a tray ceiling.

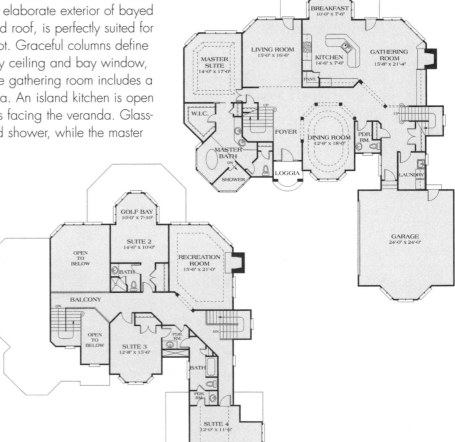

DESIGN

First Floor:
2,292 Square Feet
Second Floor:
1,465 Square Feet
Total Square Footage:
3,757
Bedrooms: 4
Bathrooms: 3½

Width: 67'-6"
Depth: 78'-0"

HPT250043

Now here is a one-of-a-kind house plan. Step down from the raised foyer into the grand gallery where columns define the living room. This area also boasts an enormous bow window with a fantastic view to the covered patio. The formal dining room is to the right and the lavish master suite is on the left. The secluded family room completes this first level. An enormous den is found on the first landing above and to the left of the foyer. Two bedroom suites and a loft are found on the second floor.

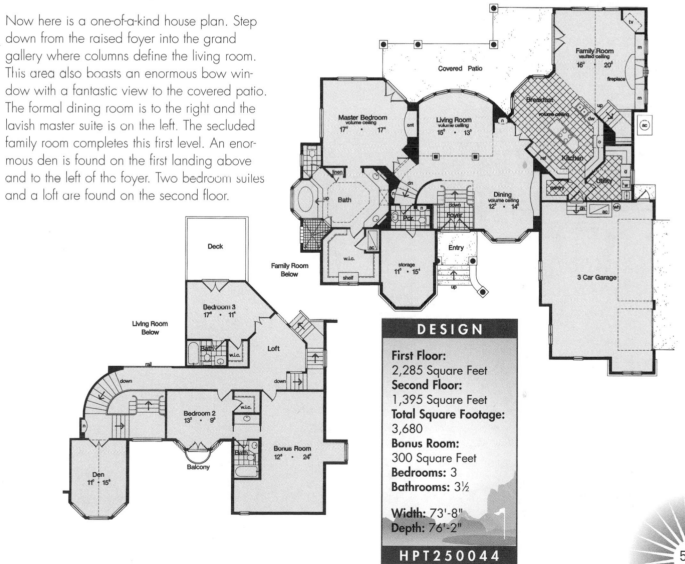

DESIGN

First Floor:
2,285 Square Feet
Second Floor:
1,395 Square Feet
Total Square Footage:
3,680
Bonus Room:
300 Square Feet
Bedrooms: 3
Bathrooms: 3½

Width: 73'-8"
Depth: 76'-2"

HPT250044

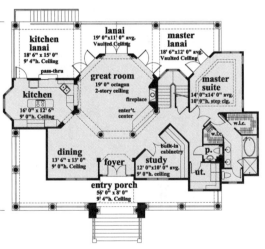

kitchen lanai
18' 6" x 15' 0"
9' 4"h. Ceiling

lanai
19' 0"x11' 0" avg.
Vaulted Ceiling

master lanai
18' 6"x12' 0" avg.
Vaulted Ceiling

pass-thru

great room
19' 0" octagon
2-story ceiling

master suite
14' 0"x14' 0" avg.
10' 0"h. step clg.

fireplace

kitchen
16' 0" x 12' 6"
9' 0"h. Ceiling

enter't. center

built-in cabinetry

w.t.c.

w.t.c.

dining
13' 6" x 13' 0"
9' 0". Ceiling

foyer

study
12' 0"x10' 0" avg.
9' 0"h. ceiling

p.

ut.

entry porch
56' 0" x 8' 0"
9' 4"h. Ceiling

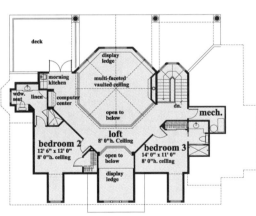

deck

morning kitchen

display ledge

wdw. seat

linen

computer center

multi-faceted vaulted ceiling

dn.

mech.

open to below

bedroom 2
12' 6" x 12' 0"
8' 0"h. ceiling

loft
8' 0"h. Ceiling

bedroom 3
14' 0" x 11' 0"
8' 0"h. ceiling

open to below

display ledge

DESIGN

First Floor:
1,855 Square Feet
Second Floor:
901 Square Feet
Total Square Footage:
2,756
Bonus Space:
1,010 Square Feet
Bedrooms: 3
Bathrooms: 3½

Width: 66'-0"
Depth: 50'-0"

HPT250045

This villa is romantically enhanced by the Italian-influenced facade. The two-story foyer opens to a study on the right and the formal dining room on the left. The octagonal great room with a vaulted ceiling offers a fireplace and three sets of double doors that lead outside to a vaulted lanai. The island kitchen is brightened by a bayed window. A U-shaped staircase winds upstairs to a loft, which overlooks the great room and the foyer. Two family bedrooms feature private baths. A computer center and a morning kitchen are located at the end of the hallway.

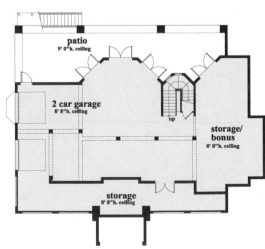

patio
9' 0"h. ceiling

2 car garage
8' 8"h. ceiling

up

storage/ bonus
8' 8"h. ceiling

storage
8' 8"h. ceiling

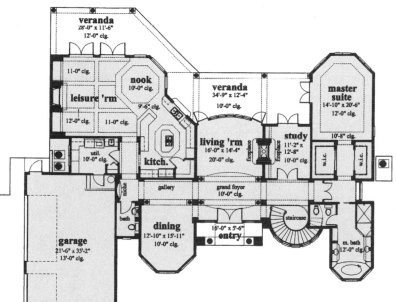

A turret, two-story bay windows and plenty of arched glass impart a graceful style to the exterior while rich amenities furnish contentment inside. A grand foyer decked with columns introduces the living room with a curve of glass windows viewing the rear gardens. The master suite fills the entire right section of the design and enjoys a tray ceiling, two walk-in closets, a separate shower and a garden tub set in a bay window.

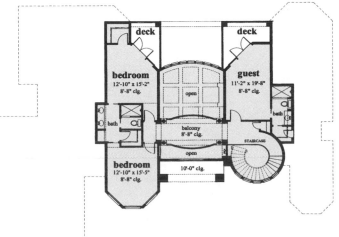

DESIGN

First Floor:
2,841 Square Feet
Second Floor:
1,052 Square Feet
Total Square Footage:
3,893
Bedrooms: 4
Bathrooms: 3½

Width: 85'-0"
Depth: 76'-8"

HPT250046

DESIGN

Entry Vestibule:
374 Square Feet
Main Level:
2,039 Square Feet
Upper Level:
1,426 Square Feet
Total Square Footage:
3,839
Bedrooms: 3
Bathrooms: 4

Width: 56'-0"
Depth: 54'-0"

HPT250047

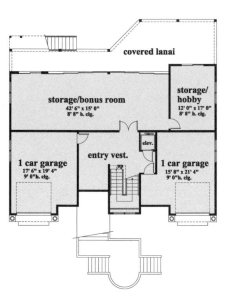

A stunning transom creates a picture-perfect entry and a glorious complement to the arch-top windows with this exquisite villa. The foyer opens to the great room, an inviting environment for crowd-size entertaining or cozy gatherings. A wet bar and three-sided fireplace help define the space. The formal dining room opens to a gourmet kitchen. The upper level is dedicated to the spacious master retreat, packed with luxury amenities. Separate garages on the lower level lead to an entry vestibule with both an elevator and stairs.

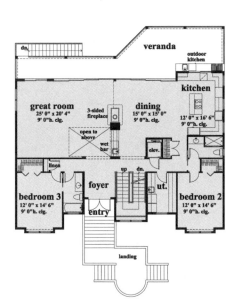

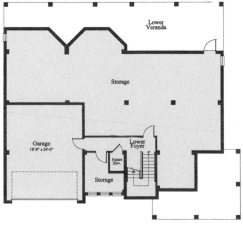

Multiple windows bring natural light to this beautiful home. Arches provide a grand entry to the beam-ceilinged great room, where built-ins flank the fireplace and three sets of French doors open to a covered veranda. Step ceilings grace the master suite and the dining room. Dazzling windows in the dining room allow enjoyment of the outdoors. Two second-floor bedrooms, one with a sun deck, feature walk-in closets and private baths.

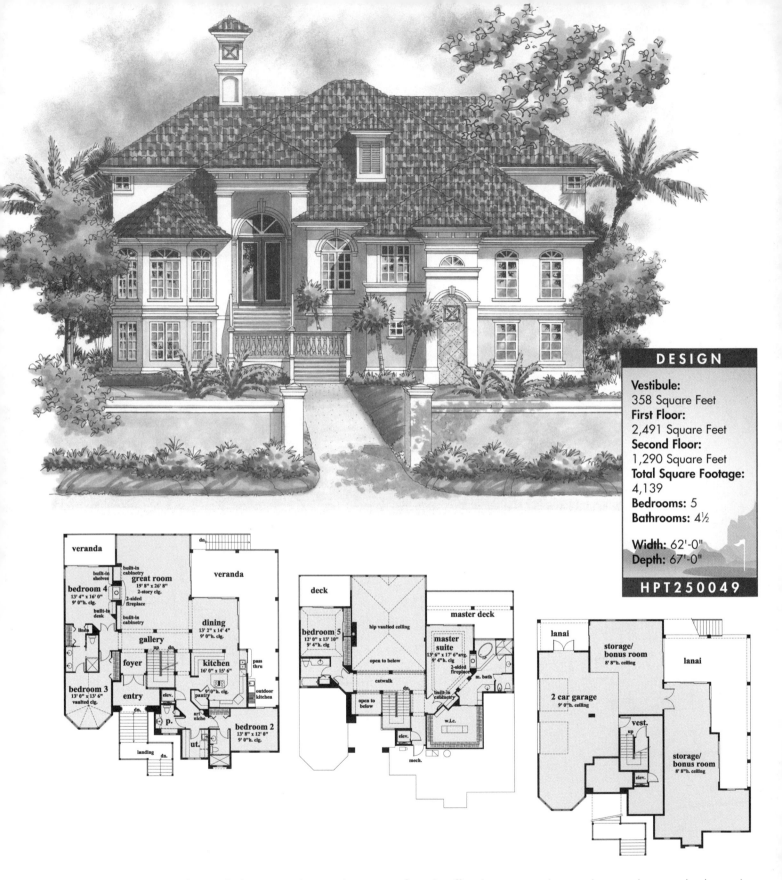

DESIGN

Vestibule:
358 Square Feet
First Floor:
2,491 Square Feet
Second Floor:
1,290 Square Feet
Total Square Footage:
4,139
Bedrooms: 5
Bathrooms: 4½

Width: 62'-0"
Depth: 67'-0"

HPT250049

Chic and glamorous, this Mediterranean facade offers keystone arches, radius windows and a hipped roof. The entry leads to the interior gallery and the great room that is warmed by a two-sided fireplace. Sliding glass doors to a wraparound veranda create great indoor/outdoor flow. The gourmet kitchen easily serves any occasion and provides a pass-through to the outdoor kitchen. The front of the plan also includes a guest suite, which features an oversized shower and ample wardrobe space. Double doors open to the master suite, which features a walk-in closet, two-sided fireplace and angled whirlpool bath.

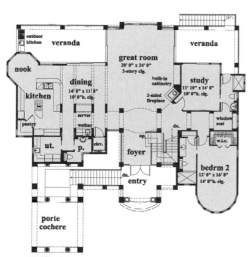

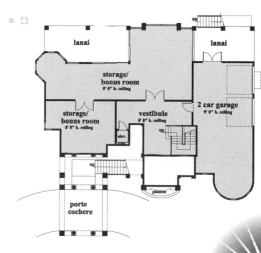

Impressive pillars, keystone lintel arches, a porte cochere and an abundance of windows are just a few of the decorative touches of this elegant design. The two-story foyer leads to a two-story great room, which enjoys built-in cabinetry, a two-sided fireplace and spectacular views to the rear property. To the left of the great room is the dining area, island kitchen and nearby bayed breakfast nook. The second-floor master suite boasts another two-sided fireplace, large walk-in closet, garden tub, separate shower and compartmented toilet.

DESIGN

First Floor:
1,383 Square Feet
Second Floor:
595 Square Feet
Total Square Footage:
1,978
Bonus Space:
617 Square Feet
Bedrooms: 3
Bathrooms: 2

Width: 48'-0"
Depth: 42'-0"

HPT250051

Those who prefer a spacious master suite set apart from the rest of the home will love this arrangement. The top story is devoted to a private master retreat complete with double doors leading to a private porch and a loft that overlooks the vaulted great room below. On the first floor, each of the two family bedrooms has an adjoining porch. The built-ins and fireplace in the great room give a feeling of casual sophistication. The mixture of grand details with a comfortable layout makes this home a perfect combination of elegance and easy living.

A keystone accent tops an elegant presentation of simple architectural details that call up the past. Simple balustrades and broad arches frame a glass-paneled entry. A vaulted foyer leads to the spacious great room. A bay window brightens the master suite and provides views of the veranda and rear property. Two walk-in closets frame a spacious dressing area and announce a luxurious bath with separate vanities and a garden tub. A hall that offers linen storage leads to a quiet study.

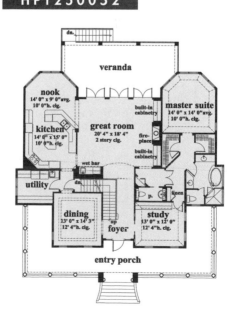

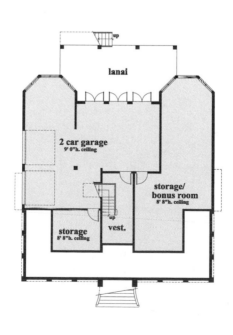

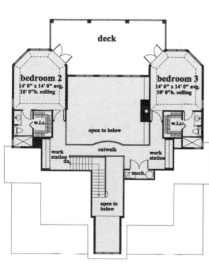

DESIGN

First Floor:
1,383 Square Feet
Second Floor:
595 Square Feet
Total Square Footage:
1,978
Bedrooms: 3
Bathrooms: 2

Width: 48'-0"
Depth: 42'-0"

HPT250053

This fabulous Key West home blends interior space with the great outdoors. Designed for a balmy climate, this home boasts expansive porches and decks—with outside access from every area of the home. The foyer leads to a splendid great room, which features a warming fireplace tucked in beside beautiful built-in cabinetry. Highlighted by a wall of glass that opens to the rear porch, this two-story living space serves as the stunning heart of the home and opens to the formal dining room and a well-appointed kitchen.

REAR VIEW

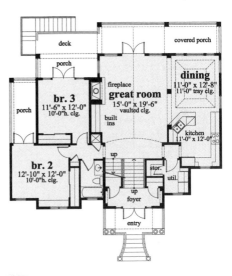

deck

porch

covered porch

porch

fireplace

built ins

great room
15'-0" x 19'-6"
vaulted clg.

dining
11'-0" x 12'-8"
11'-0" tray clg.

kitchen
11'-0" x 12'-0"

br. 3
11'-6" x 12'-0"
10'-0"h. clg.

br. 2
12'-10" x 12'-0"
10'-0"h. clg.

up

up
foyer

stor.

util.

entry

porch

master suite
12'-8" x 17'-8"
10'-0" tray clg.

open to below

w.i.c.

overlook

dn

dn

master bath

dn

porch

2 car garage

bonus/
storage

storage

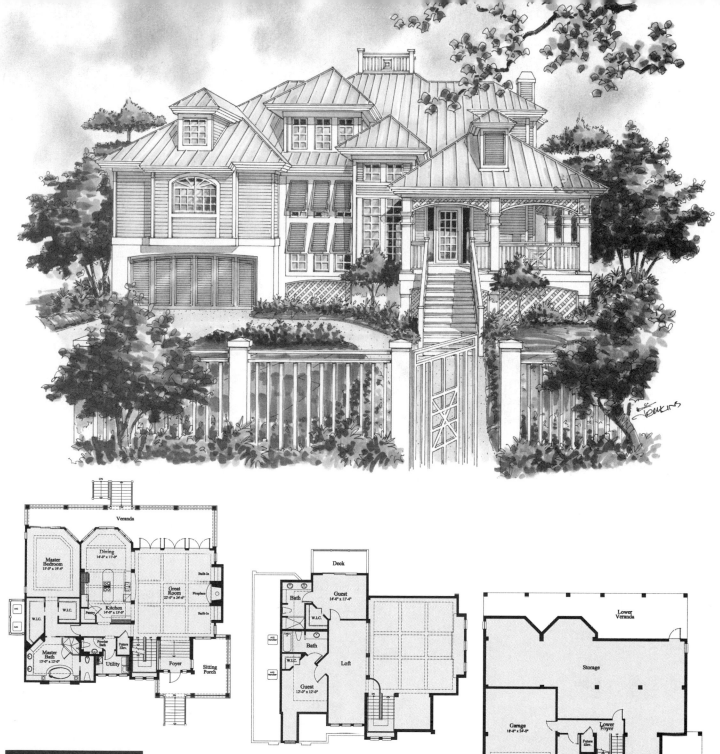

DESIGN

First Floor:
2,096 Square Feet
Second Floor:
892 Square Feet
Total Square Footage:
2,988
Storage:
1,295 Square Feet
Bedrooms: 3
Bathrooms: 3½

Width: 58'-0"
Depth: 56'-0"

HPT250054

The variety in the rooflines of this striking waterfront home will certainly make it the envy of the neighborhood. The two-story great room, with its fireplace and built-ins, is a short flight down from the foyer. The three sets of French doors give access to the covered lanai. The huge and well-equipped kitchen will easily serve the gourmet who loves to entertain. The step ceiling and bay window of the dining room will add style to every meal. The master suite completes the first level. Two bedrooms and two full baths, along with an expansive loft, constitute the second level. Bedroom 3 has an attached sun deck.

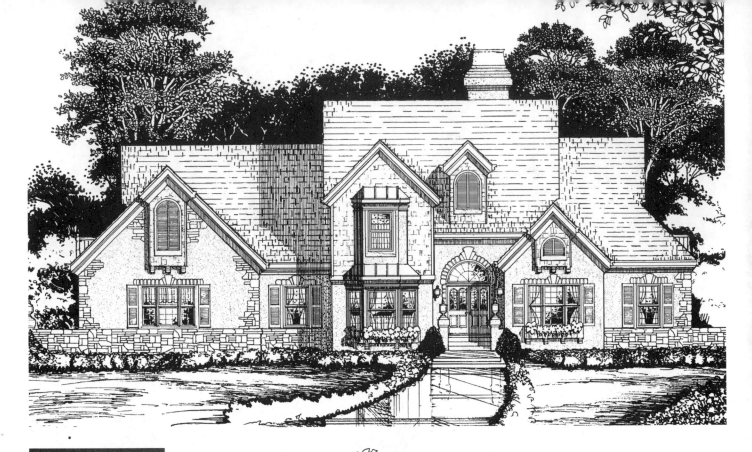

DESIGN

First Floor:
2,921 Square Feet
Second Floor:
1,640 Square Feet
Total Square Footage:
4,561
Bedrooms: 4
Bathrooms: 4½+½

Width: 85'-0"
Depth: 56'-0"

HPT250055

Corner quoins, a bay window and keystone lintels adorn this charming four-bedroom home. Inside, a tiled foyer provides a view of the living room, dining room and rear patio. Graceful columns define the dining room from the foyer and living room. The master suite and a study reside to the right of the plan. The hearth-warmed family room, bayed breakfast nook and island kitchen share an open plan. On the second level, three family bedrooms enjoy a balcony view of the living room and foyer. Note Bedroom 4 features a private bathroom—perfect for a guest or mother-in-law suite.

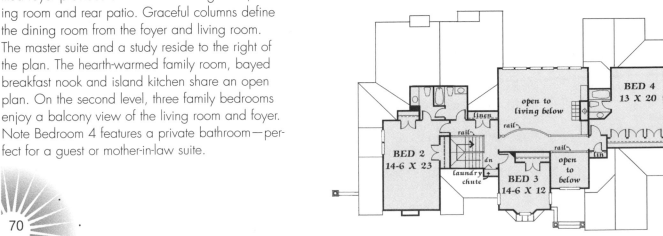

J.N. HANSEN S.D.G.

DESIGN

First Floor:
1,667 Square Feet
Second Floor:
333 Square Feet
Total Square Footage:
2,000
Bedrooms: 3
Bathrooms: 3

Width: 60'-8"
Depth: 70'-4"

HPT250056

This unique design features a touch of tradition with warm brick accents, bay windows and dormers, while its floor plan is big on entertaining spaces. The kitchen, with its huge walk-in pantry, overlooks the bayed nook, which offers wonderful views of the outdoor living space. The master suite is secluded on the right side of the home and is complete with a tray ceiling, bayed sitting area, and a well-appointed bath with His and Hers closets, a double vanity, corner spa and private toilet chamber.

REAR VIEW

With a tremendous rear porch and deck, this home is sure to please any golf-watcher in the family. From its foyer, a study/bedroom opens to the left and features access to a bath. The spacious great room offers a fireplace, built-ins, a wall of windows and access to the outdoors. Another area worth noting is the basement. The rooms here can be used as either a garage/storage area and a bedroom, office or hobby room, and also access the backyard. As for the rest of the house, amenities abound in the master suite, efficient kitchen and hobby room off of the garage. Please specify crawlspace or slab foundation when ordering.

DESIGN

Main Floor:
2,650 Square Feet
Finished Basement:
409 Square Feet
Total Square Footage:
3,059
Bedrooms: 4
Bathrooms: 4

Width: 79'-0"
Depth: 77'-8"

HPT250057

This home, as shown in the photograph, may differ from the actual blueprints.
For more detailed information, please check the floor plans carefully.

Photo by Living Concepts Home Planning

With rustic rafter tails, sturdy pillars and a siding-and-shingle facade, this welcoming bungalow offers plenty of curb appeal. Inside, the formal dining room is to the left of the foyer, and gives easy access to the angled kitchen. A spacious gathering room offers a fireplace, built-ins, a gorgeous wall of windows and access to a covered terrace. Located on the first floor for privacy, the master suite is lavish with its amenities. Upstairs, two suites offer private baths and share a linkside retreat that includes a covered veranda.

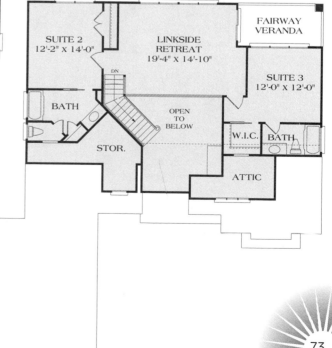

DESIGN

First Floor:
1,661 Square Feet
Second Floor:
882 Square Feet
Total Square Footage:
2,543
Bedrooms: 3
Bathrooms: 2½

Width: 59'-0"
Depth: 58'-11"

HPT250058

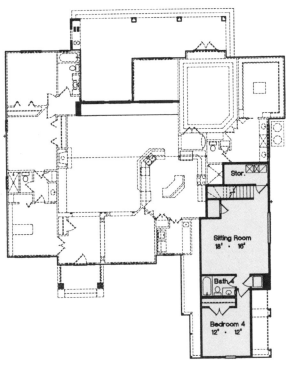

DESIGN

First Floor:
2,837 Square Feet
Second Floor:
609 Square Feet
Total Square Footage:
3,446
Bedrooms: 4
Bathrooms: 4

Width: 68'-0"
Depth: 83'-4"

HPT250059

Gable-on-gable details and an entry adorned with thick columns create a distinctly interesting exterior for this four-bedroom home. The den and formal dining room take their traditional position near the entry for this design. The great room enjoys a warming fireplace at the center of the plan. To the left are two family bedrooms and to the right is the gourmet kitchen and breakfast nook. The luxurious master suite includes many amenities, including a tray ceiling, walk-in closet, French-door access to the rear patio and a sumptuous bathroom with a corner oval soaking tub. Bedroom 4 features a full bath and a sitting room on the second floor.

DESIGN

Total Square Footage:
1,997
Bonus Room:
310 Square Feet
Bedrooms: 2/3
Bathrooms: 2½

Width: 64'-4"
Depth: 63'-0"

HPT250060

The center of this charming plan is the spacious kitchen with an island and serving bar. The nearby breakfast nook accesses the greenhouse with its wall of windows and three large skylights. A built-in media center beside a warming fireplace is the focal point of the family room. Bedroom 2 shares a full bath with the den/study, which might also be a third bedroom. The master suite features large His and Hers vanity sinks, a corner tub with an open walk-in shower, and a supersized walk-in closet. Future space over the garage can expand the living space as your family grows. Please specify basement, crawlspace or slab foundation when ordering.

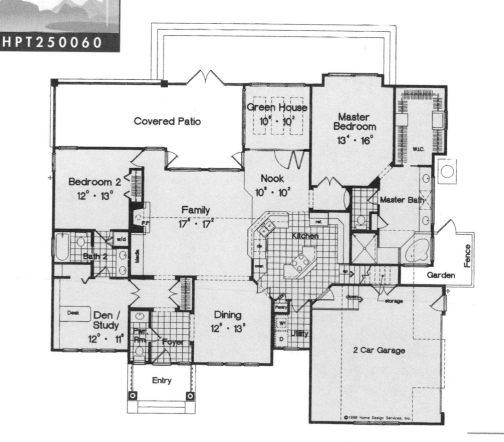

Covered Patio

Green House
10⁸ · 10²

Master Bedroom
13⁴ · 16⁰

W.I.C.

Bedroom 2
12⁰ · 13⁰

Nook
10⁸ · 10²

Family
17⁸ · 17²

Master Bath

Kitchen

Garden

Fence

w/d

Bath 2

Den / Study
12⁰ · 11⁸

Desk

Pwr. Rm.

Foyer

Dining
12⁰ · 13⁰

Pantry

Utility

storage

2 Car Garage

Entry

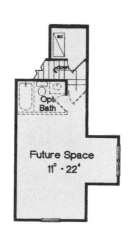

Future Space
11⁰ · 22⁴

Opt. Bath

3 SEASON PORCH
CATHEDRAL CEILING
11'8" X 11'8"

COVERED PORCH
20'0" X 9'8"

WINDOW SEAT

NK.
14'8 X 13'0"

DW
KIT.
13'4" X 13'0"
ISLAND

PANTRY

GRT.RM.
22'6" X 16'2"

DN

UP

BUTLER PAN.

D. W.

E.
2 STORY CEILING

DIN./DEN
13'4" X 15'10"

3 CAR GAR.
23'8" X 34'4"

MBR.
18'4" X 16'6"

B.R.#2
12'2" X 13'6"

DN.

B.R.#4/
BONUS RM.
16'6" X 15'4"

OPEN TO
E.

PLANT LEDGE

UP

B.R.#3
CATHEDRAL CEILING
13'0" X 12'8"

This two-story family home welcomes you from the elements with a covered front-door entrance. When entering the home, you will find a two-story foyer with an open staircase to the second floor. This home offers a den that can be converted to a formal dining room and features a butler's pantry. The enormous great room flows into the kitchen nook and includes a gorgeous window seat and fireplace. The second floor includes a total of four bedrooms and a full bath. The master suite offers a vast walk-in closet and a whirlpool tub.

DESIGN

First Floor:
1,682 Square Feet
Second Floor:
1,226 Square Feet
Total Square Footage:
2,908
Bedrooms: 3/4
Bathrooms: 2½

Width: 60'-0"
Depth: 60'-8"

HPT250061

PATIO

SCREEN PORCH
VAULTED CEILING
16'0"x16'0"

FAM. RM.
VAULTED CEILING
18'0"x20'0"

WOOD DECK
32'4"x15'8"

KIT.
15'0"x19'0"

NK
10'8"x11'0"

LIV. RM.
2-STORY CATHEDRAL CEILING
21'4"x11'6"

M.B.R.
16'4"x23'6"

2 CAR GAR.
35'8"x23'0"

DIN. RM.
13'8"x14'8"

E.
2 STORY

DEN
14'0"x17'0"

2 CAR GAR.
20'0"x24'0"

BONUS ROOM
26'6"x22'8"

B.R. #2
15'2"x13'6"

OPEN TO
LIV.

B.R. #3
13'6"x11'0"

OPEN TO
E.

DESIGN

First Floor:
3,033 Square Feet
Second Floor:
700 Square Feet
Total Square Footage:
3,733
Bedrooms: 3
Bathrooms: 3½

Width: 99'-0"
Depth: 87'-0"

HPT250062

This stunning French/country two-story home will impress you with its unique character and substantial square footage. The comfort of a fireplace is enjoyed in the den, master bedroom, living room and family room. The living room boasts a two-story cathedral ceiling and French doors that lead you to the deck. The kitchen opens to the family room for easy entertaining. The master suite offers two walk-in closets and twin vanities.

The exterior of this home is sure to get attention with its Victorian turret and ribbon of windows. The three-car garage, a tiled powder room, utility room and kitchen take up the left side of the plan. Inside the kitchen, a cooktop island and plenty of counter space provide room for meal preparation. The family room features a built-in media center and an optional fireplace. Four bedrooms, three full baths and a vaulted family room occupy the second floor. French doors open to the master bedroom where the fireplace and private balcony satisfy a high standard of living. Please specify basement or slab foundation when ordering.

78

DESIGN

First Floor:
1,474 Square Feet
Second Floor:
1,554 Square Feet
Total Square Footage:
3,028
Bedrooms: 4
Bathrooms: 3½

Width: 76'-8"
Depth: 52'-8"

HPT250063

This striking example of Gothic Victorian design features curved porches, vergeboard details and gables topped by finials. To the left of the foyer is the formal dining room; to the right is a combination living room/family room with a bay window and a fireplace. The kitchen shares a snack bar with a small sitting or media room that opens to the covered back porch. Upstairs, three bedrooms—one with a walk-in closet—share a full bath that includes double vanities and a raised corner tub. This home is designed with a basement foundation.

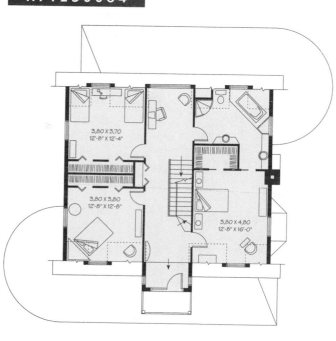

This home, as shown in the photograph, may differ from the actual blueprints.
For more detailed information, please check the floor plans carefully.

Photo by Bob Greenspan

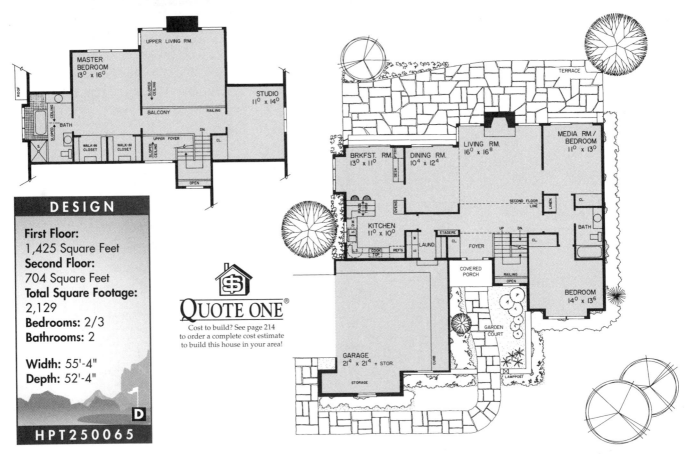

DESIGN

First Floor:
1,425 Square Feet
Second Floor:
704 Square Feet
Total Square Footage:
2,129
Bedrooms: 2/3
Bathrooms: 2

Width: 55'-4"
Depth: 52'-4"

HPT250065

QUOTE ONE®
Cost to build? See page 214
to order a complete cost estimate
to build this house in your area!

This charming Tudor adaptation features a complete second-floor master bedroom suite with a private bath, a balcony overlooking the living room, and a studio. The first floor contains a convenient kitchen with a pass-through to the breakfast room. There's also a formal dining room just steps away. An adjacent rear living room enjoys its own fireplace. Other features include a rear media room or optional bedroom. Another bedroom enjoys an excellent front view.

This home, as shown in the photograph, may differ from the actual blueprints. For more detailed information, please check the floor plans carefully.

Photo by Bob Greenspan

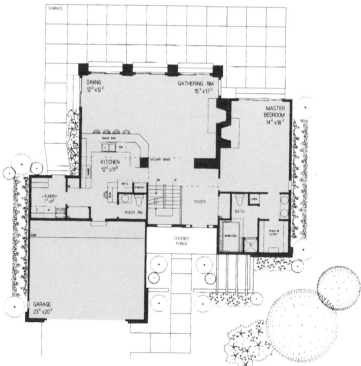

DESIGN

First Floor:
1,414 Square Feet
Second Floor:
620 Square Feet
Total Square Footage:
2,034
Bedrooms: 3
Bathrooms: 2½

Width: 53'-0"
Depth: 51'-8"

HPT250066

QUOTE ONE®
Cost to build? See page 214
to order a complete cost estimate
to build this house in your area!

Attractive, contemporary split-bedroom planning makes the most of this plan. The master suite pampers with a lavish bath and a fireplace. The living areas are open and have easy access to the rear terrace. Note, in particular, the convenient snack bar between the kitchen and the gathering room/dining room. A large laundry area and washroom separate the main house from the garage. A balcony overlook on the second floor allows views to the gathering room or to the entry foyer.

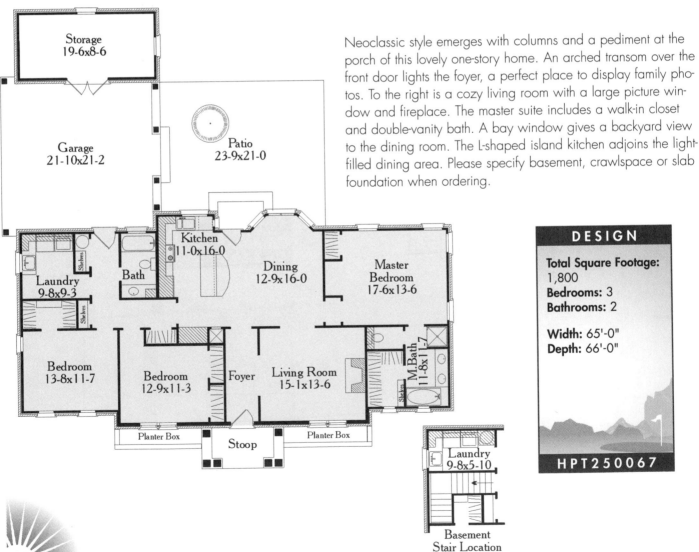

Storage
19-6x8-6

Garage
21-10x21-2

Patio
23-9x21-0

Kitchen
11-0x16-0

Dining
12-9x16-0

Master
Bedroom
17-6x13-6

Laundry
9-8x9-3

Bath

Bedroom
13-8x11-7

Bedroom
12-9x11-3

Foyer

Living Room
15-1x13-6

M.Bath
11-8x1-7

Planter Box

Stoop

Planter Box

Laundry
9-8x5-10

Basement
Stair Location

Neoclassic style emerges with columns and a pediment at the porch of this lovely one-story home. An arched transom over the front door lights the foyer, a perfect place to display family photos. To the right is a cozy living room with a large picture window and fireplace. The master suite includes a walk-in closet and double-vanity bath. A bay window gives a backyard view to the dining room. The L-shaped island kitchen adjoins the light-filled dining area. Please specify basement, crawlspace or slab foundation when ordering.

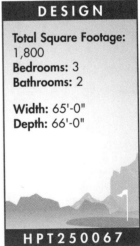

DESIGN

Total Square Footage:
1,800
Bedrooms: 3
Bathrooms: 2

Width: 65'-0"
Depth: 66'-0"

HPT250067

This elegant, symmetrical home features a gabled porch complemented by columns. The breakfast room, adjacent to the kitchen, opens to a rear porch. The spacious great room provides a fireplace and a view of the patio. A lovely bayed window brightens the master suite, which includes a walk-in closet and a bath with a garden tub and a separate shower. Two secondary bedrooms each offer a private bath. A winding staircase leads to second-level future space. Please specify basement, crawlspace or slab foundation when ordering.

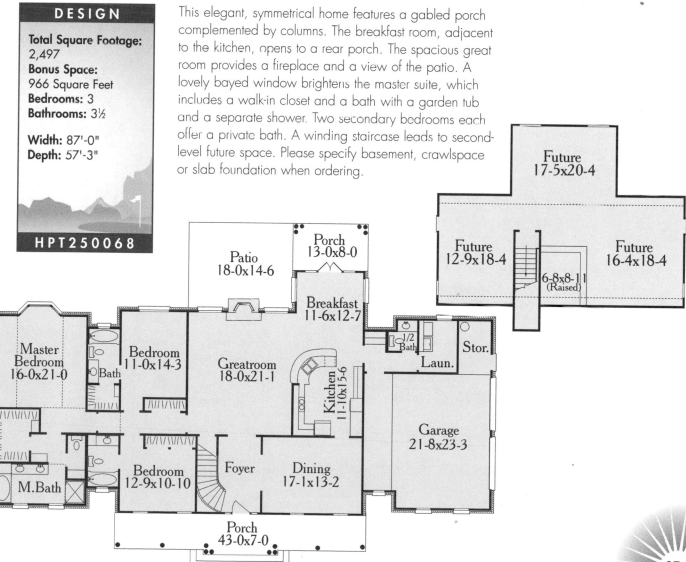

European details highlight this attractive compact exterior. The two-story foyer opens to a wide hallway with a coat closet and an elegant stairway. To the left, the den/living room features built-in cabinets. The dining room is to the right near the kitchen. Here, the family chef will appreciate a work island/snack bar combination, a walk-in pantry and a corner window sink. A bayed nook offers access to a screened porch. The great room has an impressive fireplace flanked by cabinets. The master suite boasts two closets, a garden tub and a dual-sink vanity.

SCREEN PORCH 12'6" X 16'0"

COVERED PORCH

MBR. 17'8" X 15'0"

GRT. RM. 18'8" X 14'6" CATHEDRAL CEILING

NK. 10'6" X 14'6" TRAY CEILING

KIT. 13'0 X 13'0

ISLAND

PANTRY

STOR. 1'8"X10'0"

BUILT-IN CABINETS

DEN/ LIV. 12'-1 1/8" CEILING 13'0" X 16'0"

F. 2 STORY CEILING

DIN. 12'8" X 13'0"

3 CAR GAR. 23'4" X 33'8"

ARCH

OPEN TO GRT. RM.

BR. #2 18'8" X 11'0"

STUDY AREA

OPEN TO F.

BR. #3 12'8" X 16'10"

OPTIONAL BR. #4 11'4" X 31'4"

DESIGN

First Floor: 2,172 Square Feet

Second Floor: 690 Square Feet

Total Square Footage: 2,862

Bonus Room: 450 Square Feet

Bedrooms: 3/4

Bathrooms: 2½

Width: 72'-0"

Depth: 73'-0"

HPT250069

Though designed as a grand estate, this home retains the warmth of a country manor with intimate details. A continuous vaulted ceiling follows from the family room through the kitchen and nook. The ceiling soars even higher in the bonus room with a sun deck upstairs. Two exquisitely appointed family bedrooms, with window seats and walk-in closets, share a full bath. The master suite includes pampering details such as a juice bar, a media wall and walk-in closets.

DESIGN

Total Square Footage:
2,816
Bonus Room:
290 Square Feet
Bedrooms: 3
Bathrooms: 3½ +½

Width: 94'-0"
Depth: 113'-5"

HPT250070

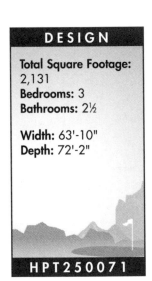

DESIGN

Total Square Footage:
2,131
Bedrooms: 3
Bathrooms: 2½

Width: 63'-10"
Depth: 72'-2"

HPT250071

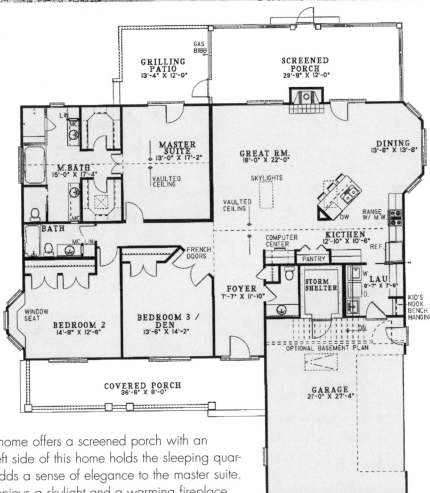

GAS BIBB

GRILLING PATIO
13'-4" X 12'-0"

SCREENED PORCH
29'-8" X 12'-0"

LIN

MC

MASTER SUITE
13'-0" X 17'-2"

GREAT RM.
18'-0" X 22'-0"

DINING
13'-8" X 13'-8"

M. BATH
15'-0" X 17'-4"

VAULTED CEILING

SKYLIGHTS

VAULTED CEILING

KICTHEN
12'-10" X 10'-6"

RANGE W/ M.W.

BATH

MC LIN

COMPUTER CENTER

PANTRY

REF.

DW

FRENCH DOORS

FOYER
7'-7" X 11'-10"

STORM SHELTER

LAU.
8'-7" X 7'-8"

KID'S NOOK BENCH / HANGING

WINDOW SEAT

BEDROOM 2
14'-8" X 12'-6"

BEDROOM 3 / DEN
13'-6" X 14'-2"

OPTIONAL BASEMENT PLAN

COVERED PORCH
36'-8" X 8'-0"

GARAGE
21'-0" X 27'-4"

This charming three-bedroom home offers a screened porch with an adjoining grilling patio. The left side of this home holds the sleeping quarters where a vaulted ceiling adds a sense of elegance to the master suite. On the right, the great room enjoys a skylight and a warming fireplace. The angled kitchen has a work island with a skylight above while the dining area has a bay window, as does one of the two family bedrooms. Please specify basement, crawlspace or slab foundation when ordering.

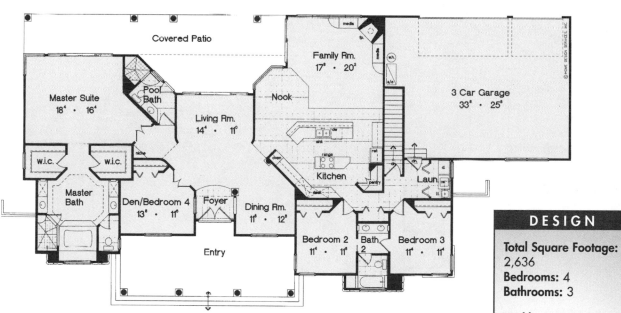

Covered Patio

Master Suite
18⁴ • 16⁴

Pool Bath

Family Rm.
17⁸ • 20²

3 Car Garage
33⁸ • 25⁸

Living Rm.
14⁴ • 11⁶

Nook

w.i.c.   w.i.c.

Master Bath

Den/Bedroom 4
13⁸ • 11⁶

Foyer

Dining Rm.
11⁸ • 12⁸

Kitchen

Laun.

Entry

Bedroom 2
11⁴ • 11⁸

Bath 2

Bedroom 3
11⁴ • 11⁸

DESIGN

Total Square Footage:
2,636

Bedrooms: 4

Bathrooms: 3

Width: 96'-6"
Depth: 52'-4"

HPT250072

This home takes up a commanding view with the country porch and stone accents. Upon entering, views throughout the home are possible as this plan reaches out in all directions. The living room has a wall of glass to the covered patio, and the dining room, with its decorative columns and angular wall, creates an impressive space. The master wing of this home sits just past the den/Bedroom 4 and pool bath, and is welcomed through double doors with a decorative niche nearby. Large glass expanses again take advantage of the rear garden areas.

DESIGN

First Floor:
1,858 Square Feet
Second Floor:
822 Square Feet
Total Square Footage:
2,680
Bonus Room:
364 Square Feet
Bedrooms: 4
Bathrooms: 3½

Width: 72'-0"
Depth: 82'-0"

HPT250073

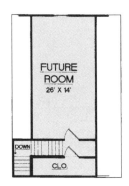

FUTURE
ROOM
26' X 14'

DOWN

CLO.

Elegance through symmetry is created with triple dormers and arch-top windows crowning a wide covered porch that is flanked by a pair of French doors—each with a fanlight window above. The entry, with the dining room to the right and a music room to the left, opens to the living room with a warming fireplace and sliding glass doors that access the rear porch and deck. The U-shaped kitchen adjoins the sunny eating area. The master suite delights with a sitting area, a lavish bath and a private patio. Please specify basement, crawlspace or slab foundation when ordering.

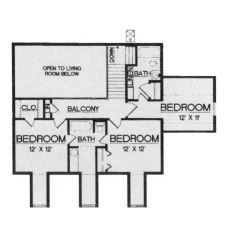

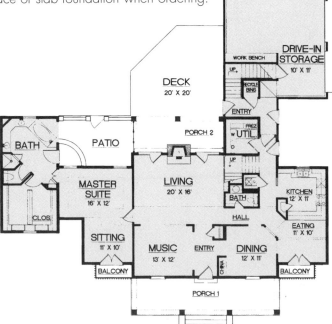

DECK

GRILLING PORCH
18'-0" X 12'-0"

BEDROOM 2
12'-2" X 12'-2"

DINING / HEARTH ROOM
13'-0" X 19'-6"

ATRIUM DOORS

LAU.
13'-8" X 6'-8"

D W

BATH

PAN

DW

REF

M. BATH
13'-8" X 7'-4"

GARAGE
20'-8" X 21'-4"

KITCHEN
14'-5" X 18'-6"

RG

CLAWFOOT TUB

BEDROOM 3
12'-2" X 12'-2"

LIVING RM.
21'-0" X 16'-0"

MASTER SUITE
13'-8" X 13'-10"

UP

MEDIA CENTER

8' COVERED PORCH

Two fireplaces bring warmth to this inviting three-bedroom home which offers an expansive wrap-around porch for a feeling of Southern hospitality. The living room has a fireplace partnered with a built-in media center. The L-shaped kitchen enjoys an angled island that boasts a snack bar for casual dining. The sunny hearth/dining room has a view of the deck and rear property. Two family bedrooms rest on the left where they share a full bath while the master suite finds seclusion and privacy on the right. Please specify basement, crawlspace or slab foundation when ordering.

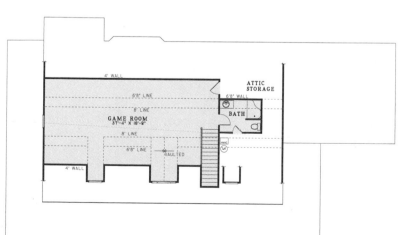

4' WALL

6'8" LINE

8' LINE

GAME ROOM
37'-4" X 18'-8"

8' LINE

6'8" LINE

VAULTED

4' WALL

ATTIC STORAGE

6'8" WALL

BATH

DESIGN

Total Square Footage:
1,921
Bonus Space:
812 Square Feet
Bedrooms: 3
Bathrooms: 3

Width: 84'-0"
Depth: 55'-6"

HPT250074

REAR VIEW

DESIGN

Main Floor:
2,711 Square Feet
Finished Basement:
948 Square Feet
Total Square Footage:
3,659
Bedrooms: 4
Bathrooms: 3½

Width: 122'-10"
Depth: 75'-5"

HPT250075

Spacious, attractive and perfect for lakeside living, this home is sure to please. A sunken great room features a warming fireplace and access to the rear covered deck. The efficient kitchen offers a breakfast room as well as easy access to the formal dining room. A sitting room nearby provides a built-in computer desk area. The lavish master suite includes two walk-in closets, a lavish bath and access to a rear deck. Downstairs, a third family bedroom is perfect for a guest suite. Please specify crawlspace or slab foundation when ordering.

High Expectations
Homes with mountain views

Once again do I behold these steep and lofty cliffs, that on a wild secluded scene impress thoughts of more deep seclusion; and connect the landscape with the quiet of the sky.

—William Wordsworth

DESIGN

Main Level:
1,635 Square Feet
Lower Level:
1,437 Square Feet
Total Square Footage:
3,072
Bedrooms: 4
Bathrooms: 3

Width: 62'-0"
Depth: 36'-0"

HPT250076

This beautiful chalet vacation home abounds with views of the outdoors and provides a grand deck, creating additional living space. With its entry on the lower level, you'll find two family bedrooms that share a full bath, an office/study and a family room with a warming fireplace. There's an extra room here which could be a third family bedroom or perhaps a library or study. Upstairs, a great room with a cathedral ceiling shares a through-fireplace with the formal dining room. This home is designed with a basement foundation.

A standing-seam metal roof, horizontal siding and a massive deck combine to create a mosaic of parallel lines on this rustic two-story home. Sunlight spills into the great room through four beautiful clerestory windows. A generous L-shaped kitchen with a work island adjoins the dining area. A bedroom and powder room are neatly tucked behind the staircase that leads to the second-floor sleeping quarters. The focal point of this design is the generous number of windows offering views of the outdoors in every direction. This home is designed with a basement foundation.

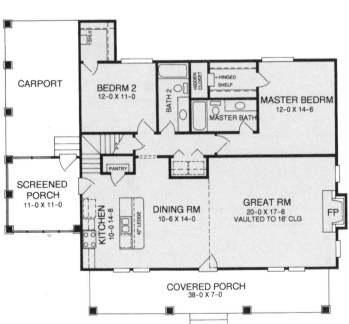

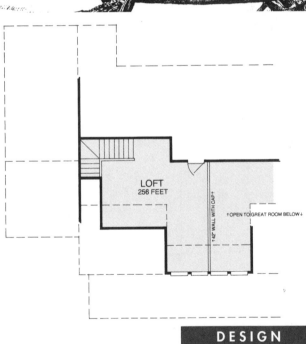

This rustic Craftsman-style cottage provides an open interior with good outdoor flow. The front covered porch invites casual gatherings, while inside, the dining area is set for both everyday and planned occasions. To the right a centered fireplace in the great room shares its warmth with the dining room. On the left, the kitchen connects to the dining room with an island pass-through and includes a vast pantry. A rear hall leads to the master suite with a full private bath and a walk-in closet.

DESIGN

Total Square Footage:
1,404
Bonus Room:
256 Square Feet
Bedrooms: 2
Bathrooms: 2

Width: 54'-7"
Depth: 46'-6"

HPT250078

This contemporary four-season cottage offers plenty of windows to take in great views. Excellent for gatherings, the living room boasts a cathedral ceiling and a cozy fireplace. The compartmented entry features a coat closet. The U-shaped kitchen includes a built-in pantry and accesses a side porch. Upstairs, two family bedrooms share a hall bath. A balcony hall leads to a sitting area with views of the front property. This home is designed with a basement foundation.

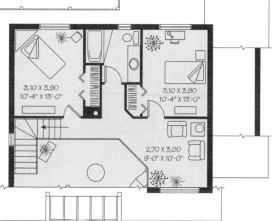

DESIGN

First Floor:
946 Square Feet
Second Floor:
604 Square Feet
Total Square Footage:
1,550
Bedrooms: 3
Bathrooms: 2

Width: 37'-0"
Depth: 30'-8"

HPT250079

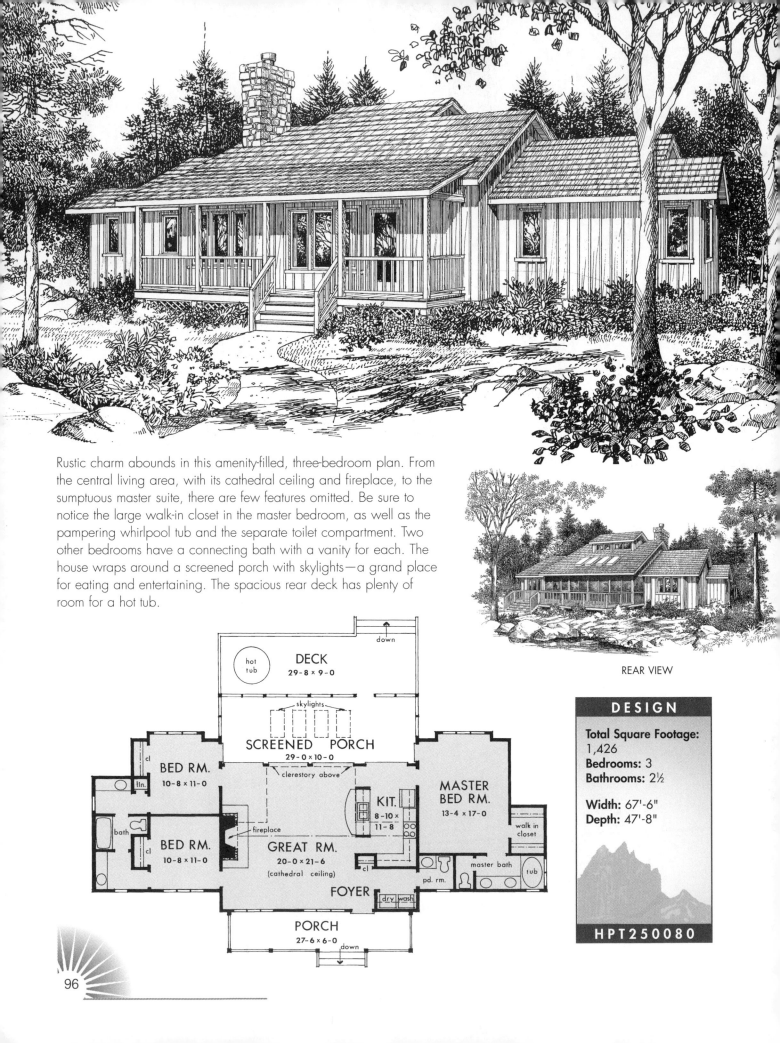

Rustic charm abounds in this amenity-filled, three-bedroom plan. From the central living area, with its cathedral ceiling and fireplace, to the sumptuous master suite, there are few features omitted. Be sure to notice the large walk-in closet in the master bedroom, as well as the pampering whirlpool tub and the separate toilet compartment. Two other bedrooms have a connecting bath with a vanity for each. The house wraps around a screened porch with skylights—a grand place for eating and entertaining. The spacious rear deck has plenty of room for a hot tub.

REAR VIEW

DECK
29-8 × 9-0
hot tub
down

skylights

SCREENED PORCH
29-0 × 10-0
clerestory above

BED RM.
10-8 × 11-0
cl
lin.

bath

BED RM.
10-8 × 11-0
cl

fireplace

KIT.
8-10 ×
11-8

MASTER BED RM.
13-4 × 17-0

walk in closet

GREAT RM.
20-0 × 21-6
(cathedral ceiling)

cl

master bath

pd. rm.

tub

FOYER

dry wash

PORCH
27-6 × 6-0
down

DESIGN

Total Square Footage:
1,426
Bedrooms: 3
Bathrooms: 2½

Width: 67'-6"
Depth: 47'-8"

HPT250080

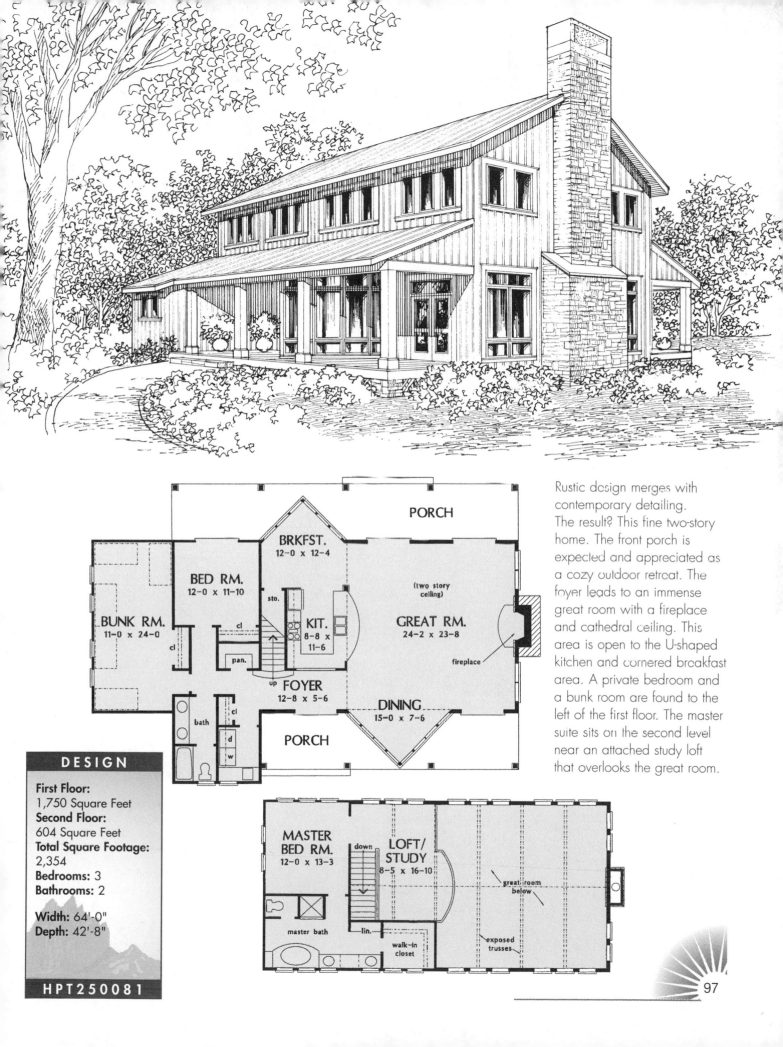

PORCH

BRKFST.
12-0 x 12-4

BED RM.
12-0 x 11-10

sto.

BUNK RM.
11-0 x 24-0

cl

cl

KIT.
8-8 x
11-6

(two story
ceiling)

GREAT RM.
24-2 x 23-8

pan.

fireplace

up FOYER
12-8 x 5-6

DINING
15-0 x 7-6

bath

cl

d

w

PORCH

Rustic design merges with contemporary detailing. The result? This fine two-story home. The front porch is expected and appreciated as a cozy outdoor retreat. The foyer leads to an immense great room with a fireplace and cathedral ceiling. This area is open to the U-shaped kitchen and cornered breakfast area. A private bedroom and a bunk room are found to the left of the first floor. The master suite sits on the second level near an attached study loft that overlooks the great room.

MASTER
BED RM.
12-0 x 13-3

down

LOFT/
STUDY
8-5 x 16-10

great room
below

master bath

lin.

walk-in
closet

exposed
trusses

DESIGN

First Floor:
1,750 Square Feet
Second Floor:
604 Square Feet
Total Square Footage:
2,354
Bedrooms: 3
Bathrooms: 2

Width: 64'-0"
Depth: 42'-8"

HPT250081

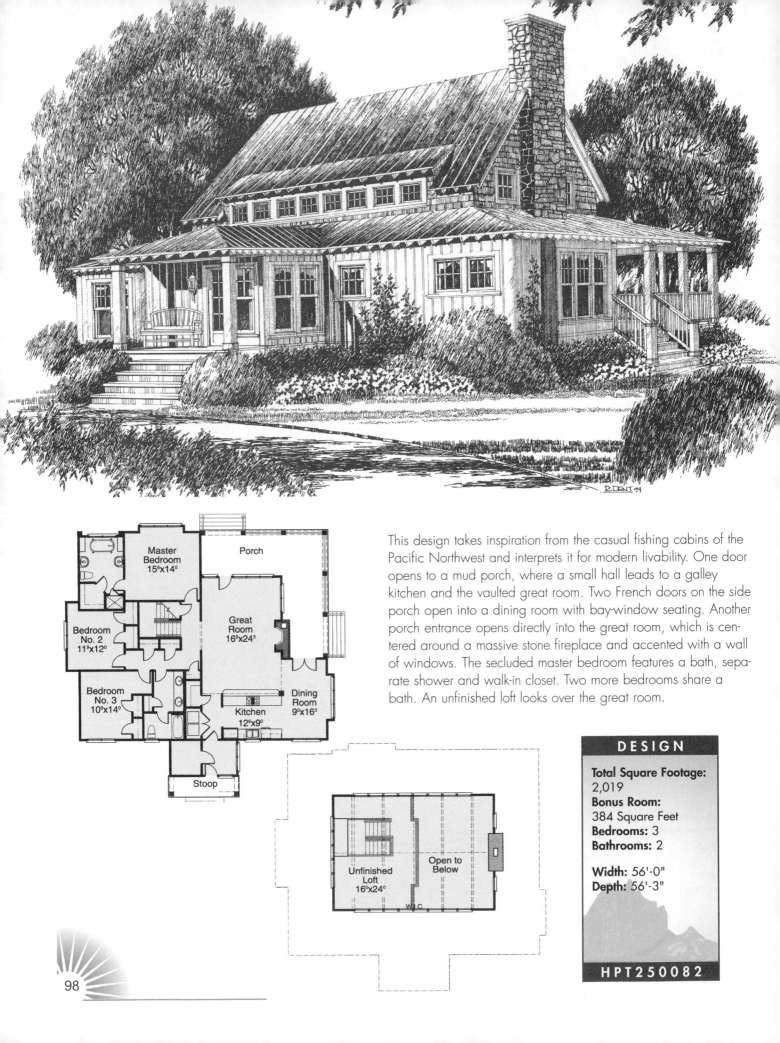

This design takes inspiration from the casual fishing cabins of the Pacific Northwest and interprets it for modern livability. One door opens to a mud porch, where a small hall leads to a galley kitchen and the vaulted great room. Two French doors on the side porch open into a dining room with bay-window seating. Another porch entrance opens directly into the great room, which is centered around a massive stone fireplace and accented with a wall of windows. The secluded master bedroom features a bath, separate shower and walk-in closet. Two more bedrooms share a bath. An unfinished loft looks over the great room.

Master Bedroom 15⁶x14⁰

Porch

Bedroom No. 2 11⁹x12⁰

Great Room 16⁹x24³

Bedroom No. 3 10⁹x14⁰

Kitchen 12⁶x9⁰

Dining Room 9⁰x16³

Stoop

Unfinished Loft 16⁰x24⁰

Open to Below

W.I.C.

DESIGN

Total Square Footage: 2,019

Bonus Room: 384 Square Feet

Bedrooms: 3

Bathrooms: 2

Width: 56'-0"

Depth: 56'-3"

HPT250082

B. NATHAN

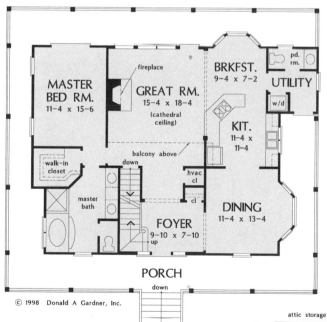

MASTER BED RM.
11-4 x 15-6

GREAT RM.
15-4 x 18-4
(cathedral ceiling)

fireplace

BRKFST.
9-4 x 7-2

pd. rm.

UTILITY

w/d

KIT.
11-4 x 11-4

walk-in closet

balcony above

down

hvac cl

cl

master bath

DINING
11-4 x 13-4

FOYER
9-10 x 7-10
up

PORCH

down

© 1998 Donald A Gardner, Inc.

great room below

attic storage

attic storage

BED RM.
11-4 x 11-2

railing

BED RM.
11-4 x 11-2

down

cl

cl

bath

cl

cl

attic sto.

foyer below

attic storage

An enchanting wraparound porch, delightful dormers and bright bay windows create excitement inside and out for this coastal home. The large center dormer brightens the vaulted foyer, while the great room with a cathedral ceiling enjoys added light from a trio of rear clerestory windows. A balcony dividing the second-floor bedrooms overlooks the great room and visually connects the two floors. The master suite is located on the first floor. The second-floor bedrooms, each with a dormer alcove, share a hall bath that includes a dual-sink vanity.

DESIGN

First Floor:
1,362 Square Feet
Second Floor:
481 Square Feet
Total Square Footage:
1,843
Bedrooms: 3
Bathrooms: 2½

Width: 49'-4"
Depth: 44'-10"

HPT250083

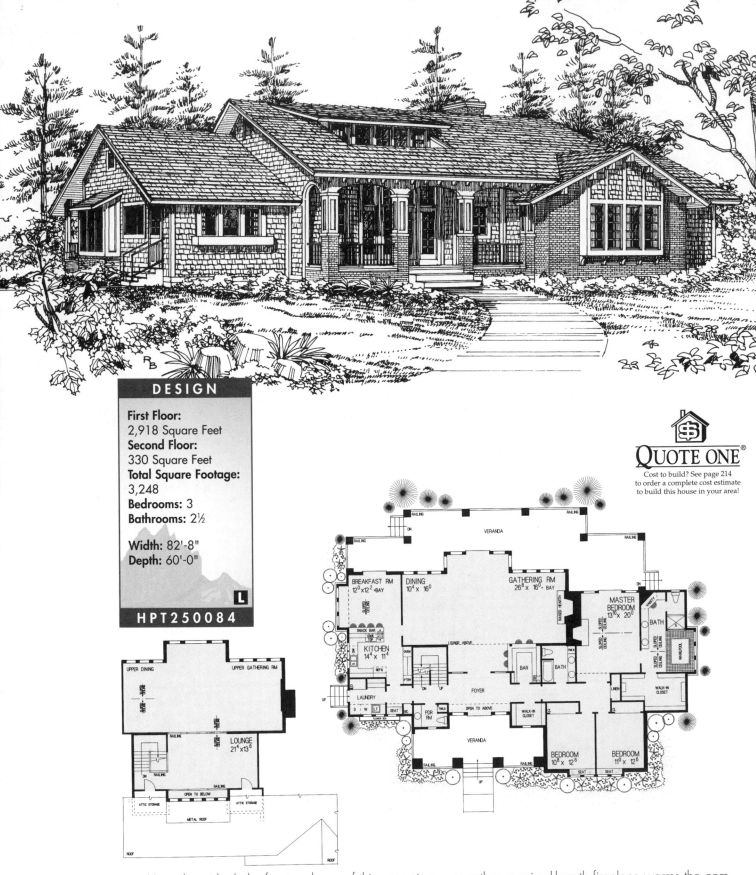

DESIGN

First Floor:
2,918 Square Feet
Second Floor:
330 Square Feet
Total Square Footage:
3,248
Bedrooms: 3
Bathrooms: 2½

Width: 82'-8"
Depth: 60'-0"

L

HPT250084

QUOTE ONE®
Cost to build? See page 214
to order a complete cost estimate
to build this house in your area!

Verandas at both the front and rear of this engaging bungalow provide outdoor enthusiasts with a front-row seat to enjoy the changing seasons. To further entice you outdoors, the master bedroom, the breakfast room and the gathering room all have French doors that open to the rear veranda. During frosty weather, a raised-hearth fireplace warms the combined gathering room and dining room and offers a friendly invitation. Bedrooms are efficiently separated from the living area. A romantic fireplace and a luxurious private bath enhance the master bedroom. Two family bedrooms share a full bath.

DECK

GREAT RM.
16/0 X 18/4
(11' CLG.)

NOOK
9/0 X 9/0
(9' CLG.)

VAULTED
MASTER
14/0 X 12/8

NICHE

BR. 2
11/4 X 10/0
(9' CLG.)

LINEN

SHLVS

PAN REF

DINING
11/4 X 12/2
(9' CLG.)

GARAGE
19/8 X 21/8

DEN/BR. 3
11/6 X 10/4
(9' CLG.)

PORCH

BENCH

SEAT

FUTURE
BR. 5
10/6 X 12/8

FUTURE
BR. 4
10/4 X 12/8

FUTURE
GAMES RM.
16/0 X 16/8 +

UP

CRAWLSPACE

CRAWLSPACE

Lower-level space adds to the compact floor plan of this home, and gives it future possibilities. The main level opens off a covered porch to a dining room on the right and a den or bedroom on the left. The great room with an attached nook opens to the rear deck. Note the amount of counter and cabinet space in the L-shaped kitchen. Two bedrooms— a master suite and a family bedroom—are on the left, as is a laundry alcove. The lower level has space for a game room, two additional bedrooms and a full bath.

DESIGN

Total Square Footage:
1,632
Basement:
1,043 Square Feet
Bedrooms: 3
Bathrooms: 2

Width: 50'-0"
Depth: 50'-0"

HPT250085

Living Room
21⁶ x 17⁶

Covered Porch

Bedroom #3
10³ x 12⁶

Kitchen
8⁹ x 11⁹

Covered Porch

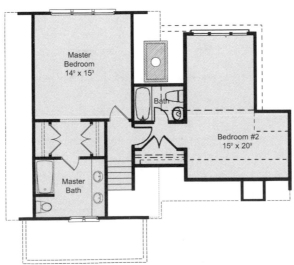

Master Bedroom
14⁹ x 15³

Bath

Master Bath

Bedroom #2
15⁰ x 20⁹

Siding, shingles and a stone chimney give rustic charm to this cozy cottage. The living room, with a fireplace, built-in shelves and a wall of windows, opens to the covered side porch for additional living space. The first-floor bedroom adjoins a full bath. On the second floor, the master suite boasts a double-sink vanity and twin closets. A second family bedroom enjoys the privacy of a private bath as well.

DESIGN

First Floor:
872 Square Feet
Second Floor:
734 Square Feet
Total Square Footage:
1,606
Bedrooms: 3
Bathrooms: 3

Width: 40'-0"
Depth: 29'-6"

HPT250086

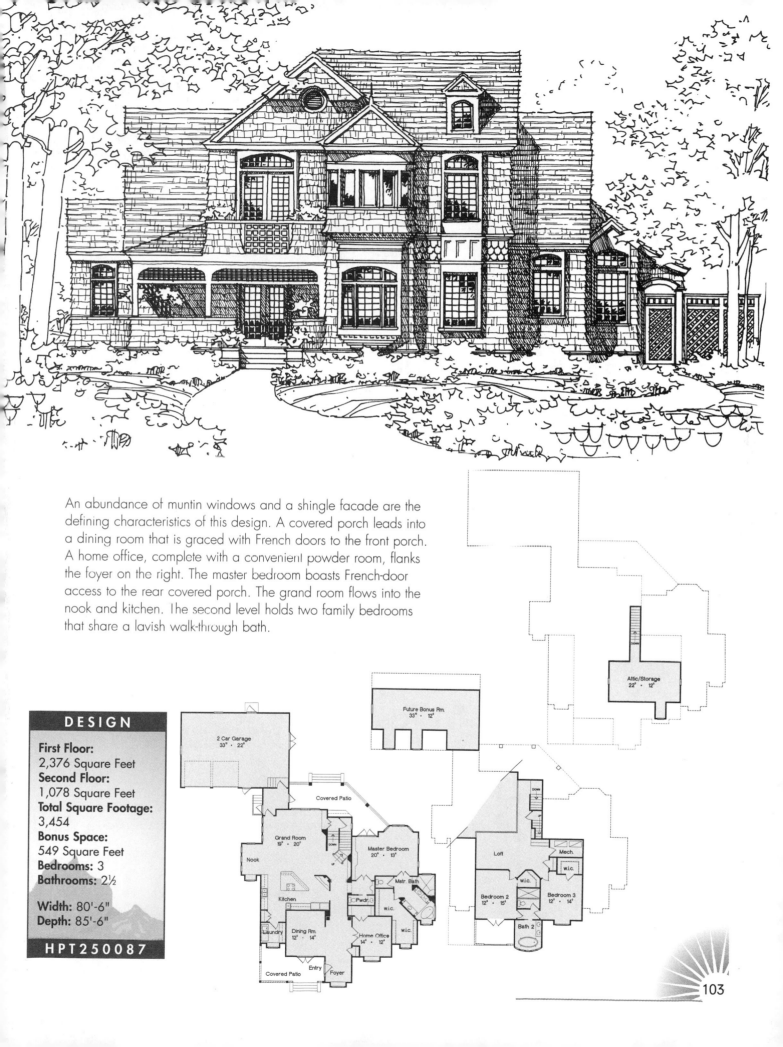

An abundance of muntin windows and a shingle facade are the defining characteristics of this design. A covered porch leads into a dining room that is graced with French doors to the front porch. A home office, complete with a convenient powder room, flanks the foyer on the right. The master bedroom boasts French-door access to the rear covered porch. The grand room flows into the nook and kitchen. The second level holds two family bedrooms that share a lavish walk-through bath.

DESIGN

First Floor:
2,376 Square Feet
Second Floor:
1,078 Square Feet
Total Square Footage:
3,454
Bonus Space:
549 Square Feet
Bedrooms: 3
Bathrooms: 2½

Width: 80'-6"
Depth: 85'-6"

HPT250087

Family
20⁸ · 15⁸

Nook

Covered Porch

Kitchen

Bedroom 2
11⁰ · 12²

Bath

Living
16⁴ · 12⁰

Bath

Master
Bedroom
14⁴ · 19⁰

Bedroom 3
11⁰ · 12²

Utility

Dining
11⁰ · 12⁴

Foyer

Den /
Study
11⁰ · 11⁰

W.I.C.

W.I.C.

Entry

Master
Bath

3 Car Garage

Bonus
Room
14⁰ · 21⁸

Bath

DESIGN

Total Square Footage:
2,713
Bonus Room:
440 Square Feet
Bedrooms: 4
Bathrooms: 3

Width: 66'-4"
Depth: 80'-8"

HPT250088

Interesting arches, columns and cantilevers adorn this shingled home. A dining room with a tray ceiling flanks the foyer to the left, while a den/study flanks it to the right. The island kitchen has an abundance of counter space and adjoins the bayed breakfast nook. The hearth-warmed family room boasts easy access to the kitchen. The master bedroom resides on the right side of the plan. Bedrooms 2 and 3 on the left side of the plan share a walk-through full bath. A three-car garage and a bonus room with a bathroom complete this plan.

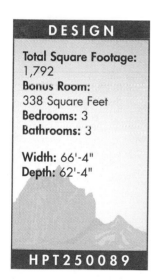

DESIGN

Total Square Footage:
1,792

Bonus Room:
338 Square Feet

Bedrooms: 3

Bathrooms: 3

Width: 66'-4"
Depth: 62'-4"

HPT250089

PORCH

DINING
12-0 x 12-4

PORCH

fireplace

GREAT RM.
18-8 x 16-0

(cathedral ceiling)

KIT.
12-0 x
13-0

PORCH

(optional 2nd master)

BED RM.
14-0 x 14-4

bath

FOYER
5-8 x
9-9

cl

cl

pan.

optional door

MASTER
BED RM.
14-0 x 14-4

master bath

walk-in
closet

BED RM./
STUDY
11-0 x 13-4

cl

bath

up

walk-in
closet

lin.

UTIL.
7-8 x
6-0

w
d

storage

PORCH

© 1998 Donald A Gardner, Inc.

GARAGE
21-4 X 22-4

down

BONUS RM.
13-0 x 21-0

attic storage   attic storage

Cedar shakes, siding and stone blend with the Craftsman details of a custom design in this stunning home. An open common area separates two master suites, great for guests or a roommate situation. Note the fireplace and direct porch access in the great room. Watch the glow of the fire from the kitchen's five-sided island. Enjoy the light-filled dining area for formal and informal dining situations. Added flexibility is found in the bedroom/study and the bonus room.

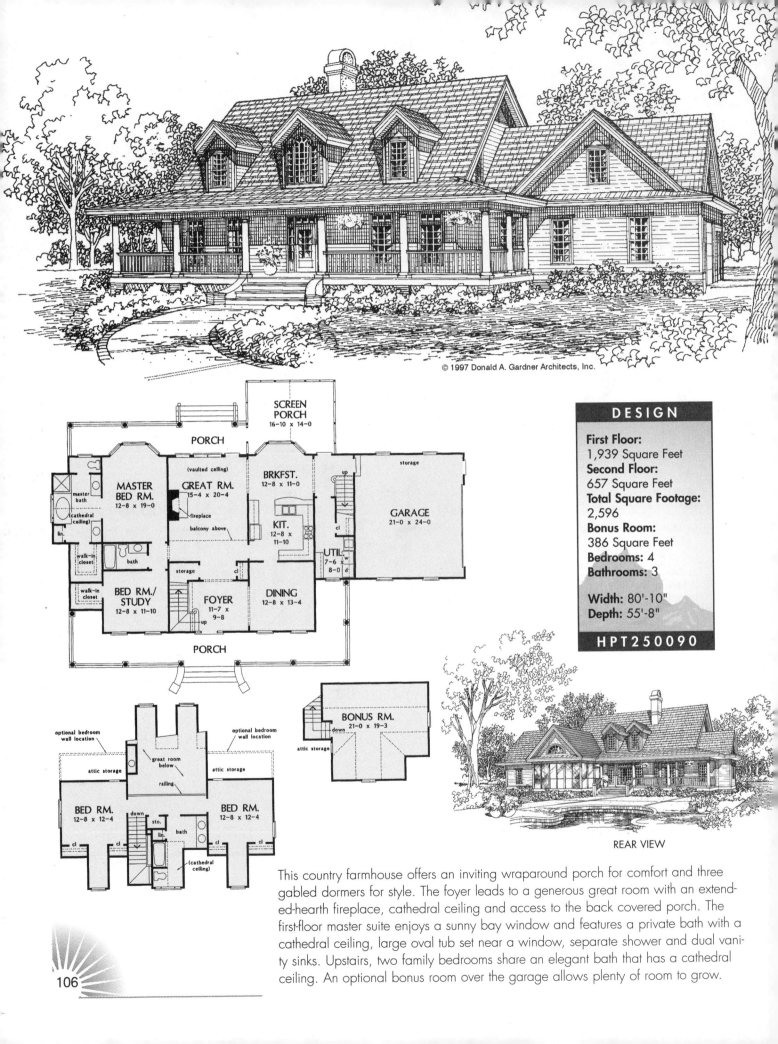

© 1997 Donald A. Gardner Architects, Inc.

SCREEN PORCH
16-10 x 14-0

PORCH

(vaulted ceiling)

BRKFST.
12-8 x 11-0

GREAT RM.
15-4 x 20-4

fireplace

balcony above

MASTER BED RM.
12-8 x 19-0

master bath

(cathedral ceiling)

lin.

KIT.
12-8 x 11-10

storage

GARAGE
21-0 x 24-0

up

cl

UTIL.
7-6 x 8-0

w d

walk-in closet

bath

storage

cl

BED RM./ STUDY
12-8 x 11-10

walk-in closet

FOYER
11-7 x 9-8

up

DINING
12-8 x 13-4

PORCH

optional bedroom wall location

optional bedroom wall location

attic storage

great room below

attic storage

railing

BED RM.
12-8 x 12-4

down

sto.

lin.

bath

(cathedral ceiling)

BED RM.
12-8 x 12-4

cl

cl

cl

cl

down

BONUS RM.
21-0 x 19-3

attic storage

DESIGN

First Floor:
1,939 Square Feet
Second Floor:
657 Square Feet
Total Square Footage:
2,596
Bonus Room:
386 Square Feet
Bedrooms: 4
Bathrooms: 3

Width: 80'-10"
Depth: 55'-8"

HPT250090

REAR VIEW

This country farmhouse offers an inviting wraparound porch for comfort and three gabled dormers for style. The foyer leads to a generous great room with an extended-hearth fireplace, cathedral ceiling and access to the back covered porch. The first-floor master suite enjoys a sunny bay window and features a private bath with a cathedral ceiling, large oval tub set near a window, separate shower and dual vanity sinks. Upstairs, two family bedrooms share an elegant bath that has a cathedral ceiling. An optional bonus room over the garage allows plenty of room to grow.

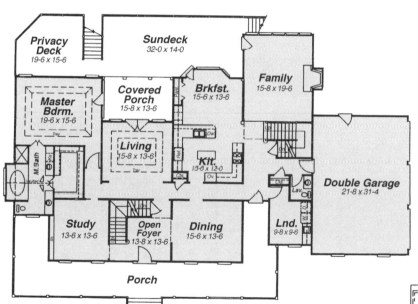

Privacy Deck
19-6 x 15-6

Sundeck
32-0 x 14-0

Covered Porch
15-8 x 13-6

Brkfst.
15-6 x 13-6

Family
15-8 x 19-6

Master Bdrm.
19-6 x 15-6

Living
15-8 x 13-6

Klt.
15-8 x 12-0

Double Garage
21-8 x 31-4

M.Bath

Study
13-6 x 13-6

Open Foyer
13-8 x 13-6

Dining
15-6 x 13-6

Lnd.
9-8 x 9-6

Porch

Shed dormers decorate the roof, while the stone-and-wood-siding facade enhances the eye-appeal of this lovely four-bedroom home. The two-story foyer opens to a study on the left and a dining room to the right. The kitchen features an island workstation, pantry and breakfast nook with a bay window. The formal living room is elegant with a tray ceiling and French-door access to the rear covered porch. The second floor includes Bedrooms 2 and 4 sharing a bath, Bedroom 3 with a private bath, a loft overlooking the family room, and a bonus room.

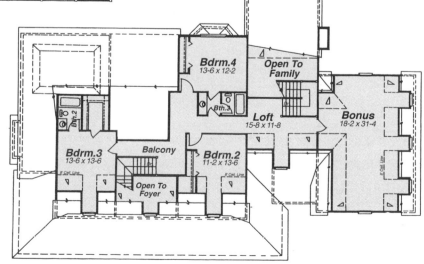

Bdrm.4
13-6 x 12-2

Open To Family

Bth.2

Bth.3

Loft
15-8 x 11-8

Bonus
18-2 x 31-4

Bdrm.3
13-6 x 13-6

Balcony

Bdrm.2
11-2 x 13-6

Open To Foyer

DESIGN

First Floor:
2,708 Square Feet

Second Floor:
1,264 Square Feet

Total Square Footage:
3,972

Bonus Room:
564 Square Feet

Bedrooms: 4

Bathrooms: 3½

Width: 90'-0"
Depth: 64'-0"

HPT250091

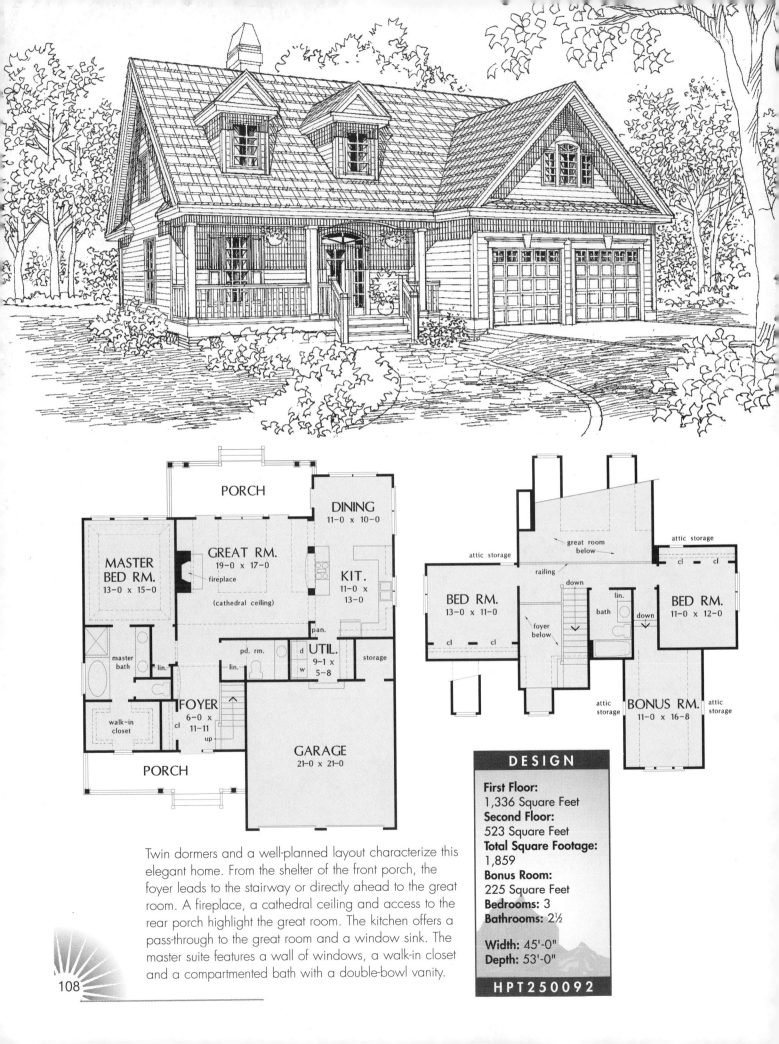

PORCH

DINING
11-0 x 10-0

MASTER BED RM.
13-0 x 15-0

GREAT RM.
19-0 x 17-0

fireplace

(cathedral ceiling)

KIT.
11-0 x 13-0

master bath

lin.

pan.

pd. rm.

lin.

UTIL.
9-1 x 5-8

storage

d
w

walk-in closet

FOYER
6-0 x 11-11

cl

up

GARAGE
21-0 x 21-0

PORCH

attic storage

great room below

attic storage

railing

down

BED RM.
13-0 x 11-0

foyer below

bath

lin.

cl

cl

down

BED RM.
11-0 x 12-0

cl

cl

cl

attic storage

BONUS RM.
11-0 x 16-8

attic storage

Twin dormers and a well-planned layout characterize this elegant home. From the shelter of the front porch, the foyer leads to the stairway or directly ahead to the great room. A fireplace, a cathedral ceiling and access to the rear porch highlight the great room. The kitchen offers a pass-through to the great room and a window sink. The master suite features a wall of windows, a walk-in closet and a compartmented bath with a double-bowl vanity.

DESIGN

First Floor:
1,336 Square Feet
Second Floor:
523 Square Feet
Total Square Footage:
1,859
Bonus Room:
225 Square Feet
Bedrooms: 3
Bathrooms: 2½

Width: 45'-0"
Depth: 53'-0"

HPT250092

DECK	seat
21-8 x 12-0	

fireplace

FAMILY RM.
13-4 x 22-0

spa

DINING
12-0 x 12-0

KIT.
9-4 x 9-8

BRKFST.

pd. rm.

UTILITY
10-4 x 6-4

up

storage

dry wash   cl

down

walk-in closet

master bath

cl

GARAGE
21-8 x 20-4

LIVING RM.
13-4 x 19-4

fireplace

up

FOYER

MASTER BED RM.
13-4 x 13-0

palladian window above

PORCH
33-8 x 6-0

down

BONUS RM.
14-4 x 23-8

bath

attic storage

down

BED RM.
13-4 x 10-8

cl   cl

BED RM.
17-0 x 10-8

cl   cl

foyer below

clerestory with palladian window

This cozy country cottage welcomes family and visitors with a covered porch to protect them from the elements. A large living room with a warming fireplace opens off the two-story foyer. The dining room is defined by two graceful columns and easily accesses the U-shaped kitchen and the rear deck. A breakfast room and family room access two separate decks. A second fireplace is found in the family room. The sleeping zone consists of a deluxe first-floor master suite, complete with a walk-in closet and a lavish bath, and two secondary bedrooms upstairs.

DESIGN

First Floor:
1,503 Square Feet
Second Floor:
542 Square Feet
Total Square Footage:
2,045
Bonus Room:
393 Square Feet
Bedrooms: 3
Bathrooms: 2½

Width: 68'-4"
Depth: 52'-8"

HPT250093

© 1998 Donald A. Gardner, Inc.

PORCH

PATIO

PORCH

fireplace

BRKFST.
9-4 x 9-0

SITTING
9-0 x 9-0

fireplace

MASTER
BED RM.
18-0 x 14-0
(cathedral ceiling)

shelves

FAMILY RM.
16-0 x 22-0
(cathedral ceiling)

fireplace

LIVING RM.
18-0 x 15-10
(cathedral ceiling)

shelves

walk-in
closet

KIT.
16-0 x 15-4

shelves

cl

lin.

pantry

up

master
bath

lin.

pd.
rm.

cl

shelves

walk-in
closet

UTIL
8-0 x
8-4

DINING
12-0 x 14-0

FOYER
10-8 x 8-0
(two story ceiling)

STUDY
12-0 x 14-4

d
w

GARAGE
22-0 x 23-0

PORCH

storage

© 1998 Donald A Gardner, Inc.

storage

living room
below

linen

bath

LIBRARY
9-10 x 9-8

down

walk-in
closet

bath

walk-in
closet

railing

BED RM.
12-0 x 13-0

foyer
below

BED RM.
12-0 x 13-0

attic
storage

BONUS RM.
13-0 x 23-0

attic
storage

attic storage

DESIGN

First Floor:
2,755 Square Feet
Second Floor:
735 Square Feet
Total Square Footage:
3,490
Bonus Room:
481 Square Feet
Bedrooms: 3
Bathrooms: 3½

Width: 92'-6"
Depth: 69'-10"

HPT250094

One can always count on a covered porch and charming dormers to bring real curb appeal, but the interior amenities of this house make it a home. The open foyer is flanked by the study and formal dining room, while the family-oriented living room separates the master suite—with its porch access and cozy sitting room—from the open kitchen, breakfast nook and family room. A library, two bedrooms, a bonus room and two full bathrooms make up the second floor.

REAR VIEW

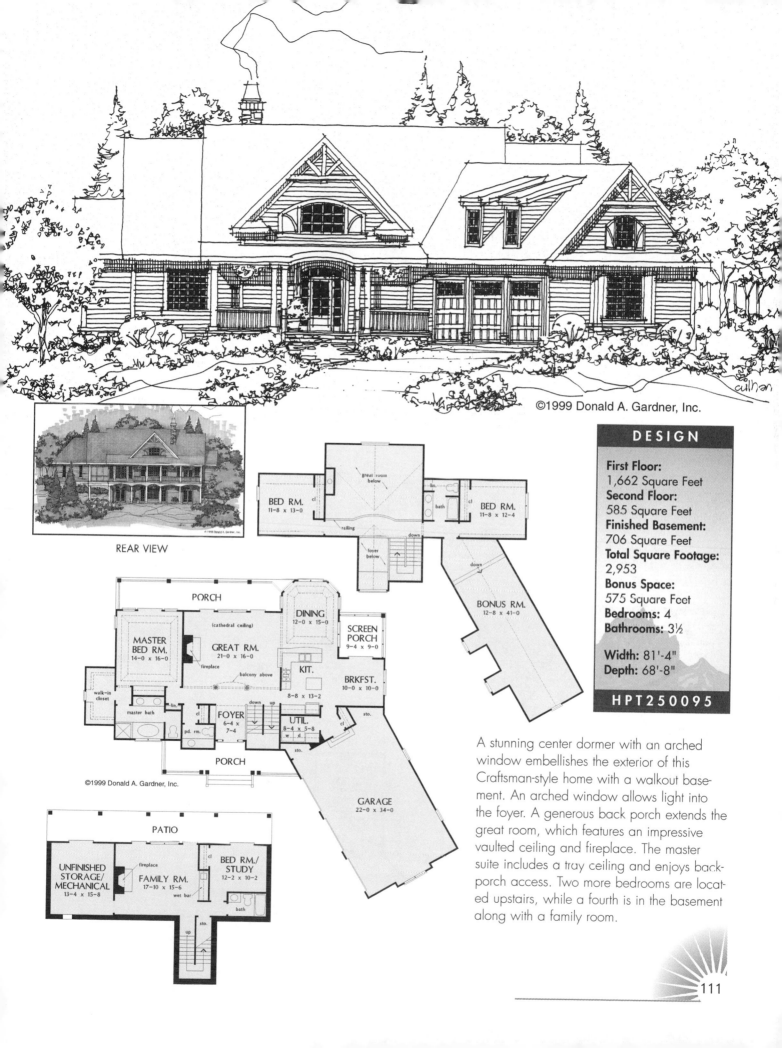

©1999 Donald A. Gardner, Inc.

REAR VIEW

©1999 Donald A. Gardner, Inc.

Floor Plans

First Floor:
- PORCH
- MASTER BED RM. 14-0 x 16-0
- GREAT RM. 21-0 x 16-0 (cathedral ceiling)
- fireplace
- balcony above
- walk-in closet
- master bath
- lin.
- cl
- pd. rm.
- FOYER 6-4 x 7-4
- DINING 12-0 x 15-0
- KIT.
- SCREEN PORCH 9-4 x 9-0
- BRKFST. 10-0 x 10-0
- 8-8 x 13-2
- down / up
- UTIL. 8-4 x 5-8
- w / d
- sto.
- cl
- sto.
- GARAGE 22-0 x 34-0
- PORCH

Second Floor:
- BED RM. 11-8 x 13-0
- great room below
- lin.
- bath
- cl
- BED RM. 11-8 x 12-4
- railing
- foyer below
- down
- BONUS RM. 12-8 x 41-0

Basement:
- PATIO
- UNFINISHED STORAGE/ MECHANICAL 13-4 x 15-8
- fireplace
- FAMILY RM. 17-10 x 15-6
- wet bar
- cl
- BED RM./ STUDY 12-2 x 10-2
- bath
- up
- sto.

DESIGN

First Floor:
1,662 Square Feet
Second Floor:
585 Square Feet
Finished Basement:
706 Square Feet
Total Square Footage:
2,953
Bonus Space:
575 Square Feet
Bedrooms: 4
Bathrooms: 3½

Width: 81'-4"
Depth: 68'-8"

HPT250095

A stunning center dormer with an arched window embellishes the exterior of this Craftsman-style home with a walkout basement. An arched window allows light into the foyer. A generous back porch extends the great room, which features an impressive vaulted ceiling and fireplace. The master suite includes a tray ceiling and enjoys back-porch access. Two more bedrooms are located upstairs, while a fourth is in the basement along with a family room.

A prominent center gable with an arched window accents the facade of this custom Craftsman home. The vaulted great room boasts a rear wall of windows and a fireplace bordered by built-in cabinets. A second-floor loft overlooks the great room for added drama. The master suite is completely secluded and enjoys a cathedral ceiling and a luxurious bath. The home includes three additional bedrooms and baths as well as a bonus room.

DESIGN

First Floor:
2,477 Square Feet
Second Floor:
819 Square Feet
Total Square Footage:
3,296
Bonus Room:
360 Square Feet
Bedrooms: 4
Bathrooms: 4

Width: 100'-0"
Depth: 66'-2"

HPT250096

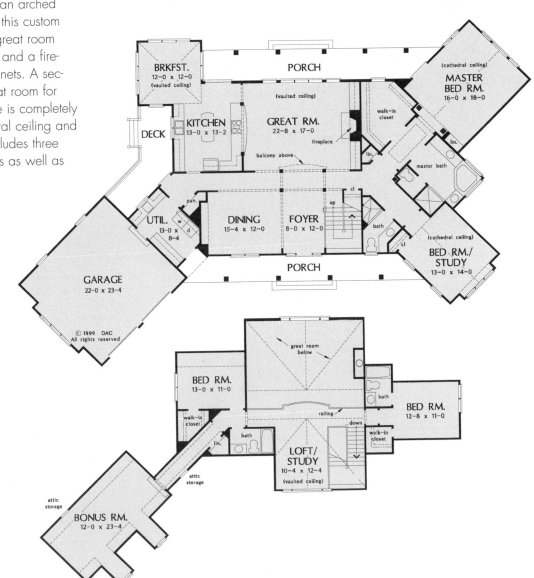

©1998 Donald A. Gardner, Inc.

Stone, siding and multiple gables combine beautifully on the exterior of this hillside home with a walkout basement. Taking advantage of rear views, the home's most oft-used rooms are oriented at the back with plenty of windows. Augmented by a cathedral ceiling, the great room features a fireplace, built-in shelves and access to the rear deck. Twin walk-in closets and a private bath infuse the master suite with luxury.

REAR VIEW

DESIGN

Main Floor:
2,065 Square Feet
Finished Basement:
1,216 Square Feet
Total Square Footage:
3,281
Bedrooms: 4
Bathrooms: 3½

Width: 82'-2"
Depth: 43'-6"

HPT250097

PATIO

BED RM.
13-0 X 12-0

fireplace

MEDIA / REC. RM.
22-6 X 16-0

BED RM.
13-0 X 12-0

bath

walk-in closet

shelves

bath

walk-in closet

wet bar

up

MECH RM.
14-0 X 6-4

(optional bath)

cl

DECK

fireplace

GREAT RM.
24-6 x 16-0

BRKFST.
13-0 x 10-0

MASTER BED RM.
13-0 x 18-0

(cathedral ceiling)

shelves

KIT.
13-0 x 13-0

sto.

walk-in closet

walk-in closet

lin.
pd. rm.
lin.

cl

down

pan.

GARAGE
22-0 x 22-0

master bath

cl

BED RM./ STUDY
12-0 x 12-0

FOYER
13-4 x 6-8

PORCH

DINING
12-0 x 14-0

d

w

cl

storage

© 1998 Donald A Gardner, Inc.

113

This quaint European cottage displays fairy-tale elegance captured from the innocence of the French countryside. To the right of the foyer, double doors open to a formal dining room. Straight ahead, the great room provides an enormous hearth and is illuminated by a wall of windows overlooking the rear wood deck. The gourmet island kitchen, which is open to the breakfast nook, features a walk-in pantry. The first-floor master suite offers private access to the rear deck, as well as a whirlpool bath and walk-in closet.

DESIGN

First Floor:
2,039 Square Feet
Second Floor:
970 Square Feet
Total Square Footage:
3,009
Bedrooms: 4
Bathrooms: 2½

Width: 69'-8"
Depth: 72'-0"

HPT250098

SCREENED PORCH

COVERED DECK

BREAKFAST
13'-0" x 10'-8"

BONUS ROOM
16'-0" x 25'-0"

MASTER SUITE
14'-0" x 19'-0"

FAMILY ROOM
22'-10" x 17'-4"

KITCHEN
13'-0" x 15'-0"

W.I.C.

W.I.C.

MASTER BATH

DINING ROOM
12'-0" x 14'-6"

P.

PDR.

LAUN.

PORCH

OFFICE

LIN.

PORTICO

DN

UP

GARAGE
23'-4" x 23'-6"

LOWER TERRACE

SUITE 2
13'-4" x 13'-0"

RECREATION ROOM
23'-0" x 17'-4"

SUITE 3
12'-0" x 14'-6"

W.I.C.

BATH

W.I.C.

BATH

WET BAR

GUEST SUITE
12'-0" x 13'-4"

MECHANICAL / STORAGE
22'-4" x 16'-6"

STOR.
10'-8" x 24'-8"

UP

DESIGN

Main Floor:
2,213 Square Feet
Finished Basement:
1,333 Square Feet
Total Square Footage:
3,546
Bonus Room:
430 Square Feet
Bedrooms: 4
Bathrooms: 3½

Width: 67'-2"
Depth: 93'-1"

HPT250099

Interesting window treatments highlight this stone-and-shake facade. Arches outline the formal dining room and the family room, both of which are convenient to the island kitchen. If your goal is relaxation, the breakfast room, screened porch and covered deck are nearby. The pampering master suite is to the left on the main level, with three more bedrooms and a recreation room on the lower level. A bonus room above the garage receives natural light from a dormer window.

This home, as shown in the photographs, may differ from the actual blueprints. For more detailed information, please check the floor plans carefully.

REAR VIEW

First-floor plan labels:

VERANDA

MORNING ROOM 13'-6" x 8'-6"

MASTER SUITE 15'-0" x 19'-0"

KITCHEN 16'-0" x 19'-6"

GATHERING ROOM 20'-4" x 21'-0"

W.I.C.

MASTER BATH

PDR.

PDR.

W.I.C.

PDR.

LAUNDRY

DINING ROOM 12'-6" x 13'-6"

FOYER

STUDY 15'-0" x 12'-6"

GARAGE 33'-6" x 23'-4"

LOGGIA

Second-floor plan labels:

SUITE 2 13'-6" x 18'-0"

STOR.

OPEN TO BELOW

BALCONY

BATH

DRESS.

SUITE 3 12'-6" x 12'-6"

OPEN TO BELOW

BATH

W.I.C.

PLANT LEDGE

GUEST LODGING 33'-6" x 13'-8"

DESIGN

First Floor:
2,660 Square Feet
Second Floor:
914 Square Feet
Total Square Footage:
3,574
Bonus Space:
733 Square Feet
Bedrooms: 3
Bathrooms: 4½

Width: 114'-8"
Depth: 75'-10"

HPT250100

Gently curved arches and dormers contrast with the straight lines of gables and wooden columns on this French-style stone exterior. Inside, a spacious gathering room, with an impressive fireplace, opens to a cheery morning room. The kitchen is a delight, with a beam ceiling, triangular work island and walk-in pantry. The first-floor master suite boasts a bay-windowed sitting nook, a deluxe bath and a handy study. The second floor includes a balcony overlooking the gathering room, two bedroom suites and a large guest area over the garage.

COVERED TERRACE

SUITE 3
15'-8" x 13'-6"

W.I.C.

BATH

RECREATION ROOM
26'-0" x 18'-0"

SUITE 2
15'-6" x 14'-0"

W.I.C.

BATH

OUTSIDE STOR.
22'-0" x 15'-0"

STOR.

UP

MECH./ STOR.
24'-0" x 15'-0"

STORAGE
26'-0" x 20'-0"

DINING ROOM
17'-0" x 14'-0"

TERRACE

COVERED TERRACE

KITCHEN
14'-8" x 13'-6"

FAMILY ROOM
26'-0" x 19'-6"

MASTER SUITE
21'-0" x 16'-0"

MASTER BATH

P.

PDR.

DESK

DN

PDR.

W.I.C.

W.I.C.

FOYER

LAUN.

OFFICE/ STUDY
14'-4" x 15'-0"

PORTICO

GARAGE
22'-4" x 34'-0"

The interior of this hillside home boasts high ceilings, a wealth of windows and interestingly shaped rooms. A covered portico leads into a roomy foyer, which is flanked by an office/study, accessible through French doors. Just beyond the foyer, a huge vaulted family room highlights columns decorating the entrance and positioned throughout the room. The island kitchen nestles closely to the beautiful dining room. The master suite enjoys two walk-in closets and a lavish bath. On the lower level, the recreation room and Suites 2 and 3 directly access the covered terrace at the rear.

DESIGN

Main Floor:
2,932 Square Feet
Finished Basement:
1,556 Square Feet
Total Square Footage:
4,488
Bedrooms: 3
Bathrooms: 3½ +½

Width: 114'-0"
Depth: 82'-11"

HPT250101

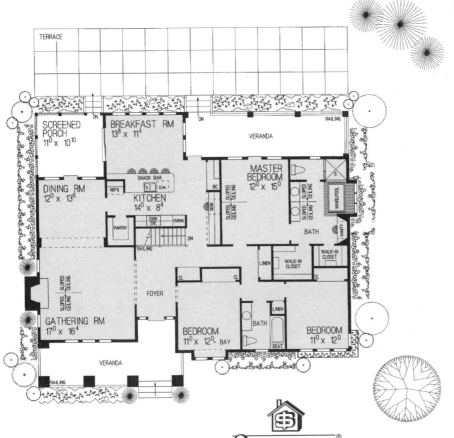

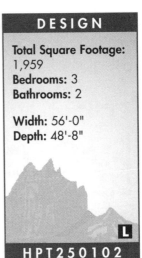

DESIGN

Total Square Footage:
1,959
Bedrooms: 3
Bathrooms: 2

Width: 56'-0"
Depth: 48'-8"

L

HPT250102

Quote One®

Cost to build? See page 214
to order a complete cost estimate
to build this house in your area!

Formal living areas in this plan are
joined by a three-bedroom sleeping
wing. One bedroom, with foyer access,
could function as a study. Two verandas
and a screened porch enlarge the plan
and enhance indoor/outdoor livability.
Notice the added extras: the abundant
storage space, walk-in pantry, built-in
planning desk, whirlpool tub and pass-
through snack bar. The sloped ceiling in
the gathering room gives this area an
open, airy quality. The breakfast room,
with its wealth of windows, will be a
cheerful and bright space to enjoy a cup
of morning coffee.

This home, as shown in the photograph, may differ from the actual blueprints.
For more detailed information, please check the floor plans carefully.

Photo by Roger Wade Studios, Inc.

DESIGN

First Floor:
2,078 Square Feet
Second Floor:
823 Square Feet
Total Square Footage:
2,901
Bedrooms: 3
Bathrooms: 2½

Width: 88'-5"
Depth: 58'-3"

HPT250103

Exposed rafters and trusses, deep eaves and low-pitched gables lend Craftsman charm to this design. Upon entering, guests are greeted with the expansive great room's cathedral ceiling and a cozy fireplace. The kitchen has a snack-counter island with a breakfast nook that opens to a deck. Located on the first floor for privacy, the master suite contains plenty of windows, two walk-in closets and a whirlpool tub with views out a bayed window.

© Stephen Fuller, Inc.

© Stephen Fuller, Inc.

Master Sitting
12³ x 7⁹

Covered Porch

Master Bedroom
15³ x 17⁹

Hers

Master Bath

His

Bedroom #4
11⁶ x 13⁹

Bedroom #3
13⁹ x 14³

Bedroom #2
13⁹ x 12⁹

Elegance and old-fashioned country charm enhance this home's good looks. Inside, the formal living and dining rooms are open to one another for easy entertaining. The dining room connects to the kitchen, which offers an abundance of counter space and an informal breakfast room. The great room dazzles with natural light from a curved wall of windows overlooking the rear porch and backyard. Upstairs, the master suite provides a sitting area, a private porch and a luxury bath flanked by His and Hers walk-in closets. This home is designed with a walkout basement foundation.

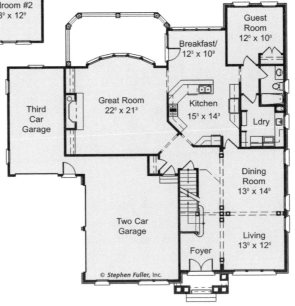

Third Car Garage

Great Room
22⁰ x 21³

Breakfast/
12³ x 10⁹

Guest Room
12⁰ x 10⁰

Kitchen
15³ x 14³

Ldry

Dining Room
13⁰ x 14⁰

Two Car Garage

Living
13⁰ x 12⁰

Foyer

© Stephen Fuller, Inc.

DESIGN

First Floor:
1,820 Square Feet
Second Floor:
1,710 Square Feet
Total Square Footage:
3,530
Bedrooms: 5
Bathrooms: 4

Width: 59'-8"
Depth: 62'-3"

HPT250104

Here's a cozy 1920s bungalow with Arts and Crafts details that flourish inside and out. The facade combines the shingles favored by Craftsman bungalows with the textural interest of brick and stone. The optional porte cochere provides covered access to the family room as well as an invitation to entertain outdoors. The deep, gabled front porch is supported by double columns on brick pedestals. The formal living room and dining room are separated from the kitchen/breakfast area and family room. This home is designed with a walkout basement foundation.

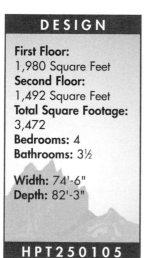

DESIGN

First Floor:
1,980 Square Feet
Second Floor:
1,492 Square Feet
Total Square Footage:
3,472
Bedrooms: 4
Bathrooms: 3½

Width: 74'-6"
Depth: 82'-3"

HPT250105

Though this home gives the impression of the Northwest, it will be the winner of any neighbor-hood. The U-shaped kitchen has a cooktop work island, an adjacent nook and easy access to the formal dining room. A spacious family room shares the fireplace with the living room, is enhanced by built-ins and also offers a quiet deck for stargazing. The upstairs consists of two family bed-rooms sharing a full bath and a vaulted master suite complete with a walk-in closet and sumptuous bath. Please specify basement or slab foundation when ordering.

DESIGN

First Floor:
1,143 Square Feet
Second Floor:
651 Square Feet
Total Square Footage:
1,794
Bonus Space:
1,114 Square Feet
Bedrooms: 2
Bathrooms: 2½

Width: 32'-0"
Depth: 57'-0"

HPT250107

This traditional country cabin is a vacationer's dream. The two-story great room visually expands the lofty interior. This room provides a warming fireplace and offers built-in cabinetry. Double doors open onto a porch that wraps around to the rear deck. The dining room opens through double doors to the porch on the left side on the plan, while the kitchen offers an efficient pantry on the right. A family bedroom with a private bath resides on this main floor. Upstairs, a vaulted ceiling enhances the master suite and its private bath. A private deck can be accessed from the master suite through a set of double doors.

REAR VIEW

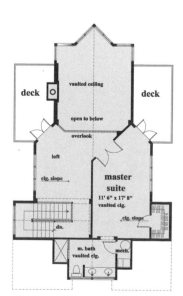

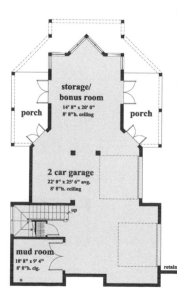

DESIGN

First Floor:
1,383 Square Feet
Second Floor:
595 Square Feet
Total Square Footage:
1,978
Bedrooms: 3
Bathrooms: 2

Width: 48'-0"
Depth: 48'-8"

HPT250108

The stone facade and woodwork detail give this home a Craftsman appeal. The foyer opens to a staircase up to the vaulted great room, which features a fireplace flanked by built-ins and French-door access to the rear covered porch. The open dining room with a tray ceiling offers conven-ience to the spacious kitchen. Two family bedrooms share a bath and enjoy private porches. An overlook to the great room below is a perfect introduction to the master suite. The second level spreads out master-suite luxury with a spacious walk-in closet, private porch and a glorious master bath with a garden tub, dual vanities and compartmented toilet.

Floor 1 (left plan):
porch
master suite
12'-8" x 17'-8"
10'-0" tray clg.
open to below
w.i.c.
overlook
dn
master bath
dn
porch

Floor 2 (center plan):
deck
covered porch
porch
br. 3
11'-6" x 12'-0"
10'-0"h. clg.
fireplace
great room
15'-0" x 19'-6"
vaulted clg.
dining
11'-0" x 12'-8"
11'-0" tray clg.
built ins
kitchen
11'-0" x 12'-0"
porch
br. 2
12'-10" x 12'-0"
10'-0"h. clg.
up
stor.
util.
up
foyer
entry

Floor 3 (right plan):
covered porch
covered porch
firewood storage
2 car garage
bonus/ storage
ski/equip. storage
mud area

Stonework and elements of Craftsman style make a strong statement on this home. The grand entry porch provides ample space for appreciating the night sky or just taking in the sights and sounds of nature. The great room offers expansive views, an extended hearth fireplace and built-in cabinetry. Nearby, a well-organized kitchen offers a pass-through to the great room and service to the formal dining room through a convenient butler's pantry. Upstairs, the master suite sports a private sitting area that opens to an upper deck through French doors. The upper-level gallery provides an overlook to the great room.

DESIGN

First Floor:
2,096 Square Feet
Second Floor:
892 Square Feet
Total Square Footage:
2,988
Storage:
1,948 Square Feet
Bedrooms: 3
Bathrooms: 3½

Width: 56'-0"
Depth: 54'-0"

HPT250110

Siding and shingles give this home a Craftsman look, while columns and gables suggest a more traditional style. The foyer opens to a short flight of stairs that leads to the great room, which features a beamed ceiling, a fireplace, built-ins and French doors to the rear veranda. To the left, the open, island kitchen enjoys a pass-through to the great room and easy service to the dining bay. The secluded master bedroom has two walk-in closets, a luxurious bath and veranda access. Upstairs, two family bedrooms enjoy their own full baths and share a loft area.

DESIGN

Vestibule:
187 Square Feet
First Floor:
2,146 Square Feet
Second Floor:
952 Square Feet
Total Square Footage:
3,285
Bedrooms: 3
Bathrooms: 3½

Width: 52'-0"
Depth: 65'-4"

HPT250111

Stately windows wrap this noble exterior with dazzling details and allow plenty of natural light inside. The two-story great room offers a fireplace, built-ins, a wet bar and three sets of French doors that open to the covered porch. A gourmet kitchen packed with amenities is prepared to serve any occasion. The master suite includes a tray ceiling and a wide bay window. The dressing area, framed by walk-in closets, leads to the lavish bath. Upstairs, two secondary suites, each with a spacious bath and walk-in closet, are separated by the balcony overlooking the great room.

TERRACE

EATING

DINING
10² X 10⁴

GATHERING RM
16⁴ X 15¹⁰

MASTER BEDROOM
12⁰ X 15⁰

KITCHEN
11⁸ X 16⁸ • EATING

PANTRY

PDR RM

LOFT ABOVE

WALK-IN CLOSET

COOK TOP

BC

DN

LAUNDRY

LOFT ABOVE

UP

DN

BATH

RAILING

FOYER

RAILING

D W

MEDIA RM
13⁸ X 10⁰

WHIRLPOOL

COVERED PORCH

RAILING

RAILING

UP

QUOTE ONE®

Cost to build? See page 214
to order a complete cost estimate
to build this house in your area!

OPEN TO
GATHERING RM
BELOW

STORAGE   LINEN

RAILING

CL

LOFT

SEAT

RAILING

DN

BEDROOM
11⁰ X 12⁰

BATH

SKYLIGHTS

CL

OPEN TO
FOYER
BELOW

BEDROOM
12² X 12⁰

PLANT LEDGE

128

DESIGN

First Floor:
1,636 Square Feet
Second Floor:
572 Square Feet
Total Square Footage:
2,208
Bedrooms: 3
Bathrooms: 2½

Width: 52'-0"
Depth: 46'-2"

L D

HPT250112

Cozy and completely functional, this 1½-story bungalow has many amenities not often found in homes its size. To the left of the foyer is a media room, and to the rear is the gathering room with a fireplace. Attached to the gathering room is a formal dining room with rear-terrace access. The kitchen features a curved casual eating area and island work station. The right side of the first floor is dominated by the master suite, which offers access to the rear terrace and a luxurious bath. Upstairs are two family bedrooms connected by a loft area overlooking the gathering room and foyer.

REAR VIEW

This stone and stucco two-bedroom home offers a multitude of windows for picturesque views of the outdoors. The formal dining room is open to the foyer and the living room where a pair of sliding glass doors opens to the rear deck. Additional deck access is found in the morning room and the master suite, for which an alternate wheelchair-accessible plan is offered. The angled galley kitchen adjoins the sunny morning room. A family bedroom resides at the front of the plan with a box-bay window and a private entry to the full bath.

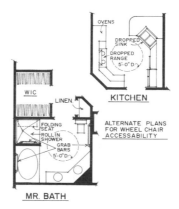

ALTERNATE PLANS FOR WHEEL CHAIR ACCESSABILITY

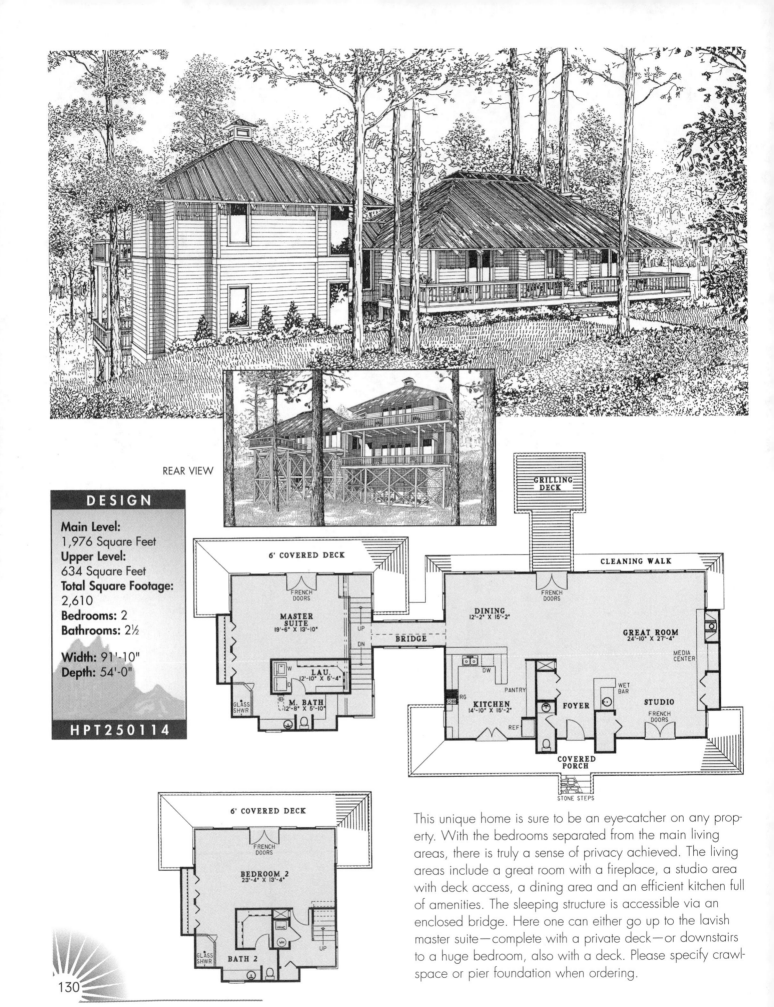

REAR VIEW

DESIGN

Main Level:
1,976 Square Feet
Upper Level:
634 Square Feet
Total Square Footage:
2,610
Bedrooms: 2
Bathrooms: 2½

Width: 91'-10"
Depth: 54'-0"

HPT250114

GRILLING DECK

6' COVERED DECK
FRENCH DOORS
MASTER SUITE 19'-6" X 13'-10"
UP
DN
BRIDGE
LAU. 12'-10" X 5'-4"
W
M. BATH 12'-8" X 5'-10"
GLASS SHWR

CLEANING WALK
FRENCH DOORS
DINING 12'-2" X 15'-2"
GREAT ROOM 24'-10" X 27'-4"
MEDIA CENTER
DW
PANTRY
WET BAR
RG
KITCHEN 14'-10" X 15'-2"
FOYER
STUDIO
FRENCH DOORS
REF
COVERED PORCH
STONE STEPS

6' COVERED DECK
FRENCH DOORS
BEDROOM 2 23'-4" X 13'-4"
HVAC
UP
GLASS SHWR
BATH 2

This unique home is sure to be an eye-catcher on any property. With the bedrooms separated from the main living areas, there is truly a sense of privacy achieved. The living areas include a great room with a fireplace, a studio area with deck access, a dining area and an efficient kitchen full of amenities. The sleeping structure is accessible via an enclosed bridge. Here one can either go up to the lavish master suite—complete with a private deck—or downstairs to a huge bedroom, also with a deck. Please specify crawl-space or pier foundation when ordering.

This four-season Cape Cod cottage is perfect for a site with great views. A sun room provides wide views and good indoor/outdoor flow. The living area boasts a corner fireplace. A well-organized kitchen serves a snack counter as well as the dining room. Two bedrooms upstairs share a full bath that includes a separate tub and shower. This home is designed with a basement foundation.

DESIGN

First Floor:
895 Square Feet
Second Floor:
565 Square Feet
Total Square Footage:
1,460
Bedrooms: 2
Bathrooms: 1½

Width: 38'-0"
Depth: 36'-0"

HPT250115

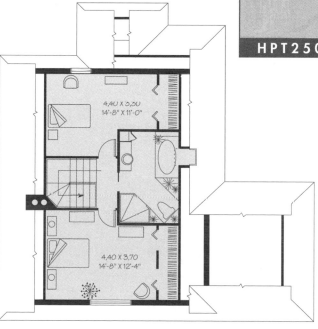

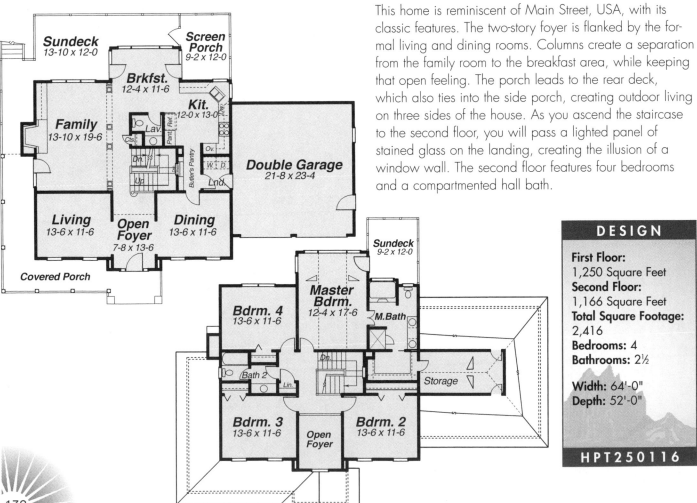

Sundeck 13-10 x 12-0

Screen Porch 9-2 x 12-0

Brkfst. 12-4 x 11-6

Kit. 12-0 x 13-0

Family 13-10 x 19-6

Pant. Ref.

Lav.

Cts.

Dn.

Up

Butler's Pantry

W/D

Lnd.

Ov.

Dw.

Double Garage 21-8 x 23-4

Living 13-6 x 11-6

Open Foyer 7-8 x 13-6

Dining 13-6 x 11-6

Covered Porch

Sundeck 9-2 x 12-0

Master Bdrm. 12-4 x 17-6

M.Bath

Bdrm. 4 13-6 x 11-6

Bath 2

Lin.

Dn.

Storage

Bdrm. 3 13-6 x 11-6

Open Foyer

Bdrm. 2 13-6 x 11-6

This home is reminiscent of Main Street, USA, with its classic features. The two-story foyer is flanked by the formal living and dining rooms. Columns create a separation from the family room to the breakfast area, while keeping that open feeling. The porch leads to the rear deck, which also ties into the side porch, creating outdoor living on three sides of the house. As you ascend the staircase to the second floor, you will pass a lighted panel of stained glass on the landing, creating the illusion of a window wall. The second floor features four bedrooms and a compartmented hall bath.

DESIGN

First Floor:
1,250 Square Feet
Second Floor:
1,166 Square Feet
Total Square Footage:
2,416
Bedrooms: 4
Bathrooms: 2½

Width: 64'-0"
Depth: 52'-0"

HPT250116

This home, as shown in the photographs, may differ from the actual blueprints.
For more detailed information, please check the floor plans carefully.

Photos by Riley & Riley Photography, Inc.

DESIGN

First Floor:
2,086 Square Feet
Second Floor:
1,077 Square Feet
Total Square Footage:
3,163
Bonus Room:
403 Square Feet
Bedrooms: 4
Bathrooms: 3½

Width: 81'-10"
Depth: 51'-8"

HPT250117

This beautiful farmhouse, with its prominent twin gables and bays, adds just the right amount of country style. The master suite is quietly tucked away downstairs with no rooms directly above. The family cook will love the spacious U-shaped kitchen and adjoining bayed breakfast nook. A bonus room is easily accessible from the back stairs or from the second floor, where three large bedrooms share two full baths. Storage space abounds with walk-ins, half-shelves and linen closets. A curved balcony borders a versatile loft/study, which overlooks the stunning two-story family room.

First Floor Plan

PORCH

MASTER BD. RM.
15-6 x 14-0

FAMILY RM.
18-8 x 23-2
(two story ceiling)
fireplace
balcony above

BRKFST.
13-4 x 13-8

pd. rm.

storage

walk-in closet

lin.

cl

KIT.
13-4 x 12-0

UTIL.
6-10 x 10-0

w d
pan.

GARAGE
21-8 x 28-4

master bath

walk-in closet

LIVING RM.
13-4 x 13-6

FOYER
8-8 x 10-2
up

DINING
13-4 x 13-6

up

© 1996 DAGA
All rights reserved

PORCH

REAR VIEW

Second Floor Plan

family room below

LOFT/ STUDY
8-8 x 10-2

railing

BED RM.
13-4 x 11-10

attic storage

cl cl

lin.

skylights

down

shelves

down
down

BONUS RM.
21-8 x 16-5

walk-in closet

bath

walk-in closet

bath

BED RM.
13-4 x 12-2

railing

balcony

BED RM.
13-4 x 13-6

down

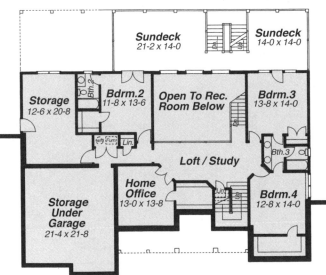

Sundeck 21-2 x 14-0

Sundeck 14-0 x 14-0

Storage 12-6 x 20-8

Bth.2

Bdrm.2 11-8 x 13-6

Open To Rec. Room Below

Bdrm.3 13-8 x 14-0

Bth.3

wh Furn Lin.

Loft / Study

Storage Under Garage 21-4 x 21-8

Home Office 13-0 x 13-8

Bdrm.4 12-8 x 14-0

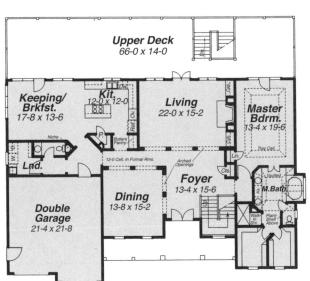

Upper Deck 66-0 x 14-0

Keeping/ Brkfst. 17-8 x 13-6

Kit. 12-0 x 12-0

Living 22-0 x 15-2

Master Bdrm. 13-4 x 19-6

Niche

Butlers Pantry

Trey Ceil.

Lnd.

12-0 Ceil. In Formal Rms.

Arched Openings

Lin.

Vaulted

Foyer 13-4 x 15-6

M.Bath

Double Garage 21-4 x 21-8

Dining 13-8 x 15-2

Walk In Clst.

Plant Shelf Above

DESIGN

Main Level:
2,153 Square Feet
Lower Level:
1,564 Square Feet
Basement Level:
794 Square Feet
Total Square Footage:
4,511
Bedrooms: 5
Bathrooms: 4½

Width: 68'-0"
Depth: 60'-0"

HPT250118

This elegant country cottage features shake siding with brick accents, charming gables and a gracious front porch. On the main level, a spacious amenity-packed master suite dominates one whole side of the house and features oversized His and Hers closets, a walk-in shower and a long vanity with angled side mirrors. The foyer looks into the formal living room with a view to the rear deck that spans the full length of the house. The kitchen opens to the cozy breakfast/keeping room that doubles as a sun room due to all the windows.

Lower Level Patio 38-6 x 14-0

Basement Storage 21-6 x 13-0

Line Of 8-0 Ceil.

2 Story Rec. Room 29-4 x 15-4

Bdrm.5 13-8 x 11-10

Lin.

Bth.4

Natural Wonders
Homes with private backyard views

I have a garden of my own,

But so with roses overgrown,

And lilies, that you would it guess

To be a little wilderness.

— Andrew Marvell

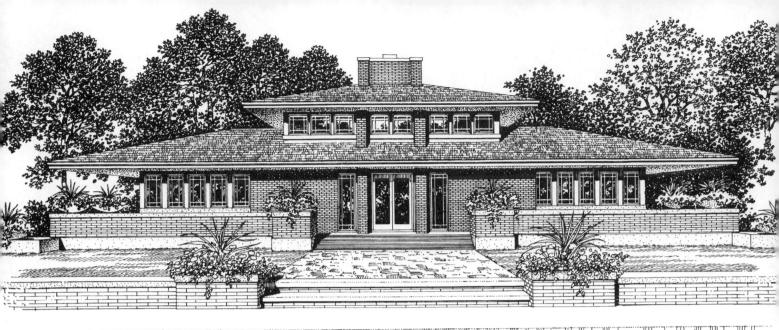

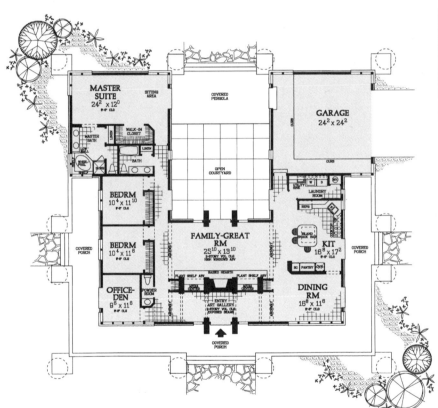

MASTER
SUITE
24² x 12⁰

SITTING
AREA

COVERED
PERGOLA

GARAGE
24² x 24²

WALK-IN
CLOSET

MASTER
BATH

LINEN
BATH

OPEN
COURTYARD

UTILITY

LAUNDRY
ROOM

REFR

BEDRM
10⁴ x 11¹⁰

FAMILY-GREAT
RM
25¹⁰ x 19¹⁰
2-STORY VOL CLG
HIGH WINDOWS ABV

ISLAND
SNACK BAR

KIT
16⁸ x 17²

COVERED
PORCH

BEDRM
10⁴ x 11⁶

PANTRY

COVERED
PORCH

OFFICE-
DEN
9⁶ x 11⁶

POWDER
ROOM

RAISED HEARTH

PLANT SHELF ABV

PLANT SHELF ABV

DINING
RM
16⁸ x 11⁶

ENTRY/
ART GALLERY/
EXPOSED BEAMS

COVERED
PORCH

DESIGN

Total Square Footage:
2,626
Bedrooms: 3
Bathrooms: 2½

Width: 75'-10"
Depth: 69'-4"

L

HPT250119

Frank Lloyd Wright had a knack for enhancing the environment with the homes he designed. This adaptation reflects his purest Prairie style complemented by a brick exterior, a multitude of windows and a low-slung hipped roof. To the right of the foyer, an archway leads to a formal dining room lined with a wall of windows. Nearby, the spacious kitchen features an island snack bar. The two-story family/great room provides an ideal setting for formal or informal gatherings. The left wing contains the sleeping quarters and an office/den. The private master suite includes a sitting area, a walk-in closet and a lavish master bath with a corner whirlpool tub.

QUOTE ONE®
Cost to build? See page 214
to order a complete cost estimate
to build this house in your area!

OPEN OVER
FAMILY-GREAT RM
2-STORY VOL CLG

OPEN OVER
ENTRY/ART GALLERY
2-STORY VOL CLG
EXPOSED BEAMS

REAR VIEW

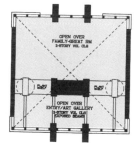

Form follows function as dual gallery halls lead from formal areas to split sleeping quarters in this Prairie adaptation. At the heart of the plan, the great room offers a raised-hearth fireplace framed by built-in cabinetry and plant shelves. Open planning combines the country kitchen with an informal dining space, and adds an island counter with a snack bar. A lavish master suite harbors a sitting area with private access to the covered pergola. The secondary sleeping wing includes a spacious guest suite with an angled whirlpool tub. A fifth bedroom or home office offers its own door to the wraparound porch.

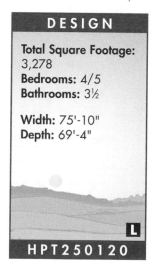

DESIGN

Total Square Footage: 3,278

Bedrooms: 4/5
Bathrooms: 3½

Width: 75'-10"
Depth: 69'-4"

L

HPT250120

Quote One®

Cost to build? See page 214
to order a complete cost estimate
to build this house in your area!

This home, as shown in the photograph, may differ from the actual blueprints.
For more detailed information, please check the floor plans carefully.

Photo by Everett & Soulé

Varying rooflines, arches and corner quoins adorn the facade of this magnificent home. A porte cochere creates a stunning prelude to the double-door entry. A wet bar serves the sunken living room and overlooks the pool area. The dining room has a tray ceiling and is located near the gourmet kitchen which boasts a preparation island and angled counter. A guest room opens off the living room. The generous family room, warmed by a fireplace, opens to the screened patio. The master bedroom has a sitting room and a fireplace that's set into an angled wall. Its luxurious bath includes a step-up tub.

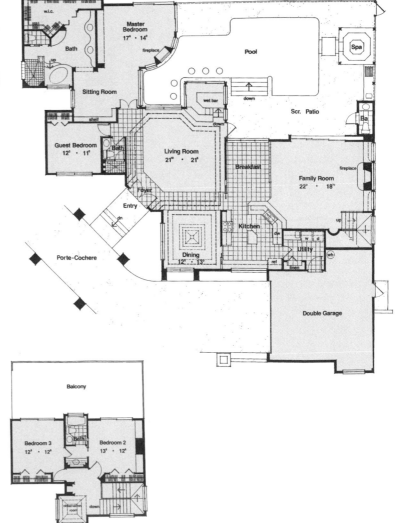

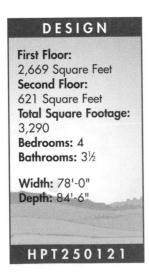

DESIGN

First Floor:
2,669 Square Feet
Second Floor:
621 Square Feet
Total Square Footage:
3,290
Bedrooms: 4
Bathrooms: 3½

Width: 78'-0"
Depth: 84'-6"

HPT250121

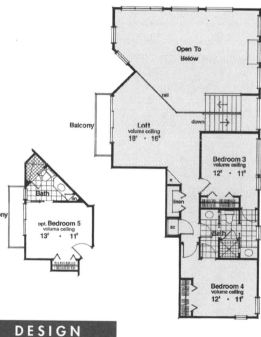

Indoor and outdoor living are enhanced by the beautiful courtyard that decorates the center of this home. A gallery provides views of the courtyard and leads to a kitchen with a center work island and adjacent breakfast room. The gallery leads to the formal living room and master suite that features a tray ceiling and double doors to a covered patio. Retreat to the master bath, where a relaxing tub awaits to pamper. The second floor contains a full bath shared by two family bedrooms and a loft that provides flexible space for an additional bedroom.

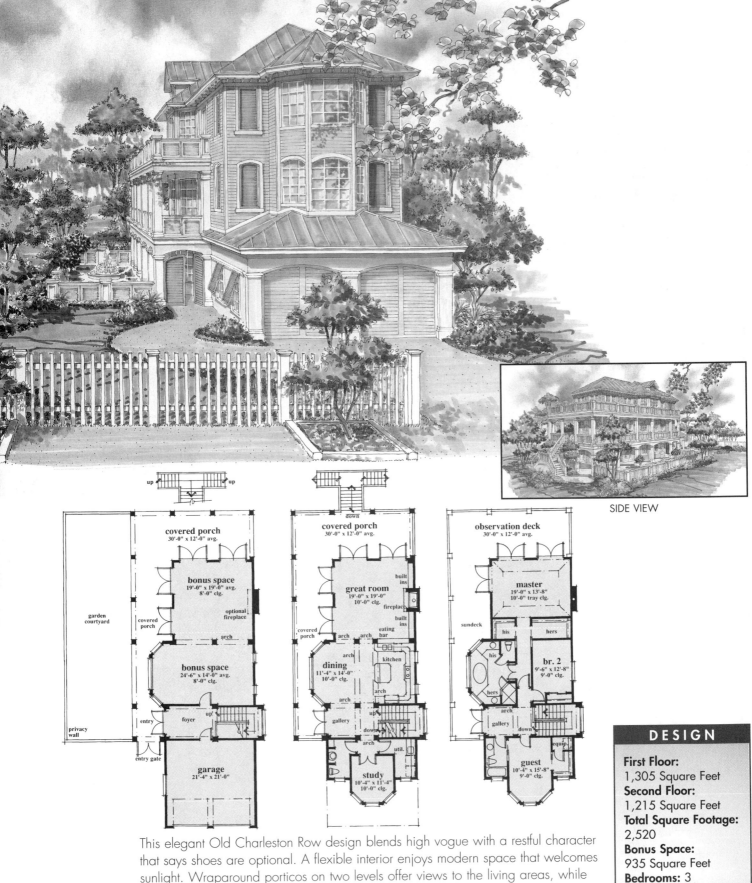

SIDE VIEW

covered porch
30'-0" x 12'-0" avg.

bonus space
19'-0" x 19'-0" avg.
8'-0" clg.

optional fireplace

covered porch

arch

bonus space
24'-6" x 14'-0" avg.
8'-0" clg.

garden courtyard

privacy wall

entry

foyer

up

entry gate

garage
21'-4" x 21'-0"

covered porch
30'-0" x 12'-0" avg.

down

built ins

great room
19'-0" x 19'-0"
10'-0" clg.

fireplace

built ins

covered porch

arch   arch

eating bar

arch

kitchen

dining
11'-4" x 14'-0"
10'-0" clg.

arch

gallery

arch

up

down

util.

arch

study
10'-4" x 11'-4"
10'-0" clg.

observation deck
30'-0" x 12'-0" avg.

master
19'-0" x 13'-8"
10'-0" tray clg.

sundeck

his   hers

his

br. 2
9'-6" x 12'-8"
9'-0" clg.

hers

arch

gallery   down

equip.

guest
10'-4" x 15'-8"
9'-0" clg.

This elegant Old Charleston Row design blends high vogue with a restful character that says shoes are optional. A flexible interior enjoys modern space that welcomes sunlight. Wraparound porticos on two levels offer views to the living areas, while an observation deck opens from the master suite. Four sets of French doors bring the outside into the great room. The second-floor master suite features a spacious bath and three sets of doors that open to the observation deck. A guest bedroom on this level leads to a gallery hall with its own access to the deck.

DESIGN

First Floor:
1,305 Square Feet
Second Floor:
1,215 Square Feet
Total Square Footage:
2,520
Bonus Space:
935 Square Feet
Bedrooms: 3
Bathrooms: 3

Width: 30'-6"
Depth: 72'-2"

HPT250123

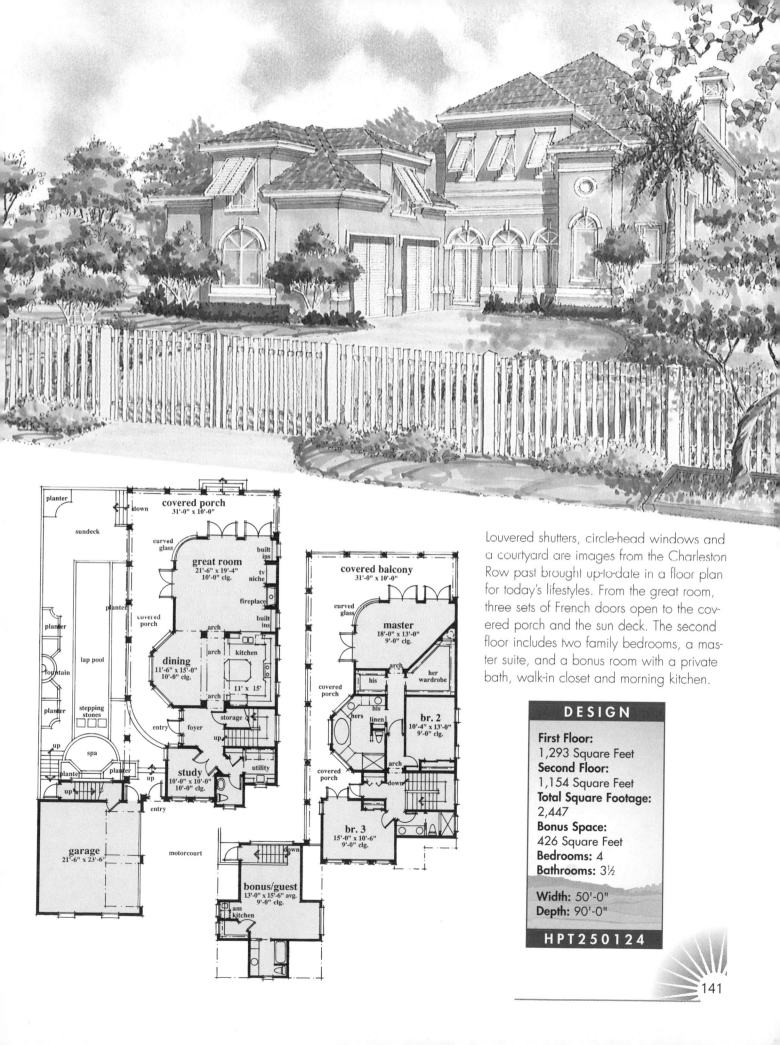

Louvered shutters, circle-head windows and a courtyard are images from the Charleston Row past brought up-to-date in a floor plan for today's lifestyles. From the great room, three sets of French doors open to the covered porch and the sun deck. The second floor includes two family bedrooms, a master suite, and a bonus room with a private bath, walk-in closet and morning kitchen.

DESIGN

First Floor:
1,293 Square Feet
Second Floor:
1,154 Square Feet
Total Square Footage:
2,447
Bonus Space:
426 Square Feet
Bedrooms: 4
Bathrooms: 3½

Width: 50'-0"
Depth: 90'-0"

HPT250124

planter

sundeck

down

covered porch
31'-0" x 10'-0"

curved glass

built ins

great room
21'-6" x 19'-4"
10'-0" clg.

tv niche

fireplace

built ins

planter

covered porch

arch

planter

lap pool

dining
11'-6" x 15'-0"
10'-0" clg.

arch

arch

kitchen

11' x 15'

fountain

planter

arch

stepping stones

entry

foyer

storage

up

up

spa

planter

planter

up

study
10'-0" x 10'-0"
10'-0" clg.

utility

up

entry

garage
21'-6" x 23'-6"

motorcourt

bonus/guest
13'-0" x 15'-6" avg.
9'-0" clg.

am kitchen

down

covered balcony
31'-0" x 10'-0"

curved glass

master
18'-0" x 13'-0"
9'-0" clg.

arch

his

her wardrobe

covered porch

hers

his

linen

br. 2
10'-4" x 13'-0"
9'-0" clg.

covered porch

arch

down

br. 3
15'-0" x 10'-6"
9'-0" clg.

DESIGN

First Floor:
2,401 Square Feet
Second Floor:
927 Square Feet
Total Square Footage:
3,328
Bedrooms: 4
Bathrooms: 3

Width: 104'-9"
Depth: 62'-5"

L

HPT250125

Honored traditions are echoed throughout this warm and inviting Santa Fe home. A large two-story gathering room with a beehive fireplace provides a soothing atmosphere for entertaining or quiet interludes. A gallery leads to the kitchen and breakfast area. A media room, with a full entertainment center, offers interesting angles. On the right side of the plan, the master suite revels in privacy. On the second floor, three bedrooms and a reading loft leave room for the kids.

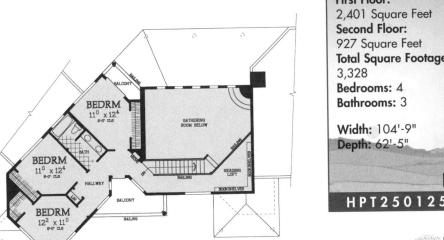

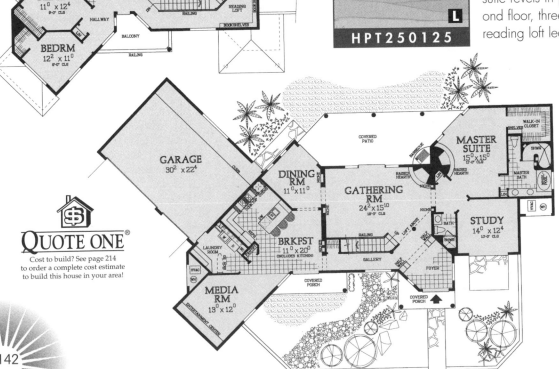

QUOTE ONE®
Cost to build? See page 214 to order a complete cost estimate to build this house in your area!

The warmth of a wraparound porch and the tasteful use of stacked fieldstone set this home apart. Upon entry, the relationship between the adult conversation area and formal dining room brings a new twist to a traditional layout, by introducing both spaces at an angle. The dining area views the pool that seems to enter the space, while the conversation area is off the front porch. Views of the pool can be had from both the kitchen and family room. The master suite enjoys generous His and Hers walk-in closets and a well-appointed bath.

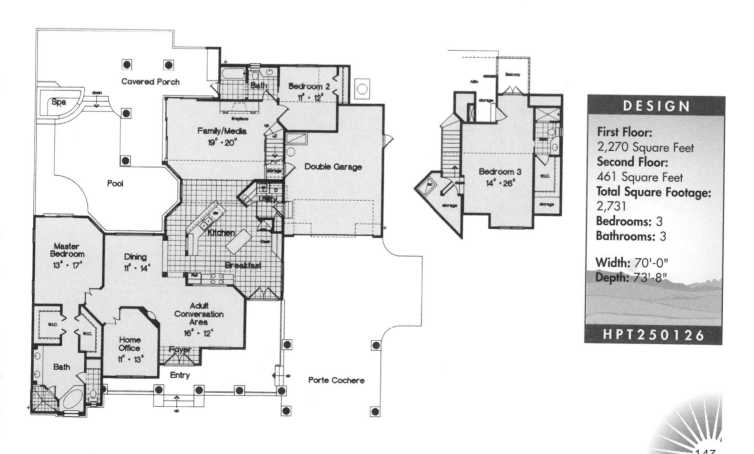

DESIGN

First Floor:
2,270 Square Feet
Second Floor:
461 Square Feet
Total Square Footage:
2,731
Bedrooms: 3
Bathrooms: 3

Width: 70'-0"
Depth: 73'-8"

HPT250126

143

DESIGN

Total Square Footage: 2,539
Bedrooms: 3
Bathrooms: 2½

Width: 75'-2"
Depth: 68'-8"

L

HPT250127

QUOTE ONE
Cost to build? See page 214
to order a complete cost estimate
to build this house in your area!

Exposed rafter tails, arched porch detailing, massive paneled front doors and stucco exterior walls
enhance the character of this Western design. The sleeping zone occupies an entire wing. The extra
room could be used for a den or study. The family dining and kitchen areas are found in the opposite
wing. A family/great room has a fireplace and media built-ins. An open courtyard is accessible from
each of the zones and leads to a quiet arbor.

An open courtyard takes center stage in this home, providing a happy marriage of indoor/outdoor relationships. Art collectors will appreciate the gallery that enhances the entry and showcases their favorite works. The centrally located great room supplies the nucleus for formal and informal entertaining. A raised-hearth fireplace flanked by built-in media centers adds a special touch. The master suite provides a private retreat where you may relax—try the sitting room or retire to the private bath for a pampering soak in the corner whirlpool tub.

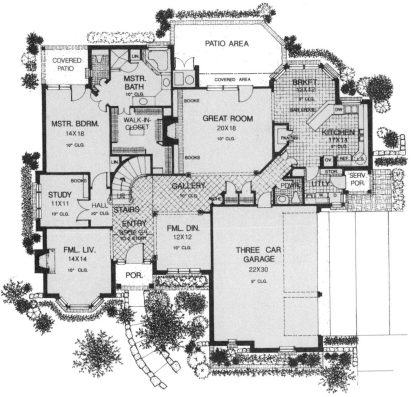

DESIGN

First Floor:
2,438 Square Feet
Second Floor:
882 Square Feet
Total Square Footage:
3,320
Bonus Room:
230 Square Feet
Bedrooms: 4
Bathrooms: 4½

Width: 70'-0"
Depth: 63'-2"

HPT250129

Wonderful rooflines top a brick exterior with cedar and stone accents and lots of English country charm. The two-story entry opens to the formal living and dining rooms. Fireplaces are found in the living room as well as the great room, which also boasts built-in bookcases and access to the rear patio. The kitchen and breakfast room add to the informal area and include a snack bar. A private patio is part of the master suite, which also offers an intriguing corner tub, twin vanities, a large walk-in closet and a nearby study. Three family bedrooms and a bonus room comprise the second floor.

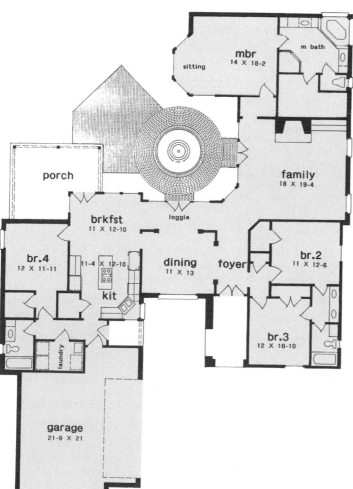

A wood-shingle roof caps this gracious stucco-and-brick home. The thoughtful design includes a back porch and a courtyard area that is visible not only from the breakfast nook, but from the family room and master bedroom as well. The foyer opens to the dining room on the left and the family room on the right. A walk-in pantry highlights the kitchen, which leads to a sunny breakfast area. Sleeping quarters include the master suite, with a bayed sitting area, and two family bedrooms—both with access to the bath. A separate fourth bedroom could serve as a home office or guest quarters.

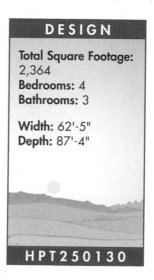

DESIGN

Total Square Footage:
2,364
Bedrooms: 4
Bathrooms: 3

Width: 62'-5"
Depth: 87'-4"

HPT250130

BATH

BEDROOM
12' X 12'
TRAY CEILING

DR.

WIC

DR.

SHOES

PLANT AREA

← FRONT

BEDROOM
12' X 11'

HALL

PORCH

WIC

BDET

BATH

HALL

FOYER

LIVING ROOM
21' X 20'

FIREPLACE

TV

BOOKS

DINETTE
12' x 11'

CLOSET

SHOWER

BATH

WIC

WIC

ENTRY

GARAGE
21' x 21'

BOOKS

BAR

PANTRY

REFRIG.

DRY WASH

UTIL.

FREEZ.

DISAP, STAIRS

PRE-FAB METAL FIREPLACE

MASTER SUITE
20' X 14'

COURTYARD

PLANTER

PORCH

DINING ROOM
13' X 12'

RANGE

KITCHEN
14' x 13'

STORAGE

BOOKS

ENTERTAINMENT CENTER – BUILT–IN

DISHWASHER

SINK

Courtyards set the mood for this aged country cottage beginning with the entry court. The narrow design of this three-bedroom plan makes it perfect for high-density areas where the owner still wants privacy. Sixteen-foot ceilings, a fireplace, an entertainment center and spacious views of the entry courtyard and dining room are all part of the amenities of the living room. The master suite has a fireplace and built-in entertainment center too! Please specify crawlspace or slab foundation when ordering.

DESIGN

Total Square Footage:
2,259
Bedrooms: 3
Bathrooms: 2½

Width: 56'-0"
Depth: 93'-0"

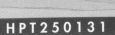
HPT250131

Wide-open windows grace this home and allow the rooms inside to enjoy natural light. Living areas are open and include a living room (or make it a study), a huge family room, a formal dining room and a breakfast room. A wonderful solarium provides light and warmth to the family room and breakfast room. Two bedrooms are split from the master suite and share a full bath that includes private vanities. An additional bedroom on the right side of the plan has a private bath.

DESIGN

Total Square Footage:
3,430
Bedrooms: 4
Bathrooms: 3½

Width: 78'-9"
Depth: 79'-4"

HPT250132

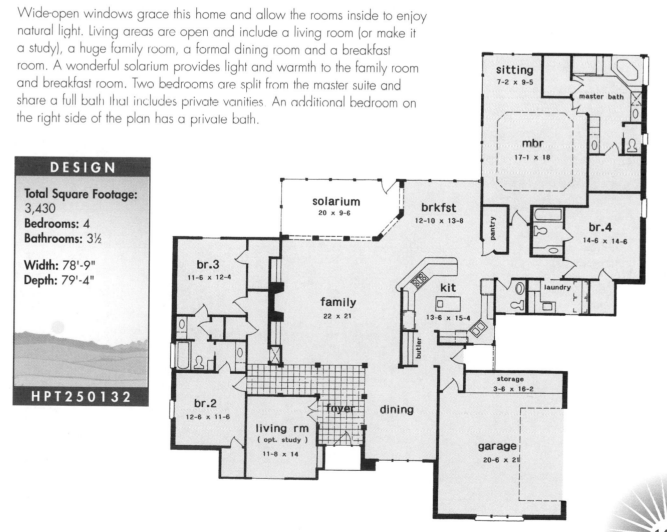

Simple Victorian detailing marks the exterior of this interesting plan. The interior surrounds a private courtyard. French doors accent the remainder of the home; they are found in the master bedroom, the dining area and on each side of the living-room fireplace. The master bathroom is a garden retreat with access to the courtyard and a planter inside next to the garden tub. Please specify crawl-space or slab foundation when ordering.

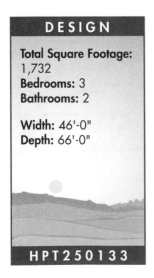

DESIGN

Total Square Footage:
1,732
Bedrooms: 3
Bathrooms: 2

Width: 46'-0"
Depth: 66'-0"

HPT250133

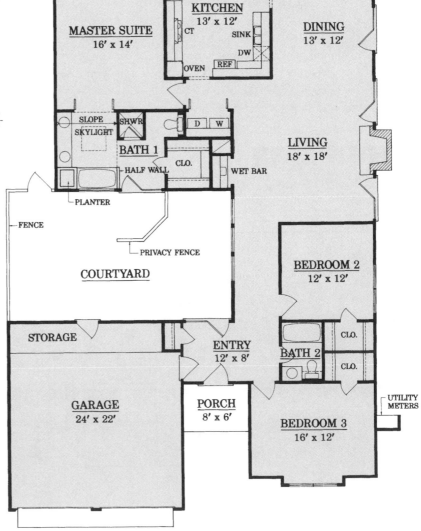

PAN

KITCHEN
13' x 12'

MASTER SUITE
16' x 14'

CT

SINK

DINING
13' x 12'

OVEN   REF
DW

SLOPE
SKYLIGHT   SHWR

D   W

LIVING
18' x 18'

BATH 1

CLO.

WET BAR

HALF WALL

PLANTER

FENCE

PRIVACY FENCE

COURTYARD

BEDROOM 2
12' x 12'

CLO.

STORAGE

ENTRY
12' x 8'

BATH 2

CLO.

CLO.

GARAGE
24' x 22'

PORCH
8' x 6'

BEDROOM 3
16' x 12'

UTILITY
METERS

Corner quoins, tall windows and multiple rooflines add a unique appeal to this design. Inside, the formal dining room features a tray ceiling and double doors that open to the kitchen. An eating nook shares a snack bar with the kitchen and overlooks the rear patio. The living room embraces a fireplace, built-in bookshelves and cabinets. Sleeping quarters consist of a master suite on the first level and three bedrooms on the second level. Walk-in closets are provided in the master suite and two of the family bedrooms. Please specify basement, crawlspace or slab foundation when ordering.

DESIGN

First Floor:
1,708 Square Feet
Second Floor:
811 Square Feet
Total Square Footage:
2,519
Bedrooms: 4
Bathrooms: 2½

Width: 52'-0"
Depth: 72'-0"

HPT250134

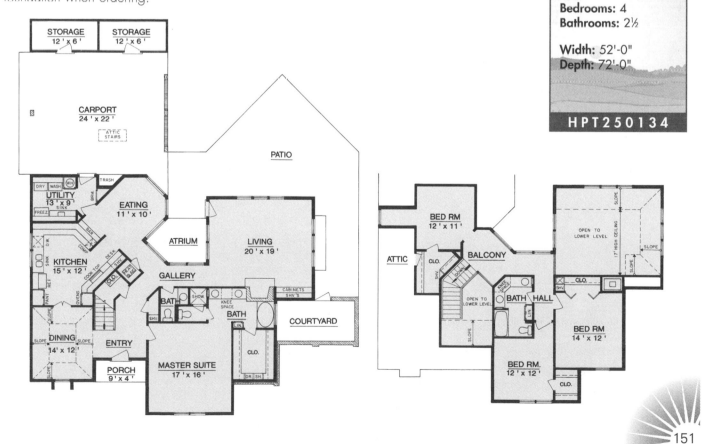

This home, as shown in the photograph, may differ from the actual blueprints. For more detailed information, please check the floor plans carefully.

Photo courtesy Design Basics, Inc.

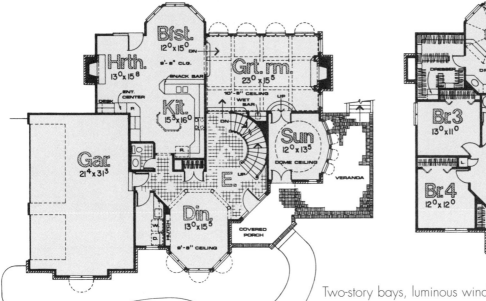

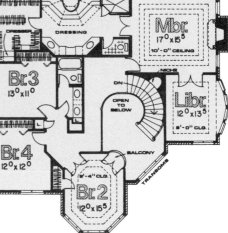

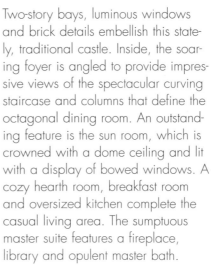

REAR ELEVATION

Two-story bays, luminous windows and brick details embellish this stately, traditional castle. Inside, the soaring foyer is angled to provide impressive views of the spectacular curving staircase and columns that define the octagonal dining room. An outstanding feature is the sun room, which is crowned with a dome ceiling and lit with a display of bowed windows. A cozy hearth room, breakfast room and oversized kitchen complete the casual living area. The sumptuous master suite features a fireplace, library and opulent master bath.

DESIGN

First Floor:
1,719 Square Feet
Second Floor:
1,688 Square Feet
Total Square Footage:
3,407
Bedrooms: 4
Bathrooms: 2½

Width: 62'-0"
Depth: 55'-4"

HPT250135

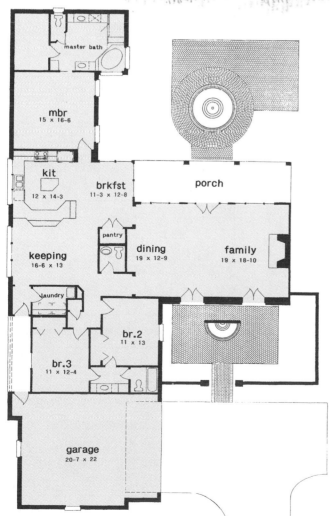

This home boasts a beautiful entry courtyard that opens to the combined dining and family rooms through two sets of double doors. Here, a cheerful fireplace and a wall of windows with another French door add to the charm. Down the hall, past the convenient powder room, is a keeping room, an island kitchen—with a snack bar—and a breakfast area. Two family bedrooms at the front of the plan share a compartmented bath between them. The secluded master suite in the back includes a large closet and a corner tub surrounded by windows.

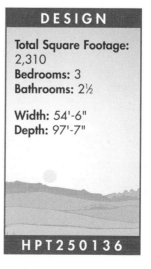

DESIGN

Total Square Footage:
2,310
Bedrooms: 3
Bathrooms: 2½

Width: 54'-6"
Depth: 97'-7"

HPT250136

This home, as shown in the photograph, may differ from the actual blueprints.
For more detailed information, please check the floor plans carefully.

DESIGN

First Floor:
2,854 Square Feet
Second Floor:
484 Square Feet
Total Square Footage:
3,338
Bedrooms: 4
Bathrooms: 3½

Width: 77'-4"
Depth: 94'-0"

HPT250137

This design garnered a grand award in the *Parade of Homes*, judged "Best in overall design and detail." The courtyard design allows for intimate poolside gatherings in complete privacy, yet golf course views are enhanced due to window walls of glass in all gathering spaces. Varied ceiling designs create more excitement as you enter through double doors, passing the paved courtyard. The master suite, with its sculptured ceilings, is generous, and the private bath is sumptuously appointed with grand arches over the spa tub.

This home, as shown in the photograph, may differ from the actual blueprints. For more detailed information, please check the floor plans carefully.

Photo by Jessie Walker

Here is a truly exquisite Tudor adaptation. Inside, the delightfully large receiving hall has a two-story ceiling and controls the flexible traffic patterns. The living and dining rooms, with the library nearby, will cater to formal living pursuits. The guest room with an adjacent full bath offers another haven for the enjoyment of peace and quiet. For the family's informal activities, there are the interactions of the family room, covered porch, nook and kitchen. The high ceiling adds to the charm of the family room. The second floor offers three family bedrooms, a lounge and a deluxe master suite.

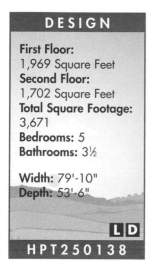

DESIGN

First Floor:
1,969 Square Feet
Second Floor:
1,702 Square Feet
Total Square Footage:
3,671
Bedrooms: 5
Bathrooms: 3½

Width: 79'-10"
Depth: 53'-6"

LD

HPT250138

DESIGN

Total Square Footage:
3,158
Bedrooms: 4
Bathrooms: 3

Width: 72'-0"
Depth: 70'-0"

HPT250139

The entry of this transitional home leads into a family room with a thirteen-foot ceiling, fireplace and built-in entertainment center. Beyond the family room are the breakfast room and sun room, where a skylight and a bar with a wine rack, sink and glass shelves can be found. The kitchen includes a pantry, skylight and snack bar. The master suite is a study in spaciousness with its large walk-in closet, sloped bathroom ceiling, skylight, linen closets, vanity and glass-surrounded spa tub. Please specify crawl-space or slab foundation when ordering.

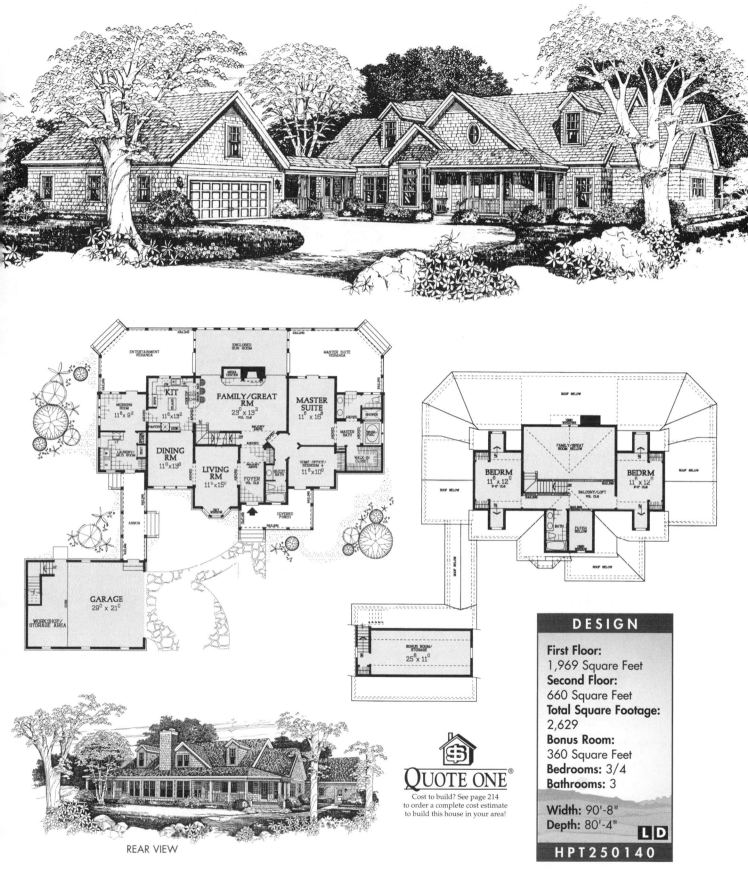

REAR VIEW

QUOTE ONE®

Cost to build? See page 214
to order a complete cost estimate
to build this house in your area!

DESIGN

First Floor:
1,969 Square Feet
Second Floor:
660 Square Feet
Total Square Footage:
2,629
Bonus Room:
360 Square Feet
Bedrooms: 3/4
Bathrooms: 3

Width: 90'-8"
Depth: 80'-4"

LD

HPT250140

Entertaining and comfortable living are the bywords for this gracious home. From the two-story foyer, enter the living room with its bay window, or the spacious family/great room with its volume ceiling, central fireplace, built-in media center and access to the enclosed sun room. The first-floor master suite includes a pampering bath with a whirlpool tub. Two additional bedrooms and a full bath are found on the second floor. The home office can also double as a fourth bedroom due to a nearby full bath.

This beautiful plan is an authentic remnant of an early
American home. Two family bedrooms on the first floor offer
access to a full bath. A fireplace warms the living room, while
a large hearth dominates the beam-ceiling family room. The
kitchen overlooks the rear covered porch. The deluxe master
bedroom located upstairs provides built-ins and a walk-in closet. An additional bedroom is available on the second floor
and can be easily converted into a study. The covered rear
porch leads to a garage and extends to a beautiful outdoor
flower court.

DESIGN

First Floor:
1,182 Square Feet
Second Floor:
708 Square Feet
Total Square Footage:
1,890
Bedrooms: 3
Bathrooms: 2

Width: 44'-0"
Depth: 64'-0"

L

HPT250141

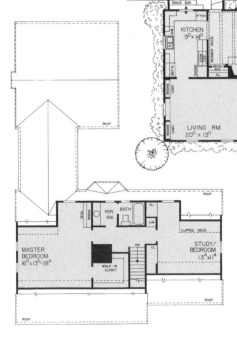

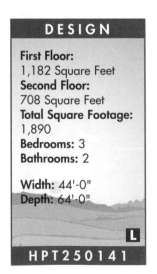

Cost to build? See page 214
to order a complete cost estimate
to build this house in your area!

158

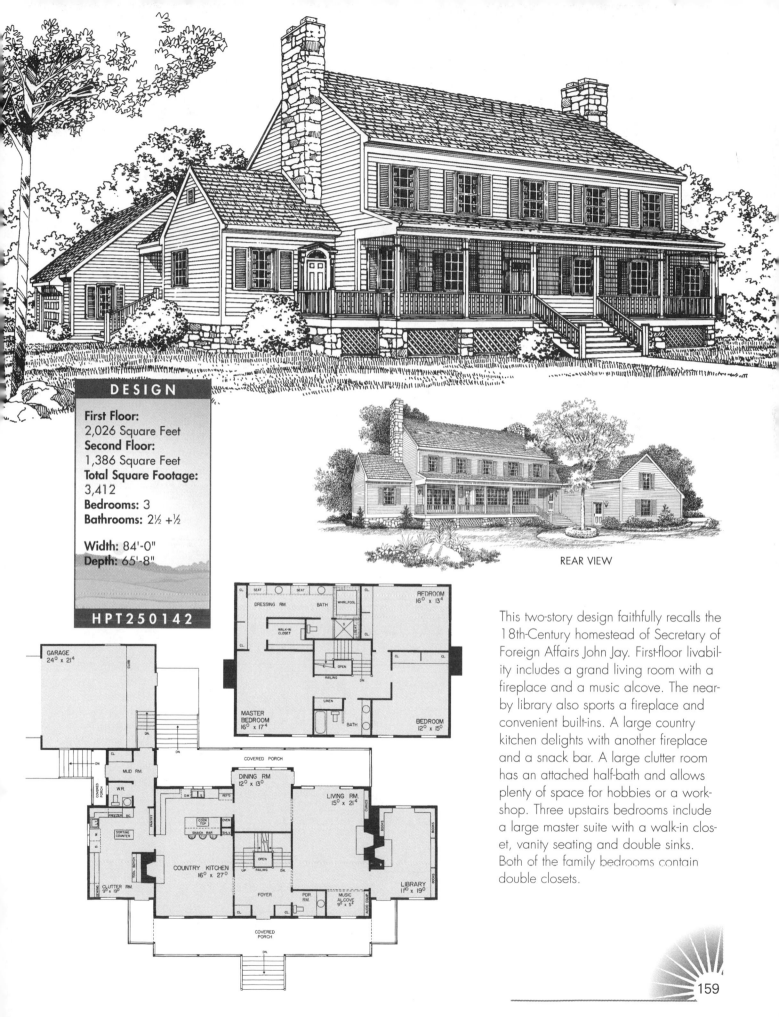

DESIGN

First Floor:
2,026 Square Feet
Second Floor:
1,386 Square Feet
Total Square Footage:
3,412
Bedrooms: 3
Bathrooms: 2½ +½

Width: 84'-0"
Depth: 65'-8"

HPT250142

REAR VIEW

This two-story design faithfully recalls the 18th-Century homestead of Secretary of Foreign Affairs John Jay. First-floor livability includes a grand living room with a fireplace and a music alcove. The nearby library also sports a fireplace and convenient built-ins. A large country kitchen delights with another fireplace and a snack bar. A large clutter room has an attached half-bath and allows plenty of space for hobbies or a workshop. Three upstairs bedrooms include a large master suite with a walk-in closet, vanity seating and double sinks. Both of the family bedrooms contain double closets.

This home, as shown in the photographs, may differ from the actual blueprints. For more detailed information, please check the floor plans carefully.

Photos by Riley & Riley Photography, Inc.

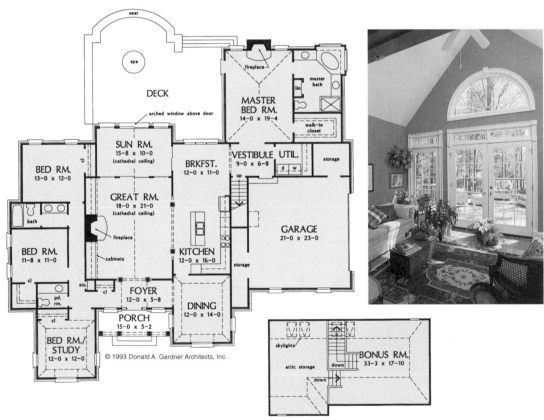

© 1993 Donald A. Gardner Architects, Inc.

This home features large arched windows, round columns, a covered porch and brick veneer siding. The arched window in the clerestory above the entrance provides natural light to the interior. The great room boasts a cathedral ceiling, a fireplace and built-in cabinets and bookshelves. Sliding glass doors lead to the sun room. The L-shaped kitchen services the dining room, the breakfast area and the great room. The master suite, with a fireplace, uses a private passage to the deck and its spa. Three additional bedrooms—one could serve as a study—are at the other end of the house for privacy.

Let The Sun Shine In
Homes with panoramic windows and glass walls

Far away there in the sunshine are my highest aspirations. I may not reach them, but I can look up and see their beauty, believe in them, and follow where they lead.

—Louisa May Alcott

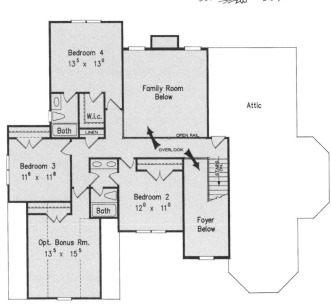

First Floor:
Breakfast — French Door — FPL. — SEAT — SHWR — LINEN — His — M.Bath 11'-10" HIGH TRAY CLG. — Island — DW. — RANGE — Kitchen — REF. — Two Story Family Room 15⁸ x 20² — Pwdr. — Hers — W. D. — Laund. — Pantry — Coats — DECORATIVE COLUMNS — STAIRS DN — STAIRS UP — FRENCH DOOR — Dining Room 12⁰ x 13² — Master Suite 18⁵ x 14⁷ — TRAY CLG — Garage 20⁵ x 23⁷ — Two Story Foyer — Living Room 12⁵ x 13⁶ — RADIUS WINDOW

Second Floor:
Bedroom 4 13⁵ x 13⁰ — Bath — W.i.c. — LINEN — Family Room Below — Attic — Bedroom 3 11⁶ x 11⁸ — OPEN RAIL — OVERLOOK — STAIRS DN — Bath — Bedroom 2 12⁰ x 11⁰ — Opt. Bonus Rm. 13⁵ x 15⁵ — Foyer Below

DESIGN

First Floor:
1,839 Square Feet

Second Floor:
842 Square Feet

Total Square Footage:
2,681

Bonus Room:
254 Square Feet

Bedrooms: 4

Bathrooms: 3½

Width: 60'-0"
Depth: 52'-0"

HPT250144

Keystone arches dominate the facade of this two-story plan which gets its inspiration from the homes of the European countryside. The two-story foyer is flanked on the left by the formal dining room, with its decorative columns, and on the right, by the living room where the bay window floods the interior with sunlight. The two-story family room is open to the dining room and the sunny breakfast area that conveniently adjoins the elaborate kitchen. Three family bedrooms are tucked away on the second floor while the lavish master suite finds seclusion on the first floor. Please specify basement or crawlspace foundation when ordering.

This captivating exterior is accentuated by handsome stone columns and a dramatic cantilevered bay. Inside, formal elegance is captured in the living room that has a volume ceiling, bowed windows and a fireplace. The kitchen is enhanced with a prep island, snack bar and pantry. Informal gatherings will be enjoyed in the breakfast nook or the sun room. The master suite has an adjoining sitting room and a luxury bath. Upstairs, at the landing level, is a den with a spider-beam ceiling. The second floor houses three bedrooms—two share a bath and one has a private bath.

DESIGN

First Floor:
2,804 Square Feet
Second Floor:
961 Square Feet
Total Square Footage:
3,765
Bedrooms: 4
Bathrooms: 3½

Width: 70'-8"
Depth: 73'-4"

HPT250145

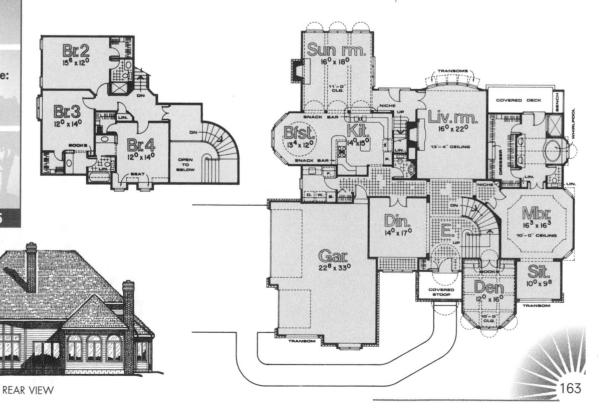

REAR VIEW

DECK

MASTER BEDROOM
13'-4" X 15'-3"

GREAT ROOM
13'-4" X 16'-7"

BREAKFAST
10'-6" X 10'-6"

GUEST BEDROOM
13'-4" X 12'-0"

MASTER BATH

W.I.C.

GUEST BATH

KITCHEN
10'-6" X 15'-0"

UP

DN

LAUNDRY
9'-4" X 6'-0"

W.I.C.

FOYER
6'-8" X 17'-4"

DINING ROOM
12'-0" X 13'-4"

STUDY
13'-4" X 11'-2"

TWO CAR GARAGE
21'-4" X 21'-4"

Wood shingles add a cozy touch to the exterior of this home; the arched covered front porch adds its own bit of warmth. Interior rooms include the great room with a bay window and a fireplace, the formal dining room, and the study with another fireplace. A guest room on the first floor contains a full bath and walk-in closet. The relaxing master suite is also on the first floor and features a pampering master bath with His and Hers walk-in closets, dual vanities, a separate shower and a whirlpool tub. This home is designed with a walkout basement foundation.

DESIGN

First Floor:
2,070 Square Feet
Second Floor:
790 Square Feet
Total Square Footage:
2,860
Bedrooms: 4
Bathrooms: 3½

Width: 57'-6"
Depth: 54'-0"

HPT250146

Bedroom No. 3
12'0 x 11'6

Gallery

Bath

Loft
12'0 x 9'10

Bedroom No. 2
12'0 x 12'0

REAR VIEW

DECK

BREAKFAST
9'-4" X 10'-6"

TWO STORY
GREAT ROOM
16'-8" X 15'-4"

MEDIA ROOM
12'-0" X 12'-0"

KITCHEN
15'-8" X 14'-0"

STORAGE

UP   DN.

LAUNDRY
6'-2" X 7'-6"

POWDER   WET BAR

TWO-CAR GARAGE
21'-4" X 21'-4"

DINING ROOM
12'-0" X 13'-0"

UP

TWO STORY
FOYER
10'-6" X 13'-0"

LIVING ROOM
12'-0" X 12'-2"

PORCH

SITTING

MASTER
BEDROOM
16'-0" X 13'-0"

OPEN TO BELOW

BEDROOM NO. 2
12'-0" X 11'-4"

BALCONY

BATH

MASTER
BATH

BATH

OPEN TO
BELOW

BEDROOM NO. 3
12'-0" X 11'-4"

DN.

DN.

W.I.C.

BEDROOM NO. 4
11'-2" X 12'-0"

SECRET
ROOM

QUOTE ONE®

Cost to build? See page 214
to order a complete cost estimate
to build this house in your area!

DESIGN

First Floor:
1,475 Square Feet
Second Floor:
1,460 Square Feet
Total Square Footage:
2,935
Bedrooms: 4
Bathrooms: 3½

Width: 57'-6"
Depth: 46'-6"

HPT250147

Quaint keystones and shutters offer charming accents to the stucco-and-stone exterior of this stately English country home. The two-story foyer opens through decorative columns to the formal living room, which offers a wet bar. The nearby media room shares a through-fireplace with the two-story great room, which has double doors that lead to the rear deck. A breakfast bay shares its light with an expansive gourmet kitchen that features an angled cooktop counter. The master suite boasts unusual amenities—angled walls, a tray ceiling and a bayed sitting area. This home is designed with a walkout basement foundation.

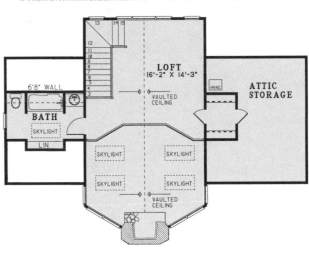

COVERED PORCH
16'-10" X 5'-0"

KITCHEN
10'-7" X 11'-10"

FRENCH DOORS

STACKED W/D

GRILLING PORCH
11'-0" X 5'-0"

FOYER

BALCONY LINE

GREAT RM.
16'-2" X 17'-8"
OPEN TO ABOVE

STONE FIREPLACE

FRENCH DOORS   FRENCH DOORS

LIN

MASTER SUITE
11'-6" X 17'-0"

FRENCH DOORS

DECK

6'8" WALL

BATH

SKYLIGHT

LIN

SKYLIGHT

SKYLIGHT

LOFT
16'-2" X 14'-3"

VAULTED CEILING

HVAC

ATTIC STORAGE

SKYLIGHT

SKYLIGHT

VAULTED CEILING

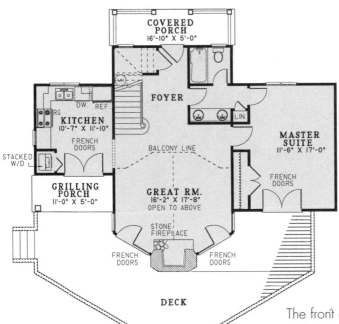

REAR VIEW

The front of this two-bedroom home is sweet and simple, while the rear is dedicated to fun and sun. Inside, the foyer opens to the two-story great room, where sunlight pours into the room not only from the wall of windows but also from four skylights. A large stone fireplace dominates the window wall and offers warmth on cool spring evenings. The L-shaped kitchen features French doors out to the grilling porch. On the opposite side of the home, a large master suite offers a second set of French doors leading out to the deck. Please specify crawlspace or slab foundation when ordering.

DESIGN

First Floor:
862 Square Feet
Second Floor:
332 Square Feet
Total Square Footage:
1,194
Bedrooms: 2
Bathrooms: 2

Width: 42'-0"
Depth: 36'-2"

HPT250148

DESIGN

First Floor:
1,395 Square Feet
Second Floor:
1,210 Square Feet
Total Square Footage:
2,605
Bonus Room:
225 Square Feet
Bedrooms: 3
Bathrooms: 2½

Width: 47'-0"
Depth: 49'-6"

HPT250149

BEDROOM NO. 2
12'-0" X 12'-0"

OPEN TO BELOW

SITTING

MASTER BEDROOM
19'-8" X 13'-6"

BALCONY

W.I.C. W.I.C.

BATH

DN

MASTER BATH

BEDROOM NO. 3
12'-0" X 12'-6"

OPEN TO BELOW

W.I.C.

UNFIN. BONUS
12'-0" X 11'-4"

DECK

MEDIA ROOM
12'-0" X 15'-6"

TWO STORY
GREAT ROOM
14'-0" X 18'-0"

BREAKFAST
10'-0" X 10'-0"

KITCHEN
12'-6" X 11'-6"

LAUNDRY

POWDER

UP

DN

UP

DINING ROOM
12'-0" X 11'-6"

TWO STORY
FOYER
10'-6" X 10'-8"

LIVING ROOM
13'-4" X 10'-6"

TWO CAR GARAGE
21'-10" X 22'-0"

STOOP

The well-balanced use of stucco and stone combined with box-bay window treatments and a covered entry make this English country home especially inviting. The two-story foyer opens on the right to formal living and dining rooms, bright with natural light. A spacious U-shaped kitchen adjoins a breakfast nook with views of the outdoors. This area flows nicely into the two-story great room, which offers a through-fireplace to the media room. A plush retreat awaits the homeowner upstairs with a master suite that offers a quiet windowed sitting area with views to the rear grounds. Two family bedrooms share a full bath and a balcony hall that has a dramatic view of the great room below. This home is designed with a walkout basement foundation.

QUOTE ONE®
Cost to build? See page 214
to order a complete cost estimate
to build this house in your area!

REAR VIEW

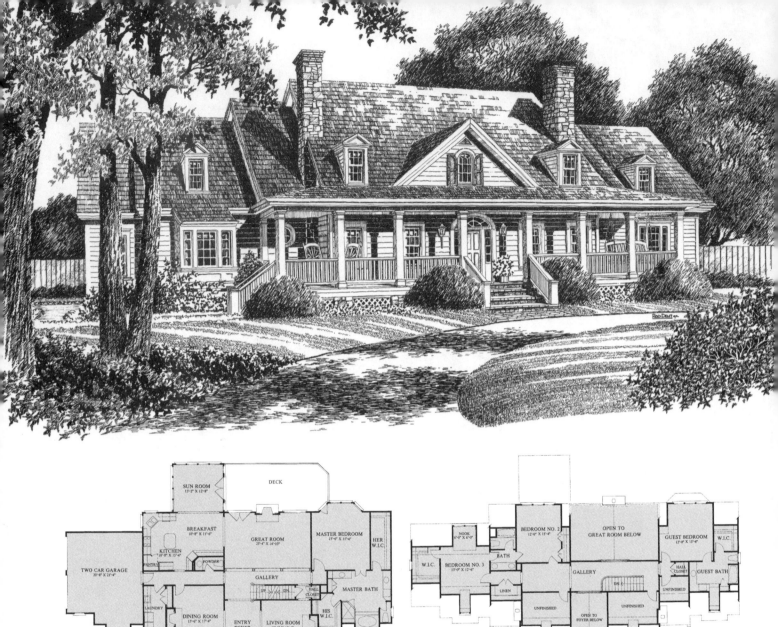

A symmetrical facade with twin chimneys makes a grand statement. A covered porch welcomes visitors and provides a pleasant place to spend a mild evening. The entry foyer is flanked by formal living areas: a dining room and a living room, each with a fireplace. A third fireplace is the highlight of the expansive great room to the rear. An L-shaped kitchen offers a work island and a walk-in pantry as amenities and easily serves the nearby breakfast and sun rooms. This home is designed with a walkout basement foundation.

QUOTE ONE®
Cost to build? See page 214
to order a complete cost estimate
to build this house in your area!

REAR VIEW

DESIGN

First Floor:
2,565 Square Feet
Second Floor:
1,375 Square Feet
Total Square Footage:
3,940
Bedrooms: 3
Bathrooms: 3½

Width: 88'-6"
Depth: 58'-6"

HPT250150

This home, as shown in the photographs, may differ from the actual blueprints.
For more detailed information, please check the floor plans carefully.

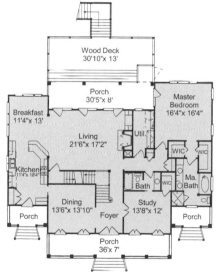

Wood Deck
30'10"x 13'

Porch
30'5"x 8'

Master
Bedroom
16'4"x 16'4"

Breakfast
11'4"x 13'

Living
21'6"x 17'2'

Util.

WIC   WIC

Kitchen
11'4" 18'4"

Dining
13'6"x 13'10"

Foyer

Bath

WIC

Ma.
Bath

Study
13'8"x 12'

Porch

Porch

Porch
36'x 7'

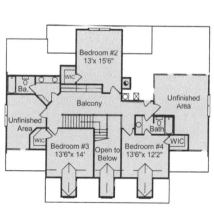

Bedroom #2
13'x 15'6"

WIC

Ba.

Balcony

Unfinished
Area

Unfinished
Area

Bedroom #3
13'6"x 14'

Open to
Below

Bedroom #4
13'6"x 12'2"

Bath

WIC

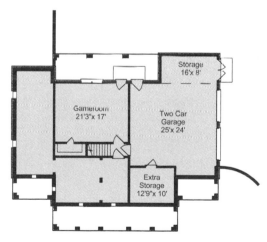

Storage
16'x 8'

Gameroom
21'3"x 17'

Two Car
Garage
25'x 24'

Extra
Storage
12'9"x 10'

DESIGN

First Floor:
2,129 Square Feet
Second Floor:
1,206 Square Feet
Finished Basement:
435 Square Feet
Total Square Footage:
3,770
Bedrooms: 4
Bathrooms: 4

Width: 59'-4"
Depth: 64'-0"

HPT250151

French style embellishes this dormered country home. Stepping through French doors to the foyer, the dining area is immediately to the left. To the right are double doors leading to a study or secondary bedroom. A lavish master suite provides privacy and plenty of storage space. The living room sports three doors to the rear porch and a lovely fireplace with built-ins. A secluded breakfast nook adjoins an efficient kitchen. Upstairs, two of the three family bedrooms boast dormer windows. Plans include a basement-level garage that adjoins a game room and two handy storage areas.

REAR VIEW

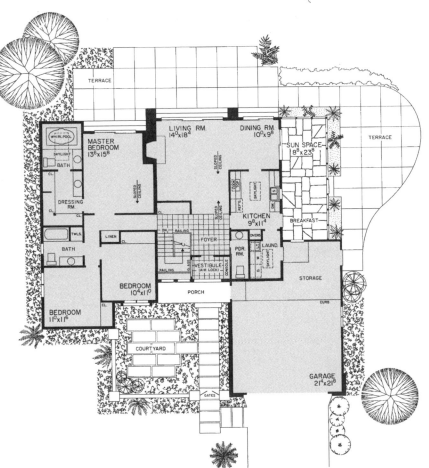

DESIGN

Total Square Footage:
1,632

Bedrooms: 3

Bathrooms: 2½

Width: 59'-0"
Depth: 56'-8"

L

HPT250152

Quote One®

Cost to build? See page 214
to order a complete cost estimate
to build this house in your area!

A sun space highlights this passive solar design. It features access from the kitchen, the dining room and the garage and will be a great place to enjoy meals. Three skylights highlight the interior—in the kitchen, laundry and master bath. An air-locked vestibule helps this design's energy efficiency. Interior livability is excellent. The living/dining room rises with a sloped ceiling and enjoys a fireplace and two sets of sliding glass doors to the terrace. Three bedrooms are in the sleeping wing. The master bedroom will delight with its private bath and luxurious whirlpool tub.

This cleverly designed Southwestern-style home takes its cue from the California Craftsman and Bungalow styles that have seen such an increase in popularity lately. Nonetheless, it is suited to just about any climate. Its convenient floor plan includes living and working areas on the first floor in addition to a master suite. The second floor holds two family bedrooms and a guest bedroom. Note the abundance of window areas to the rear of the plan.

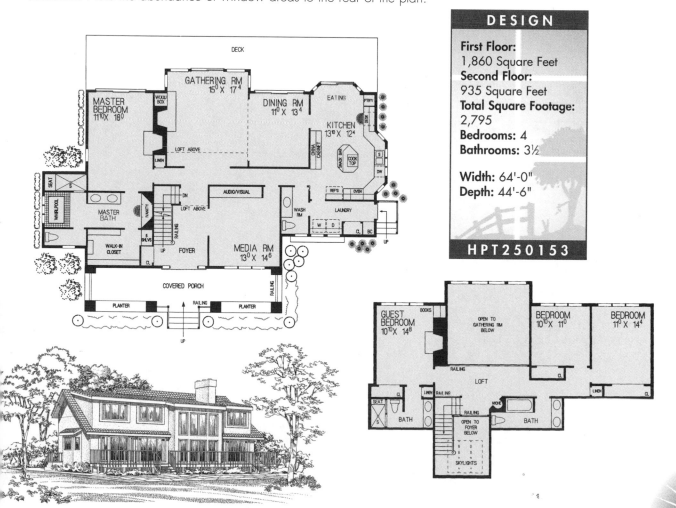

DESIGN

First Floor:
1,860 Square Feet
Second Floor:
935 Square Feet
Total Square Footage:
2,795
Bedrooms: 4
Bathrooms: 3½

Width: 64'-0"
Depth: 44'-6"

HPT250153

REAR VIEW

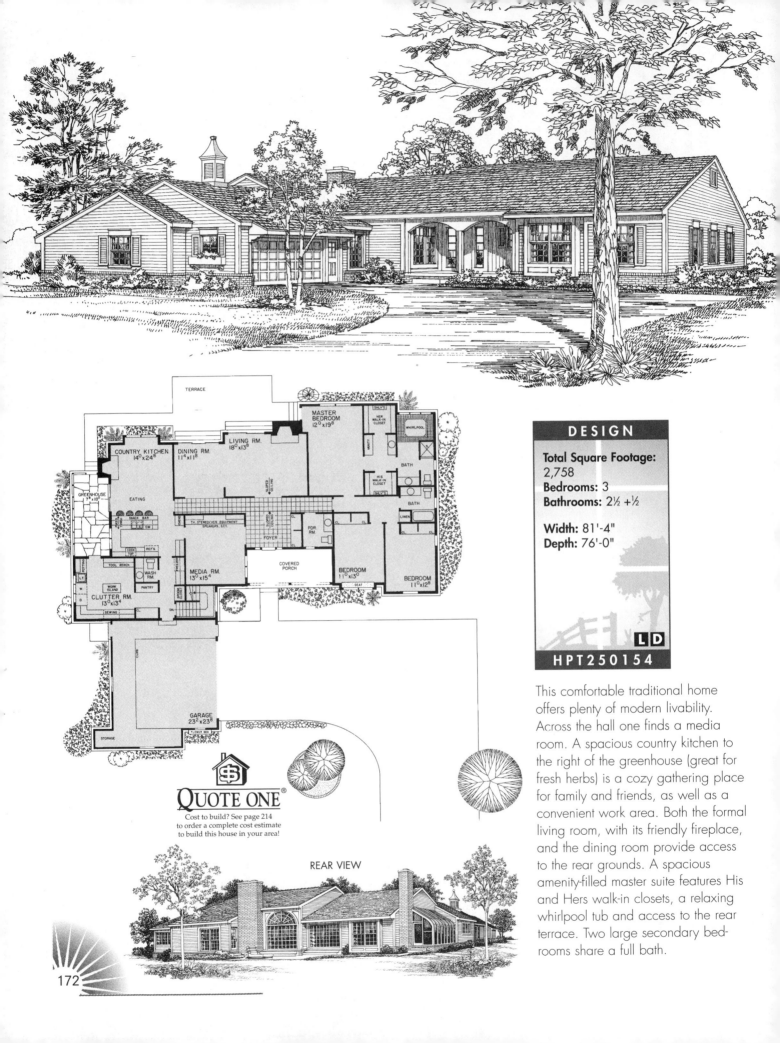

TERRACE

COUNTRY KITCHEN
14⁰x24⁸

DINING RM.
11⁴x11⁸

LIVING RM.
18⁰x13⁴

MASTER
BEDROOM
12⁰x19⁶

HER
WALK-IN
CLOSET

SHLV'S

VANITY

WHIRLPOOL

BATH

GREENHOUSE
7⁰x18⁰

EATING

SNACK BAR

HIS
WALK-IN
CLOSET

SHLV'S

BATH

LINEN

TV, STEREO/VCR EQUIPMENT
SPEAKERS, ECT.

SLOPED CEILING

PDR.
RM.

FOYER

REF'S
COOK
TOP

TOOL BENCH

WASH
RM.

WORK
ISLAND

PANTRY

MEDIA RM.
13⁰x15⁴

CLUTTER RM.
13⁰x13⁴

SEWING

COVERED
PORCH

BEDROOM
11⁰x13⁰

SEAT

BEDROOM
11⁰x12⁸

GARAGE
23²x23⁸

STORAGE

FLOWER BOX

QUOTE ONE
Cost to build? See page 214
to order a complete cost estimate
to build this house in your area!

REAR VIEW

172

DESIGN

Total Square Footage:
2,758
Bedrooms: 3
Bathrooms: 2½ +½

Width: 81'-4"
Depth: 76'-0"

L D

HPT250154

This comfortable traditional home
offers plenty of modern livability.
Across the hall one finds a media
room. A spacious country kitchen to
the right of the greenhouse (great for
fresh herbs) is a cozy gathering place
for family and friends, as well as a
convenient work area. Both the formal
living room, with its friendly fireplace,
and the dining room provide access
to the rear grounds. A spacious
amenity-filled master suite features His
and Hers walk-in closets, a relaxing
whirlpool tub and access to the rear
terrace. Two large secondary bedrooms share a full bath.

REAR VIEW

DESIGN

First Floor:
2,655 Square Feet
Second Floor:
820 Square Feet
Total Square Footage:
3,475
Bedrooms: 4
Bathrooms: 4½

Width: 74'-0"
Depth: 78'-0"

HPT250155

French opulence is the theme of this classical European cottage. The foyer is flanked on either side by a study with a fireplace and a formal living room with another fireplace. Straight ahead, a sun room views the rear porch where privacy abounds. The kitchen is set between the formal dining room and the casual eating area. On the opposite side of the home, the master suite features a private bath with a bayed tub and His and Hers walk-in closets. The guest bedroom with a walk-in closet is placed next to a full hall bath.

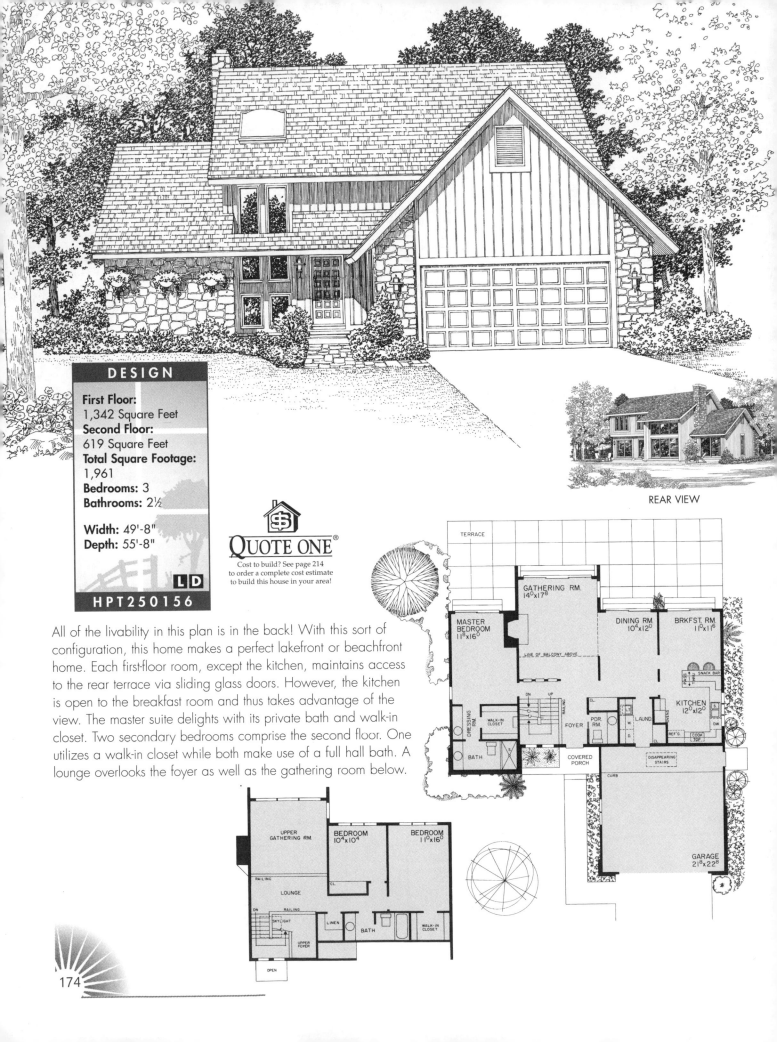

DESIGN

First Floor:
1,342 Square Feet
Second Floor:
619 Square Feet
Total Square Footage:
1,961
Bedrooms: 3
Bathrooms: 2½

Width: 49'-8"
Depth: 55'-8"

LD

HPT250156

QUOTE ONE®
Cost to build? See page 214
to order a complete cost estimate
to build this house in your area!

REAR VIEW

All of the livability in this plan is in the back! With this sort of configuration, this home makes a perfect lakefront or beachfront home. Each first-floor room, except the kitchen, maintains access to the rear terrace via sliding glass doors. However, the kitchen is open to the breakfast room and thus takes advantage of the view. The master suite delights with its private bath and walk-in closet. Two secondary bedrooms comprise the second floor. One utilizes a walk-in closet while both make use of a full hall bath. A lounge overlooks the foyer as well as the gathering room below.

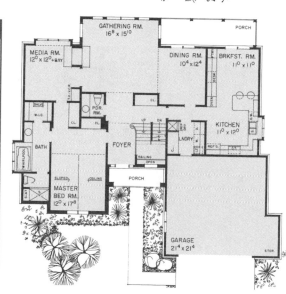

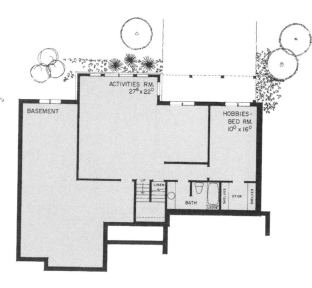

There is much more to this design than meets the eye. While it may look like a 1½-story plan, bonus recreation and hobby space in the walkout basement adds almost 1,000 square feet. The first floor holds living and dining areas as well as the deluxe master suite. Two family bedrooms share a full bath on the second floor and are connected by a balcony that overlooks the gathering room below. Notice the covered porch beyond the breakfast and dining rooms.

REAR VIEW

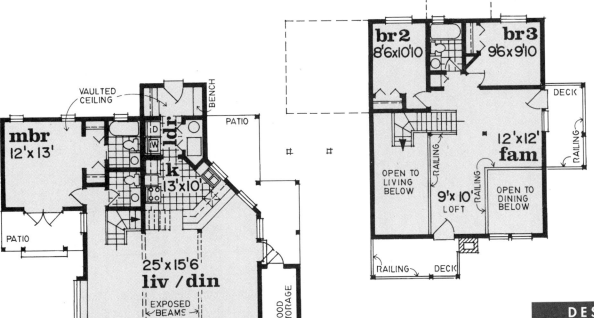

Stone and siding work in complement for this cozy design with chalet features. The vaulted living and dining rooms, with exposed beam ceilings, are open to the loft above. A wood storage area is found off the living room to feed the warm hearth inside. The kitchen features a pass-through counter to the dining area and leads to a laundry room with a work bench. The master suite has a private patio and bath on the first floor. An additional half-bath is located in the main hall. The second floor holds a family room with a deck and two family bedrooms with a shared bath.

DESIGN

First Floor:
1,036 Square Feet
Second Floor:
630 Square Feet
Total Square Footage:
1,666
Bedrooms: 3
Bathrooms: 2½

Width: 45'-6"
Depth: 44'-0"

HPT250158

This home, as shown in the photographs, may differ from the actual blueprints.
For more detailed information, please check the floor plans carefully.

Photos by Allen Maertz

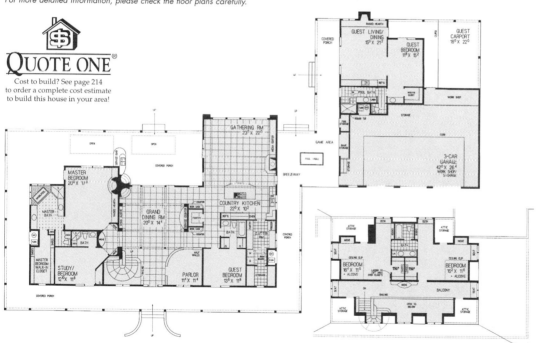

QUOTE ONE®

Cost to build? See page 214
to order a complete cost estimate
to build this house in your area!

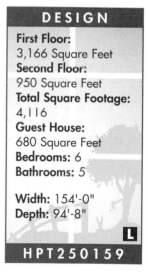

DESIGN

First Floor:
3,166 Square Feet
Second Floor:
950 Square Feet
Total Square Footage:
4,116
Guest House:
680 Square Feet
Bedrooms: 6
Bathrooms: 5

Width: 154'-0"
Depth: 94'-8"

L

HPT250159

REAR VIEW

A long low-pitched roof distinguishes this Southwestern-style farmhouse design. The tiled entrance leads to a grand dining room and opens to a formal parlor secluded by half-walls. A country kitchen with a cooktop island overlooks the two-story gathering room with its full wall of glass, fireplace and built-in media shelves. The master suite satisfies the most discerning tastes with a raised hearth, an adjacent study or exercise room, access to the wraparound porch, and a bath with a corner whirlpool tub. Rooms upstairs can serve as secondary bedrooms for family members, or can be converted to home office space or used as guest bedrooms.

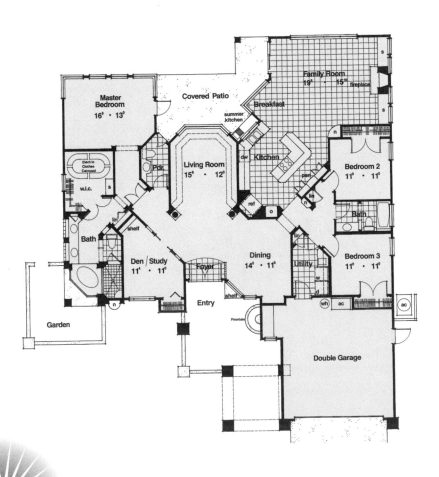

Low-slung, hipped rooflines and an abundance of glass enhance the unique exterior of this sunny, one-story home. Inside, the use of soffits and tray ceilings heighten the distinctive style of the floor plan. To the left, double doors lead to the private master suite, which is bathed in natural light. Convenient planning of the gourmet kitchen places everything at minimum distances and serves the outdoor summer kitchen, breakfast nook and family room with equal ease.

DESIGN

Total Square Footage: 2,397

Bedrooms: 3

Bathrooms: 2½

Width: 60'-0"
Depth: 71'-8"

HPT250160

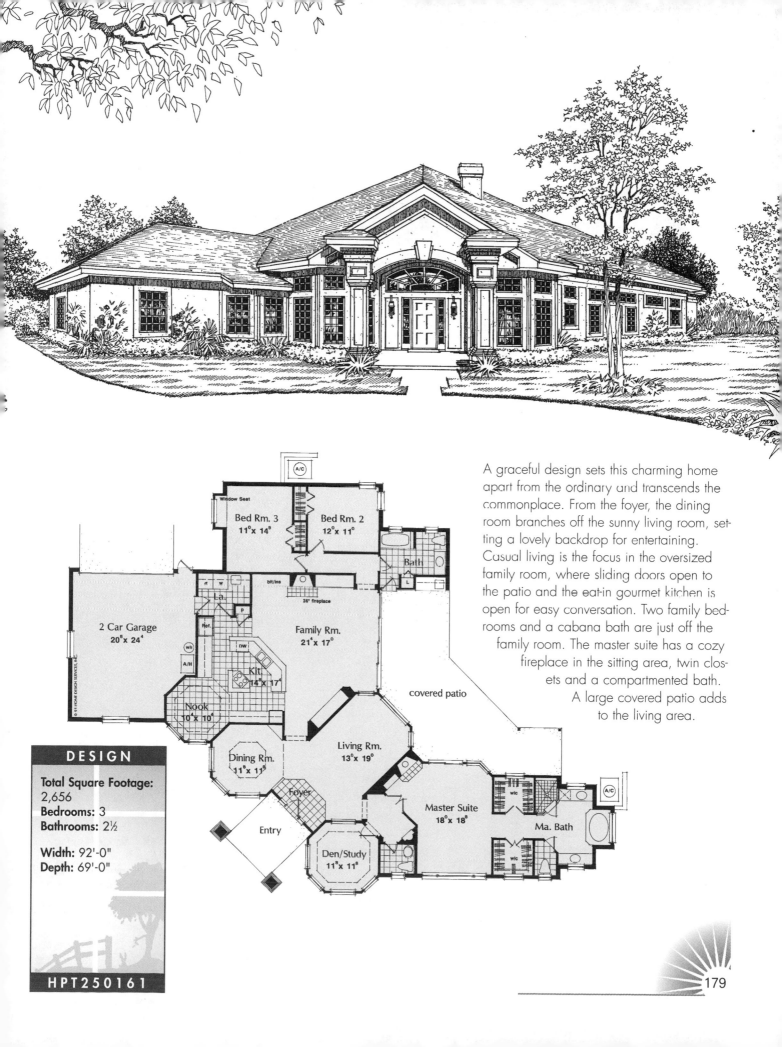

A graceful design sets this charming home apart from the ordinary and transcends the commonplace. From the foyer, the dining room branches off the sunny living room, setting a lovely backdrop for entertaining. Casual living is the focus in the oversized family room, where sliding doors open to the patio and the eat-in gourmet kitchen is open for easy conversation. Two family bedrooms and a cabana bath are just off the family room. The master suite has a cozy fireplace in the sitting area, twin closets and a compartmented bath. A large covered patio adds to the living area.

DESIGN

Total Square Footage:
2,656

Bedrooms: 3

Bathrooms: 2½

Width: 92'-0"
Depth: 69'-0"

HPT250161

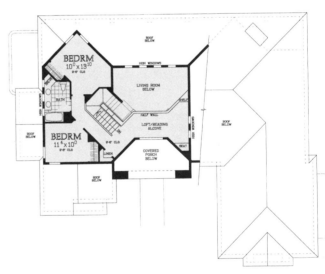

Quote One®

Cost to build? See page 214
to order a complete cost estimate
to build this house in your area!

This stucco home provides a wealth of livability for the entire family. Inside, formal areas grab your attention with a dining room and an elegant living room that opens to a covered entertainment area outside. The family room delights with open views to the kitchen and breakfast nook. The two-car garage opens off this area. On the left side of the plan, the master suite delights with a full, private bath and a lanai that's perfect for a spa. A large den could easily double as a study. Two bedrooms and a full bath are located upstairs.

DESIGN

First Floor:
2,137 Square Feet
Second Floor:
671 Square Feet
Total Square Footage:
2,808
Bedrooms: 3
Bathrooms: 2½

Width: 75'-6"
Depth: 62'-6"

L

HPT250162

This stucco-and-stone chateau offers five bedrooms and a second-floor activity room within a European facade. Two front towers hold the formal dining room and a study on the first floor and two family bedrooms on the second floor. The great room is at the back of the plan and features sliding doors to the rear terrace and a cozy hearth. The master bedroom is also hearth-warmed.

REAR VIEW

DESIGN

First Floor:
2,960 Square Feet
Second Floor:
1,729 Square Feet
Total Square Footage:
4,689
Bedrooms: 5
Bathrooms: 3½ + ½

Width: 117'-4"
Depth: 59'-3"

HPT250163

MASTER BEDRM
18⁰ x 14⁰
9'-0" CLG

COVERED DECK

MASTER BATH

SHOWER

WALK-IN CLOSET

LIVING RM
20² x 19⁰
12'-0" VGA CLG

BATH

HALF WALL

BEDRM
12⁰ x 12⁶

LAUNDRY

HALF WALL

FOYER
10'-0" VGA CLG

DINING
13⁴ x 11⁸
10'-0" VGA CLG

RAILING

COVERED PORCH

PANTRY

KIT
10⁴ x 9⁰

BRKFST
8⁰ x 8⁰

GARAGE
20⁰ x 29¹⁰

QUOTE ONE®

Cost to build? See page 214
to order a complete cost estimate
to build this house in your area!

BEDRM
13⁸ x 12⁸

BEDRM
10⁰ x 19⁰

COVERED PATIO

GREAT RM
20² x 18⁰

HALF WALL

STORAGE

BATH

REAR VIEW

The simple, Pueblo-style lines borrowed from early Native American dwellings combine with contemporary planning to create a sensation, highlighted by an angled master suite. Half-walls border the entrance to the formal living room, which is warmed by a beehive fireplace. An angled master wing harbors a retreat with a spacious bath that offers a generous walk-in closet and dressing area. The lower level includes a great room for casual activities as well as two family bedrooms and a hall bath.

DESIGN

Main Level:
1,946 Square Feet
Lower Level:
956 Square Feet
Total Square Footage:
2,902
Bedrooms: 4
Bathrooms: 3

Width: 51'-6"
Depth: 70'-2"

L

HPT250164

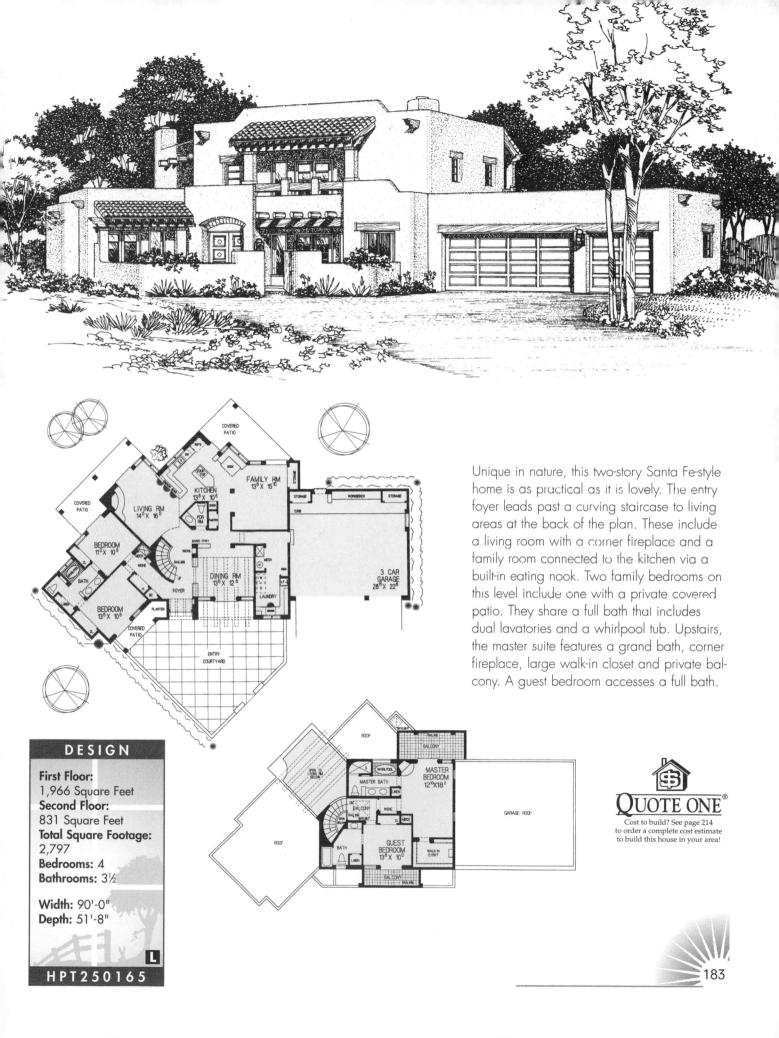

Unique in nature, this two-story Santa Fe-style home is as practical as it is lovely. The entry foyer leads past a curving staircase to living areas at the back of the plan. These include a living room with a corner fireplace and a family room connected to the kitchen via a built-in eating nook. Two family bedrooms on this level include one with a private covered patio. They share a full bath that includes dual lavatories and a whirlpool tub. Upstairs, the master suite features a grand bath, corner fireplace, large walk-in closet and private balcony. A guest bedroom accesses a full bath.

QUOTE ONE®

Cost to build? See page 214
to order a complete cost estimate
to build this house in your area!

DESIGN

First Floor:
1,966 Square Feet
Second Floor:
831 Square Feet
Total Square Footage:
2,797
Bedrooms: 4
Bathrooms: 3½

Width: 90'-0"
Depth: 51'-8"

L

HPT250165

Floor Plan Labels

First Floor:
- COVERED PATIO
- NOOK 9⁶ x 9⁰ / 12'-0" CLG
- SHWR
- MASTER BATH
- WHIRL POOL
- PATIO
- FAMILY RM 14⁴ x 13¹⁰ / 15'-0" CLG
- KIT 9⁶ x 11⁸ / 12'-0" CLG
- WALK-IN CLOSET
- MASTER SUITE 15⁰ x 13⁰ / 11'-0" CLG
- 2-CAR GARAGE 21⁰ x 23⁸
- PDR.
- DEN/SITTING 12⁸ x 10⁰ / 11'-0" CLG
- LAUNDRY ROOM
- WALK-IN PANTRY
- 1-CAR GARAGE 20¹⁰ x 11⁶
- FOYER 10'-0" CLG
- DINING RM 11⁸ x 12⁰ / 12'-0" CLG
- LIVING RM 14⁴ x 14⁰ / 15'-0" CLG
- COVERED PORCH
- BANCO
- HALF WALL

Second Floor:
- ROOF BELOW
- BEDRM 12⁶ x 10² / 9'-10" CLG
- LIVING ROOM BELOW
- HALL
- BEDRM 12⁰ x 13² / 9'-10" CLG
- BATH
- BALCONY
- GUEST 12⁶ x 11⁸ / 9'-10" CLG
- LIVING ROOM BELOW

QUOTE ONE®
Cost to build? See page 214
to order a complete cost estimate
to build this house in your area!

Tame the Wild West with this handsome adobe-style home. Suitable for side-sloping lots, it contains a wealth of livability. A beehive fireplace graces the living room to enhance formal entertaining. The dining room is to the right of the foyer. A den or sitting room is located near the master bedroom suite. Enjoy the family room, which opens to the covered patio. Four bedrooms include a guest room. Split styling puts the master suite on the right side of the plan. Here, a walk-in closet, curved shower and dual vanities bring a touch of luxury.

DESIGN

First Floor:
2,024 Square Feet
Second Floor:
800 Square Feet
Total Square Footage:
2,824
Bedrooms: 3
Bathrooms: 3½

Width: 80'-10"
Depth: 54'-0"

L

HPT250166

DESIGN

Total Square Footage:
2,226
Bedrooms: 3
Bathrooms: 2½

Width: 103'-2"
Depth: 78'-0"

L

HPT250167

The impressive, double-door entry to the walled courtyard sets the tone for this Santa Fe masterpiece home. The expansive great room shows off its casual style with a centerpiece fireplace and abundant windows overlooking the patio. Joining the great room is the formal dining room, also graced with windows and patio doors. The large gourmet kitchen has an eat-in snack bar. Family-room extras include a fireplace, entertainment built-ins and double doors to the front courtyard. The relaxing master suite is located off the great room and has double doors to the back patio.

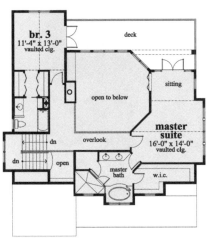

br. 3
11'-4" x 13'-0"
vaulted clg.

deck

sitting

open to below

master
suite
16'-0" x 14'-0"
vaulted clg.

overlook

dn

open

dn

master
bath

w.i.c.

bonus/
storage

2 car garage

storage

storage

br. 2
11'-4" x 13'-0"
10'-0"h. clg.

covered porch

built
ins

great room
19'-0" x 18'-0"
2-story clg.

fireplace

built
ins

dining
12'-0" x 14'-0"
10'-0" h. clg.

up

up

foyer

kitchen
10'-8" x 13'-6"

butler
pantry

util.

built
ins

study
13'-4" x 12'-0"
vaulted clg.

entry porch

DESIGN

First Floor:
1,542 Square Feet
Second Floor:
971 Square Feet
Total Square Footage:
2,513
Bedrooms: 4
Bathrooms: 3

Width: 46'-0"
Depth: 51'-0"

HPT250168

Stately and elegant, this home displays fine Tuscan columns, fanlight windows, hipped gables and a detailed balustrade that splash its facade with a subtle European flavor. The foyer opens to the two-story great room. With imaginative angles and a multitude of windows and French doors, the great room holds a magnificent fireplace nestled with built-in cabinetry. The private master suite boasts a dual-sink vanity, compartmented toilet, separate shower, garden tub and walk-in closet. The sitting area allows marvelous views and provides French doors to the deck.

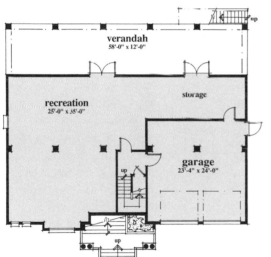

verandah
58'-0" x 12'-0"

recreation
25'-0" x 35'-0"

storage

garage
23'-4" x 24'-0"

up

up

The dramatic arched entry of this Southampton-style cottage borrows freely from its Southern coastal past. The foyer and central hall open to the grand room. The kitchen is flanked by the dining room and the morning nook, which opens to the lanai. On the left side of the plan, the master suite also accesses the lanai. Two walk-in closets and a compartmented bath with a separate tub and shower and a double-bowl vanity complete this opulent retreat. The right side of the plan includes two secondary bedrooms and a full bath.

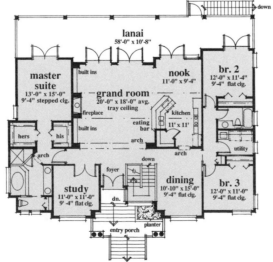

lanai
58'-0" x 10'-8"

down

master suite
13'-0" x 15'-0"
9'-4" stepped clg.

built ins

nook
11'-0" x 9'-4"

br. 2
12'-0" x 11'-4"
9'-4" flat clg.

grand room
20'-0" x 18'-0" avg.
tray ceiling

fireplace

built ins

kitchen
11' x 11'

eating bar

hers

his

arch

arch

utility

down

study
11'-0" x 11'-0"
9'-4" flat clg.

dn.

foyer

dining
10'-10" x 15'-0"
9'-4" flat clg.

br. 3
12'-0" x 11'-0"
9'-4" flat clg.

entry porch

planter

REAR VIEW

DESIGN

Total Square Footage:
2,190

Bedrooms: 3

Bathrooms: 2

Width: 58'-0"

Depth: 54'-0"

HPT250169

porch

sitting

keeping
16-2 x 18-2

brkfst
12-8 x 15

mbr
18 x 21

kit
16-6 x 11-8

family
20-5 x 14

m bath

br.2
14-8 x 11

desk

study
12-6 x 14

foyer

dining
12-6 x 14

laundry

br.3
12 x 11

garage
31-9 x 20-10

This country estate is bedecked with all the details that pronounce its French origins. They include the study, family room and keeping room. Dine in one of two areas—the formal dining room or the casual breakfast room. A large porch to the rear can be reached through the breakfast room or the master suite's sitting area. All three bedrooms in the plan have walk-in closets. Bedrooms 2 and 3 share a full bath that includes private vanities.

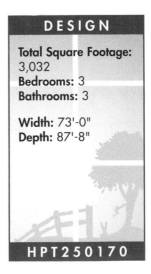

DESIGN

Total Square Footage: 3,032

Bedrooms: 3

Bathrooms: 3

Width: 73'-0"
Depth: 87'-8"

HPT250170

A mini-estate with French country details, this home preserves the beauty of historical design without sacrificing modern convenience. Through double doors, the floor plan opens from a central foyer flanked by a dining room and a study. The family room offers windows overlooking the rear yard and a fireplace. The master suite features a sitting room and a bath fit for royalty. A smaller family bedroom has a full bath nearby. A third bedroom also enjoys a full bath.

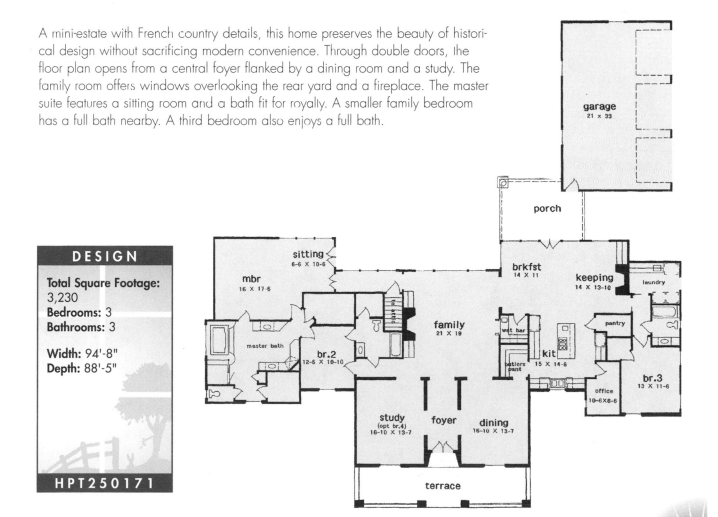

DESIGN

Total Square Footage:
3,230
Bedrooms: 3
Bathrooms: 3

Width: 94'-8"
Depth: 88'-5"

HPT250171

This home has a comfortable European design with a chateau spirit. Open casual space and formal rooms invite gatherings of friends and family. The tiled foyer opens to the family room, which has a fireplace and floor-to-ceiling windows that look out to the backyard. The breakfast room features access to a private porch. The master suite offers its own fireplace, a spacious bath and two walk-in closets.

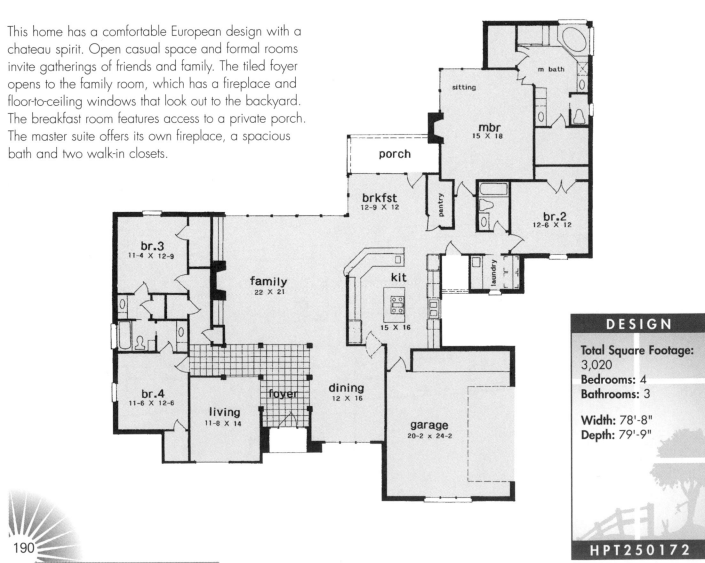

DESIGN

Total Square Footage: 3,020
Bedrooms: 4
Bathrooms: 3

Width: 78'-8"
Depth: 79'-9"

HPT250172

Upon The Water
Homes for living near the ocean, lake or river

A lake is the landscape's most beautiful and expressive feature. It is earth's eye; looking into which the beholder measures the depth of his own nature.

—*Henry David Thoreau*

REAR VIEW

3,60 X 3,60
12'-0" X 12'-0"

6,00 X 4,20
20'-0" X 14'-0"

4,20 X 3,90

3,90 X 2,70
13'-0" X 9'-0"

This fine brick home features a bay-windowed sun room, perfect for admiring the view. Inside this open floor plan, a family room features a fireplace and a spacious eat-in kitchen with access to the sun room. There are also a bedroom, a full bath and laundry facilities on this floor. Upstairs, two more bedrooms share a compartmented bath, as well as an overlook to the family room below. This home is designed with a basement foundation.

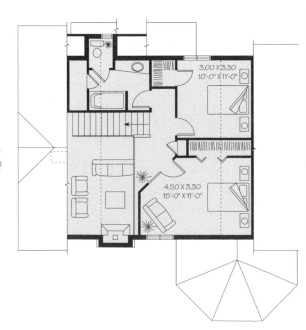

3,00 X 3,30
10'-0" X 11'-0"

4,50 X 3,30
15'-0" X 11'-0"

DESIGN

First Floor:
858 Square Feet
Second Floor:
502 Square Feet
Total Square Footage:
2,218
Bedrooms: 3
Bathrooms: 2

Width: 35'-0"
Depth: 29'-8"

HPT250173

3,30 X 5,70
11'-0" X 19'-0"

4,20 X 4,80
14'-0" X 16'-0"

2,40 X 2,70
8'-0" X 9'-0"

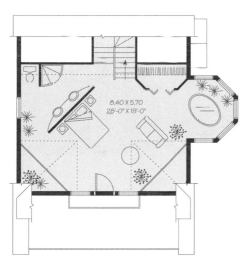

8,40 X 5,70
28'-0" X 19'-0"

3,60 X 3,60
12'-0" X 12'-0"

3,60 X 4,20
12'-0" X 14'-0"

OPTIONAL SECOND FLOOR

DESIGN

First Floor:
737 Square Feet
Second Floor:
587 Square Feet
Total Square Footage:
1,324
Bedrooms: 1
Bathrooms: 1½

Width: 33'-0"
Depth: 26'-0"

HPT250174

This home is absolutely full of windows, and a large deck enhances the outdoor living possibilities. Picture the wall of windows facing the seashore, with the sound of waves lulling you into a calm, comfortable feeling. Inside, an open floor plan includes a family/dining room, an L-shaped kitchen with a snack bar, and a full bath with laundry facilities. A special treat is the bumped-out hot tub room, almost entirely surrounded by windows. Upstairs, choose either the one- or two-bedroom plan. Both include a full bath and access to the upper balcony. This home is designed with a basement foundation.

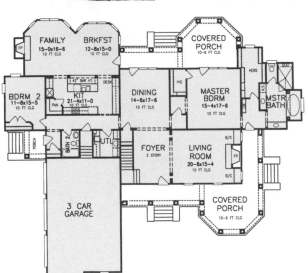

REAR VIEW

Dormer windows complement classic square columns on this country estate home, gently flavored with a Southern-style facade. A two-story foyer opens to traditional rooms. Two columns announce the living room, which has a warming hearth. The formal dining room opens to the back covered porch, decked out with decorative columns. The first-floor master suite has His and Hers walk-in closets, an oversized shower, a whirlpool tub and a windowed water closet, plus access to the covered porch. A well-appointed kitchen features a corner walk-in pantry and opens to a double-bay family room and breakfast area.

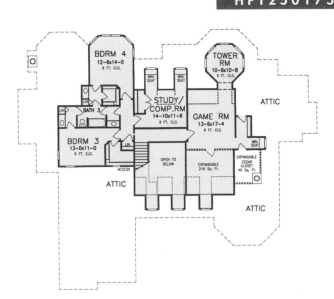

Large windows, a covered porch and an upper balcony make this home perfect for waterfront living. Inside, find a very comfortable plan, including a family room, a dining room with French-door access to the patio, and an L-shaped kitchen with a breakfast area. A convenient powder room and laundry facilities also reside on this floor. Upstairs, the two bedrooms share a full bath that contains a separate tub and shower. French doors opening to the balcony enhance the larger bedroom. This home is designed with a basement foundation.

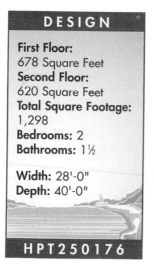
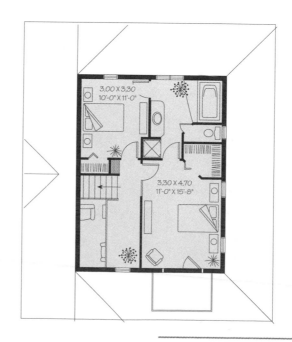

This nostalgic country design will bring a breath of fresh air to any neighborhood—in grand style. Past the wrap-around porch, the open foyer expands to the stunning living area, with a central fireplace and views from all three sides. Steps away from the cheery breakfast nook, an angled breakfast bar also provides additional counter space for the amenity-filled kitchen. The master suite offers a sizable walk-in closet, twin lavatories with a vanity, and a windowed whirlpool tub.

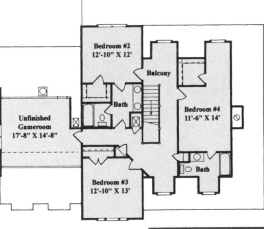

Bedroom #2
12'-10" X 12'

Balcony

Bath

Unfinished Gameroom
17'-8" X 14'-8"

Bedroom #4
11'-6" X 14'

Bedroom #3
12'-10" X 13'

Bath

Storage
19'-8" X 7'-4"

Carport
20'-3" X 22'

Breakfast
12'-10" X 11'

Covered Porch

Util.

Ba.

Ma. Bath

Kitchen
12'-10" X 12'

Living
15'-3" X 25'

Master Bedroom
17'-8" X 13'

Dining
12'-10" X 14'

Foyer

Porch

DESIGN

First Floor:
1,729 Square Feet
Second Floor:
1,123 Square Feet
Total Square Footage:
2,852
Bonus Room:
261 Square Feet
Bedrooms: 4
Bathrooms: 3½

Width: 60'-0"
Depth: 67'-6"

HPT250177

DINING
12/0 X 15/0
(13' 6" CLG.)

BR. 2
10/10 X 12/0
(9' CLG.)

21/0 X 10/8 +/-
(10' CLG.)

BR. 3
11/0 X 11/0
(9' CLG.)

LINEN

NOOK
9/6 X 11/6
(9' CLG.)

TWO STORY
GREAT RM.
21/0 X 20/6 +/-

TERRACE

This stunning facade is ready for an ocean view or a beautiful suburb. Two story windows with transoms allow natural light to fill the great room, which opens to the formal dining room. A grand kitchen has wrapping counters and a morning nook opening to a terrace. The upper-level master suite provides a double-bowl vanity, walk-in closet and fireplace. A nearby den boasts its own fireplace and plenty of space for computers and books. The lower-level four-car garage offers additional storage.

DEN
15/0 X 10/8 +/-
(9' CLG.)

GREAT RM.
BELOW

MASTER
19/6 X 13/0 +/-
(9'-10" CLG.)

SPA

DECK

UNEXCAVATED

UNEXCAVATED

UP

GARAGE
20/8 X 28/8

GARAGE
19/4 X 26/8

DESIGN

First Floor:
1,765 Square Feet
Second Floor:
907 Square Feet
Total Square Footage:
2,672
Bedrooms: 4
Bathrooms: 2

Width: 65'-0"
Depth: 42'-6"

HPT250178

This home, as shown in the photographs, may differ from the actual blueprints.
For more detailed information, please check the floor plans carefully.

LOWER DECK

STEPS

DINING ROOM
15'X11'4

SUN ROOM
11'X11'

MIDDLE DECK

DN.

DN.

STEPS

BAR

KITCHEN
15'X12'

DN.

UPPER DECK

PANTRY

GREAT ROOM
20'X18'

FP.

2 CAR GARAGE

DN.

FOYER

BATH

STEPS

GUEST
BEDROOM
12'X12'

PORCH

MASTER BATH

DECK

SHWR.

BALCONY

MASTER CLO.
11'4"X10'4"

OPEN TO
LIVING BELOW

MASTER
BEDROOM
13'4"X17'10"

FP.

STORAGE

UTIL.

BALCONY

OFFICE
15'4"X14'

LOFT
9'8"X9'8"

BATH 3

DECK

BEDROOM 3
11'8"X12'4"

Clean, contemporary lines, a unique floor plan and a metal roof with a cupola set this farmhouse apart. Remote-control transoms in the cupola open to create an airy and decidedly unique foyer. The great room, sun room, dining room and kitchen flow from one to another for casual entertaining with flair. The rear of the home is fashioned with plenty of windows overlooking the multi-level deck. A front bedroom and bath would make a comfortable guest suite. The master bedroom and bath upstairs are bridged by a pipe-rail balcony that also gives access to a rear deck. An additional bedroom, home office and bath complete this very special plan.

DESIGN

First Floor:
1,309 Square Feet
Second Floor:
1,343 Square Feet
Total Square Footage:
2,652
Bedrooms: 3
Bathrooms: 3

Width: 44'-4"
Depth: 58'-2"

L

HPT250179

REAR VEIW

Horizontal siding, plentiful windows and a wraparound porch grace this comfortable home. The great room is aptly named, with a fireplace, built-in seating and access to the rear deck. Meal preparation is a breeze with a galley kitchen designed for efficiency. A screened porch is available for sipping lemonade on warm summer afternoons. The first floor contains two bedrooms and a unique bath to serve family and guests. The second floor offers a private getaway with a master suite that supplies panoramic views from its adjoining sitting area.

Deck

Great Room
25⁹ x 19³

Porch

Bedroom No. 2
10⁹ x 12³

Kitchen
14³ x 9⁹

Foyer

Bedroom No. 3
10⁹ x 12³

Porch

Open To Below

Deck

Sitting Area

Master Bedroom
14³ x 14³

REAR VIEW

DESIGN

First Floor:
1,341 Square Feet
Second Floor:
598 Square Feet
Total Square Footage:
1,939
Bedrooms: 3
Bathrooms: 2

Width: 50'-3"
Depth: 46'-3"

HPT250180

J.N. HANSEN S.D.G.

DESIGN

First Floor:
1,073 Square Feet
Second Floor:
470 Square Feet
Total Square Footage:
1,543
Bedrooms: 4
Bathrooms: 2

Width: 30'-0"
Depth: 71'-6"

HPT250181

This spectacular coastal wonder is wrapped with windows and plenty of outdoor living space. The intricate details on this home's facade and decking make it a treat to view. The entry leads to the spacious family room and to the breakfast nook and kitchen area. Double doors open to the rear deck from the breakfast nook. A family bedroom and master suite are located on the first level while two more family bedrooms are on the second level.

Bedroom 4
13⁰ • 11⁸

Bedroom 3
10⁸ • 11⁸

Nook   Kitchen

Utility

Bedroom 2
9² • 10³

Family
13⁴ • 14¹⁰

W.I.C.

Foyer

Master Bedroom
15⁴ • 11¹⁰

Entry

© 1998 Donald A. Gardner, Inc.

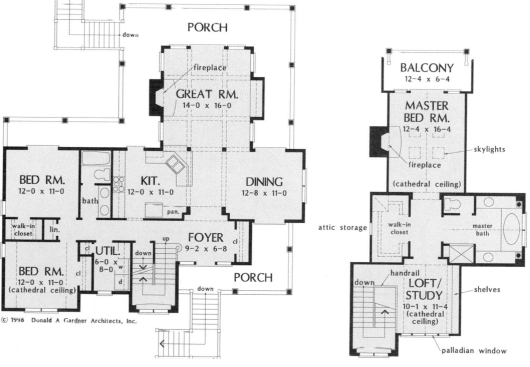

PORCH

fireplace

GREAT RM.
14-0 x 16-0

down

BED RM.
12-0 x 11-0

bath

KIT.
12-0 x 11-0

DINING
12-8 x 11-0

walk-in closet

lin.

pan.

cl

UTIL.
6-0 x 8-0

w

d

cl

up

down

FOYER
9-2 x 6-8

cl

BED RM.
12-0 x 11-0
(cathedral ceiling)

down

PORCH

(c) 1998 Donald A Gardner Architects, Inc.

BALCONY
12-4 x 6-4

MASTER BED RM.
12-4 x 16-4

skylights

fireplace

(cathedral ceiling)

attic storage

walk-in closet

master bath

handrail

down

LOFT/ STUDY
10-1 x 11-4
(cathedral ceiling)

shelves

palladian window

B. NATHAN

With an elevated pier foundation, this stunning home is perfect for waterfront properties. Magnificent porches, a balcony and a plethora of picture windows take advantage of the beach or lakeside views. The great room features a ten-foot beam ceiling, a fireplace and a space-saving built-in entertainment center. The master suite is the essence of luxury with skylights, a fireplace, cathedral ceiling, balcony, vaulted bath and oversized walk-in closet. Family bedrooms on the first floor share a full bath. Note the front and rear wrapping porches.

A lovely sun room opens from the dining room and allows great views from this home. An angled hearth warms the living and dining areas. Three lovely windows brighten the dining space, which leads out to a stunning sun porch. The gourmet kitchen has an island counter with a snack bar. The first-floor master bedroom enjoys a walk-in closet and a nearby bath. Upstairs, a spacious bath with a whirlpool tub is thoughtfully placed between two bedrooms. A daylight basement allows a lower-level portico.

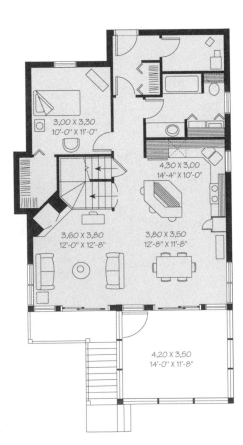

3,00 X 3,30
10'-0" X 11'-0"

4,30 X 3,00
14'-4" X 10'-0"

3,60 X 3,80
12'-0" X 12'-8"

3,80 X 3,50
12'-8" X 11'-8"

4,20 X 3,50
14'-0" X 11'-8"

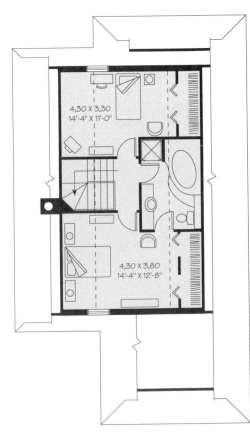

4,30 X 3,30
14'-4" X 11'-0"

4,30 X 3,80
14'-4" X 12'-8"

DESIGN

First Floor:
1,182 Square Feet
Second Floor:
838 Square Feet
Total Square Footage:
2,020
Bedrooms: 4
Bathrooms: 3

Width: 34'-0"
Depth: 52'-0"

HPT250184

This coastal two-story home finds its gable-ornamented inspiration in the Craftsman style. Open planning is the key—the living and dining areas share the front of the first floor with the U-shaped kitchen and stairway. Both the dining room and the living room access the second porch. The master suite boasts a walk-in closet and private vanity and tub. The utility room is efficiently placed between the kitchen and bath. Bedrooms 2 and 3 share a bath while Bedroom 4 enjoys a private bath.

With its wide windows and wraparound porch, this traditional design is ideal for a site with splendid views. Families will also enjoy special features designed with teenagers in mind. On the lower level, they will find their own bedroom and bathroom, access to a private patio and their own living area on the main floor—stairs are located in front of the bedrooms. Direct access to a shower and toilet from the backyard make this home perfect for outdoor pursuits.

DESIGN

Main Level:
1,099 Square Feet
Lower Level:
822 Square Feet
Total Square Footage:
1,921
Bedrooms: 3
Bathrooms: 3½

Width: 60'-0"
Depth: 39'-0"

HPT250185

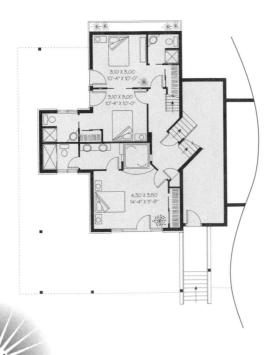

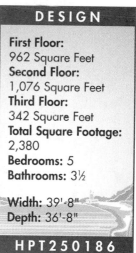

DESIGN

First Floor:
962 Square Feet
Second Floor:
1,076 Square Feet
Third Floor:
342 Square Feet
Total Square Footage:
2,380
Bedrooms: 5
Bathrooms: 3½

Width: 39'-8"
Depth: 36'-8"

HPT250186

This three-level beach house will offer spectacular views all around. With three deck levels accessible from all living areas, the outside sea air will surround you. The first level enjoys a living room, three bedrooms, a full bath and a laundry area. The second level expands to a family area, dining room and kitchen with an island snack bar and half-bath nearby. The master suite enjoys a walk-through closet and an amenity-filled bath with dual vanities and a separate tub and shower. The third level is a private haven—perfect for another bedroom—complete with a bath, walk-in closet and sitting area.

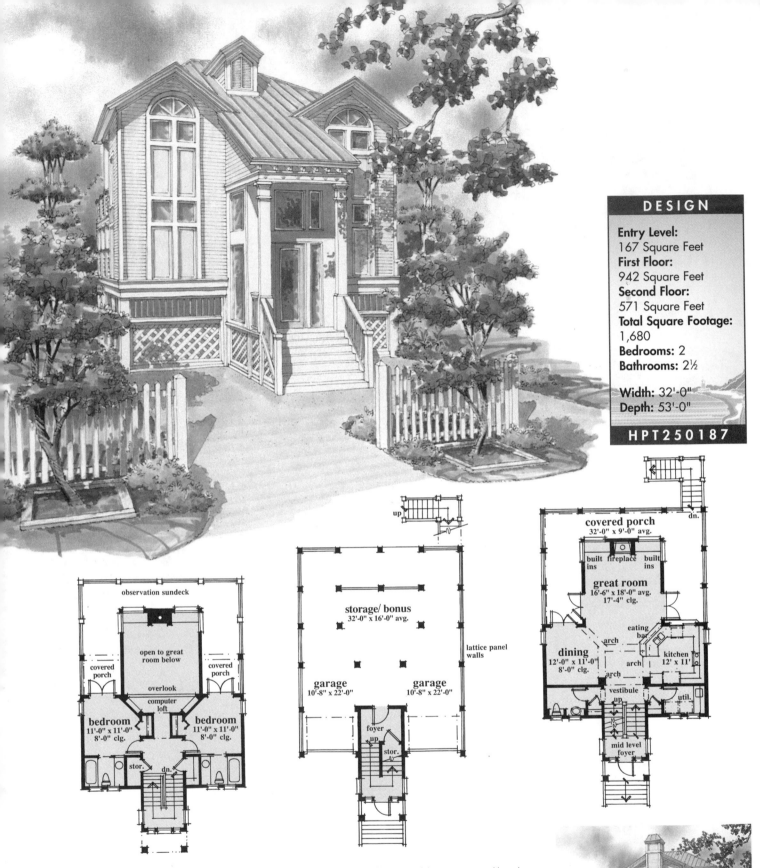

DESIGN

Entry Level:
167 Square Feet
First Floor:
942 Square Feet
Second Floor:
571 Square Feet
Total Square Footage:
1,680
Bedrooms: 2
Bathrooms: 2½

Width: 32'-0"
Depth: 53'-0"

HPT250187

observation sundeck

covered porch

covered porch

open to great room below

overlook

computer loft

bedroom
11'-0" x 11'-0"
8'-0" clg.

bedroom
11'-0" x 11'-0"
8'-0" clg.

stor.

dn.

up

storage/ bonus
32'-0" x 16'-0" avg.

lattice panel walls

garage
10'-8" x 22'-0"

garage
10'-8" x 22'-0"

foyer
up

stor.

up

dn.

covered porch
32'-0" x 9'-0" avg.

built ins   fireplace   built ins

great room
16'-6" x 18'-0" avg.
17'-4"

eating bar

arch

dining
12'-0" x 11'-0"
8'-0" clg.

arch

arch

kitchen
12' x 11'

vestibule

up

util.

mid level foyer

The modest detailing of Greek Revival style gives rise to this grand home. A mid-level foyer eases the trip from ground level to the raised living area, where an arched vestibule announces the great room. The formal dining room offers French-door access to the covered porch. Built-ins, a fireplace and two ways to access the porch make the great room truly great. A well-appointed kitchen serves a casual eating bar as well as the dining room. This home is designed with a pier foundation.

REAR VIEW

DESIGN

Foyer
242 Square Feet
First Floor:
874 Square Feet
Second Floor:
880 Square Feet
Total Square Footage:
1,996
Bedrooms: 3
Bathrooms: 2½

Width: 34'-0"
Depth: 43'-0"

HPT250188

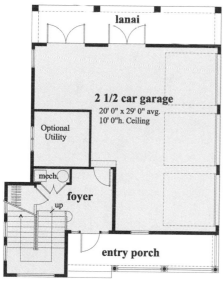

lanai

2 1/2 car garage
20' 0" x 29' 0" avg.
10' 0"h. Ceiling

Optional Utility

mech.

foyer

up

entry porch

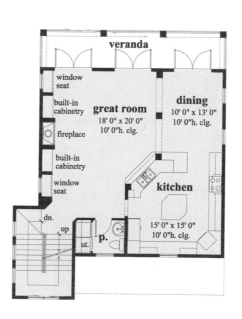

veranda

window seat

built-in cabinetry

fireplace

built-in cabinetry

window seat

great room
18' 0" x 20' 0"
10' 0". clg.

dining
10' 0" x 13' 0"
10' 0"h. clg.

kitchen
15' 0" x 15' 0"
10' 0"h. clg.

dn.

up

ut.

p.

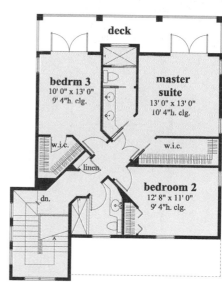

deck

bedrm 3
10' 0" x 13' 0"
9' 4"h. clg.

master suite
13' 0" x 13' 0"
10' 4"h. clg.

w.i.c.

linen

w.i.c.

dn.

bedroom 2
12' 8" x 11' 0"
9' 4"h. clg.

With irresistable charm and quiet curb appeal, this enchanting cottage conceals a sophisticated interior that's prepared for busy lifestyles. Built-in cabinetry frames a massive fireplace in the great room. An open kitchen provides an island with a double sink and snack counter. Planned events are easily served in the formal dining room. On the upper level, a central hall with linen storage connects the sleeping quarters. The master suite boasts a walk-in closet and a roomy bath with a dual-sink vanity. A compartmented bath and an oversized shower complete this relaxing retreat. Each of two secondary bedrooms has plenty of wardrobe space.

DESIGN

First Floor:
878 Square Feet
Second Floor:
1,245 Square Feet
Total Square Footage:
2,123
Bedrooms: 3
Bathrooms: 2½

Width: 27'-6"
Depth: 64'-0"

HPT250189

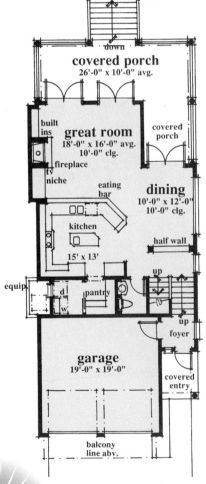

covered porch
26'-0" x 10'-0" avg.

down

built ins

great room
18'-0" x 16'-0" avg.
10'-0" clg.

covered porch

fireplace

tv niche

eating bar

dining
10'-0" x 12'-0"
10'-0" clg.

kitchen
15' x 13'

half wall

equip

d w

pantry

up

up
foyer

garage
19'-0" x 19'-0"

covered entry

balcony line abv.

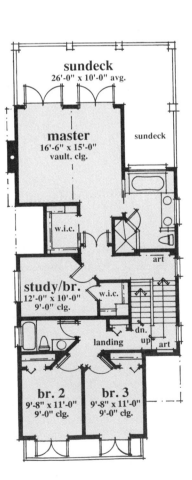

sundeck
26'-0" x 10'-0" avg.

master
16'-6" x 15'-0"
vault. clg.

sundeck

w.i.c.

art

study/br.
12'-0" x 10'-0"
9'-0" clg.

w.i.c.

landing

dn.

up

art

br. 2
9'-8" x 11'-0"
9'-0" clg.

br. 3
9'-8" x 11'-0"
9'-0" clg.

A captivating front balcony draws attention to this picturesque design. Inside, the great room offers a fireplace and built-ins and accesses the rear covered porch through French doors. The island kitchen features a large pantry and shares an eating bar with the dining room and great room. Upstairs, the master suite features a private bath and walk-in closet and opens to a private sun deck. Two secondary bedrooms access the front balcony. The study could be used as a fourth bedroom.

REAR VIEW

DESIGN

Foyer:
150 Square Feet
First Floor:
1,642 Square Feet
Second Floor:
1,165 Square Feet
Total Square Footage:
2,957
Bedrooms: 3
Bathrooms: 3½

Width: 44'-6"
Depth: 58'-0"

HPT250190

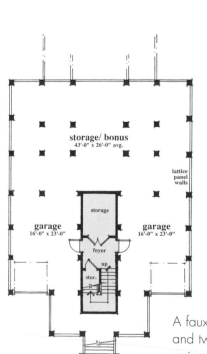

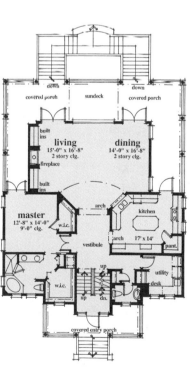

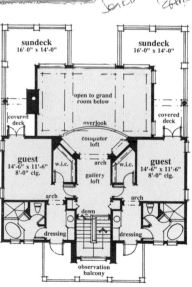

A faux widow's walk creates a stunning complement to the observation balcony and two sun decks. Inside, the open living and dining area is defined by two pairs of French doors that frame a two-story wall of glass, and built-ins flank the living-room fireplace. The efficient kitchen features a walk-in pantry, a work island and a door to the covered porch. Split sleeping quarters offer privacy to the first-floor master suite. Upstairs, two guest suites provide private baths. A gallery loft leads to a computer area with a built-in desk and a balcony overlook. This home is designed with a pier foundation.

PLANS ONLINE

*A new Web site, **www.eplans.com**, provides a way for you to*

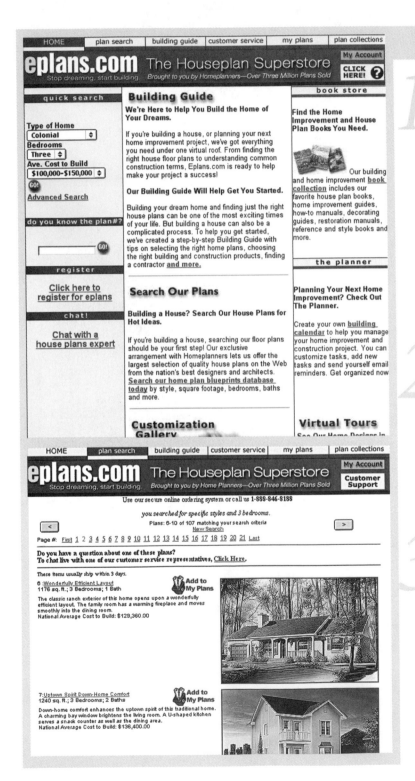

THE EPLANS SITE

1 SEARCH FOR PLANS

The heart of the site is the Plan Search feature that offers an extensive database of plans for your consideration. Do a simplified search by style, number of bedrooms and approximate cost to build in order to find appropriate homes in your range. Or, choose a more advanced search that includes choices for square footage, number of floors, number of bedrooms and baths, width and depth, style, amenities, garage size and, if you prefer, a specified designer.

Either way, you gain access to a selection of homes that meets your specifications, allowing you to easily make comparisons. The site shows front perspectives as well as detailed floor plans for each of your choices. You can even look at enlarged versions of the drawings to make more serious analyses.

2 SAVE FAVORITE PLANS

As you're doing your searches, you can save favorite plans to a personal portfolio called My Plans so that you can easily recall them for future reference and review. This feature stores summary information for each of the plans you select and allows you to review details of the plan quickly without having to re-search or re-browse. You can even compare plans, deleting those that don't measure up and keeping those that appeal, so you can narrow down your search more quickly.

3 PURCHASE PLANS

Once you've made your final choice, you can proceed to purchase your plan, either by checking out through our secure online ordering process or by calling the toll-free number offered in the site. If you choose to check out online, you'll receive information about foundation options for your chosen plan, plus other helpful products such as a building cost estimator to help you gauge costs to build the plan in your zip code area, a materials list specific to your plan, color and line renderings of the plan, and mirror and full reverses. Information relating to all of these products can also be reviewed with a customer service representative if you choose to order by phone.

search for home plans that is as simple as pointing and clicking.

also on the EPLANS site...

VIRTUAL TOURS

In order to help you more completely visualize the homes as built, eplans offers virtual tours of a select group of homes. Showing both interior and exterior features of the homes, the virtual tour gives you a complete vision of how the floor plans for the home will look when completed. All you have to do is choose a home in the Virtual Tour gallery, then click on an exterior or interior view. The view pops up and immediately begins a slow 360º rotation to give you the complete picture. Special buttons allow you to stop the rotation anywhere you like, reverse the action, or move it up or down, and zoom in on a particular element. There's even a large-screen version to allow you to review the home in greater detail.

CUSTOMIZATION GALLERY

For a special group of plans, a customization option allows you to try out building product selections to see which looks the best and to compare styles, colors, and textures. You'll start with an eplans design rendering and then be given options for such elements as roofing, columns, siding, and trim, among others. A diverse grouping of materials and color options is available in each product category. As you choose each option, it will appear on the rendering, allowing you to mix and match options and try out various design ideas. When you're satisfied with your choices, you can enlarge the view, print it out or save it in your personalized Home Project Folder for future reference.

The eplans site is convenient and contains not only the best home plans in the business, but also a host of other features and services. Like Home Planners handy books and magazines, it speaks your language in user-friendly fashion.

In fact, if you want or need more help, there is a Live Person, real-time chat opportunity available with one of our customer service representatives right on the site to answer questions and help you make plans selections.

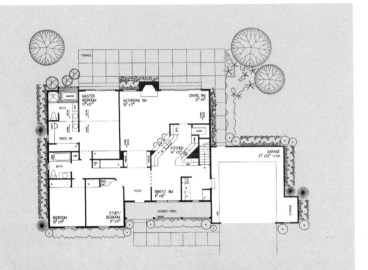

Customize your plan—without spending a penny or hammering a nail! The Customization Gallery lets you "try on" various material colors and styles before you make decisions.

The **eplans.com** Advantage

also on the EPLANS site...

BUILDING GUIDE AND TASK PLANNER

Because building a home is a complicated process, eplans gets you started with a step-by-step Building Guide. Covering everything from choosing a lot to settling into your new home, the Building Guide gives tips and valuable information to help you understand the entire process of constructing your new home. Learn about the steps in framing your home, different foundation types and which might work best for your building situation, financing your project, home products such as appliances, and much, much more. A handy glossary is available in each section that helps define terms that relate to the information in that section.

Within the Building Guide is a unique Task Planner outlining each of the various tasks involved in residential construction over the entire 16-week (average) life of the project. Simply tell Task Planner when you plan to start construction or when you plan to move into the finished home, and it will create a calendar that shows each of the many steps involved in building your home. You can customize tasks, add new tasks, and send yourself email reminders that help you manage the building project. In addition, each task in the calendar is linked to a tip or information piece in the Building Guide to help make the process easier to follow and understand. Choose the Calendar View, which shows a month-by-month progression of construction, or the Task View, which lists each task by category and shows its due date.

While there are hundreds of home plans sites on the Web, only eplans.com offers the variety, quality, and ease of use you want when doing a search for the perfect home. From expert advice to online ordering of plans, eplans gives you a full complement of services, information, home plans, and planning tools to make your building experience easy and enjoyable. Log on to www.eplans.com to begin your search for the home you've always wanted.

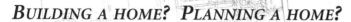

LET US SHOW YOU OUR HOME BLUEPRINT PACKAGE.

BUILDING A HOME? PLANNING A HOME?

OUR BLUEPRINT PACKAGE HAS NEARLY EVERYTHING YOU NEED TO GET THE JOB DONE RIGHT,

whether you're working on your own or with help from an architect, designer, builder or subcontractors. Each Blueprint Package is the result of many hours of work by licensed architects or professional designers.

QUALITY

Hundreds of hours of painstaking effort have gone into the development of your blueprint set. Each home has been quality-checked by professionals to insure accuracy and buildability.

VALUE

Because we sell in volume, you can buy professional quality blueprints at a fraction of their development cost. With our plans, your dream home design costs substantially less than the fees charged by architects.

SERVICE

Once you've chosen your favorite home plan, you'll receive fast, efficient service whether you choose to mail or fax your order to us or call us toll free at 1-800-521-6797. For customer service, call toll free 1-888-690-1116.

SATISFACTION

Over 50 years of service to satisfied home plan buyers provide us unparalleled experience and knowledge in producing quality blueprints.

ORDER TOLL FREE
1-800-521-6797

After you've looked over our Blueprint Package and Important Extras, call toll free on our Blueprint Hotline: 1-800-521-6797, for current pricing and availability prior to mailing the order form on page 221. We're ready and eager to serve you. For customer service, call toll free 1-888-690-1116.

Each set of blueprints is an interrelated collection of detail sheets which includes components such as floor plans, interior and exterior elevations, dimensions, cross-sections, diagrams and notations. These sheets show exactly how your house is to be built.

SETS MAY INCLUDE:

FRONTAL SHEET
This artist's sketch of the exterior of the house gives you an idea of how the house will look when built and landscaped. Large floor plans show all levels of the house and provide an overview of your new home's livability, as well as a handy reference for deciding on furniture placement.

FOUNDATION PLANS
This sheet shows the foundation layout including support walls, excavated and unexcavated areas, if any, and foundation notes. If slab construction rather than basement, the plan shows footings and details for a monolithic slab. This page, or another in the set, may include a sample plot plan for locating your house on a building site.

DETAILED FLOOR PLANS
These plans show the layout of each floor of the house. Rooms and interior spaces are carefully dimensioned and keys are given for cross-section details provided later in the plans. The positions of electrical outlets and switches are shown.

HOUSE CROSS-SECTIONS
Large-scale views show sections or cut-aways of the foundation, interior walls, exterior walls, floors, stairways and roof details. Additional cross-sections may show important changes in floor, ceiling or roof heights or the relationship of one level to another. Extremely valuable for construction, these sections show exactly how the various parts of the house fit together.

INTERIOR ELEVATIONS
Many of our drawings show the design and placement of kitchen and bathroom cabinets, laundry areas, fireplaces, bookcases and other built-ins. Little "extras," such as mantelpiece and wainscoting drawings, plus molding sections, provide details that give your home that custom touch.

EXTERIOR ELEVATIONS
These drawings show the front, rear and sides of your house and give necessary notes on exterior materials and finishes. Particular attention is given to cornice detail, brick and stone accents or other finish items that make your home unique.

INTRODUCING EIGHT IMPORTANT

PLANNING AND CONSTRUCTION AIDS DEVELOPED BY

OUR PROFESSIONALS TO HELP YOU SUCCEED IN YOUR HOME-BUILDING PROJECT

MATERIALS LIST

(Note: Because of the diversity of local building codes, our Materials List does not include mechanical materials.)

For many of the designs in our portfolio, we offer a customized materials take-off that is invaluable in planning and estimating the cost of your new home. This Materials List outlines the quantity, type and size of materials needed to build your house (with the exception of mechanical system items). Included are framing lumber, windows and doors, kitchen and bath cabinetry, rough and finish hardware, and much more. This handy list helps you or your builder cost out materials and serves as a reference sheet when you're compiling bids. A Materials List cannot be ordered before blueprints are ordered.

SPECIFICATION OUTLINE

This valuable 16-page document is critical to building your house correctly. Designed to be filled in by you or your builder, this book lists 166 stages or items crucial to the building process. It provides a comprehensive review of the construction process and helps in choosing materials. When combined with the blueprints, a signed contract, and a schedule, it becomes a legal document and record for the building of your home.

QUOTE ONE®

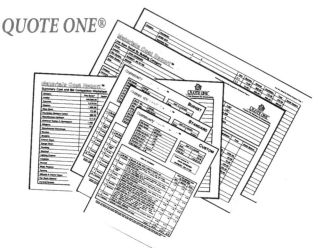

SUMMARY COST REPORT   **MATERIALS COST REPORT**

A product for estimating the cost of building select designs, the Quote One® system is available in two separate stages: The Summary Cost Report and the Materials Cost Report.

The **Summary Cost Report** is the first stage in the package and shows the total cost per square foot for your chosen home in your zip-code area and then breaks that cost down into various categories showing the costs for building materials, labor and installation. The report includes three grades: Budget, Standard and Custom. These reports allow you to evaluate your building budget and compare the costs of building a variety of homes in your area.

Make even more informed decisions about your home-building project with the second phase of our package, our **Materials Cost Report.** This tool is invaluable in planning and estimating the cost of your new home. The material and installation (labor and equipment) cost is shown for each of over 1,000 line items provided in the Materials List (Standard grade), which is included when you purchase this estimating tool. It allows you to determine building costs for your specific zip-code area and for your chosen home design. Space is allowed for additional estimates from contractors and subcontractors, such as for mechanical materials, which are not included in our packages. This invaluable tool includes a Materials List. A Materials Cost Report cannot be ordered before blueprints are ordered. Call for details. In addition, ask about our Home Planners Estimating Package.

If you are interested in a plan that is not indicated as Quote One®, please call and ask our sales reps. They will be happy to verify the status for you. To order these invaluable reports, use the order form on page 221 or call 1-800-521-6797 for availability.

CONSTRUCTION INFORMATION

*IF YOU WANT TO KNOW MORE ABOUT TECHNIQUES—
and deal more confidently with subcontractors —
we offer these useful sheets. Each set is an excellent
tool that will add to your understanding of these
technical subjects. These helpful details provide
general construction information and
are not specific to any single plan.*

PLUMBING
The Blueprint Package includes locations for all the plumbing fix-tures, including sinks, lavatories, tubs, showers, toilets, laundry trays and water heaters. However, if you want to know more about the complete plumbing system, these Plumbing Details will prove very useful. Prepared to meet requirements of the National Plumbing Code, these fact-filled sheets give general information on pipe schedules, fittings, sump-pump details, water-softener hookups, septic system details and much more. Sheets also include a glossary of terms.

ELECTRICAL
The locations for every electrical switch, plug and outlet are shown in your Blueprint Package. However, these Electrical Details go further to take the mystery out of household electrical systems. Prepared to meet requirements of the National Electrical Code, these comprehensive drawings come packed with helpful information, including wire sizing, switch-installa-tion schematics, cable-routing details, appliance wattage, door-bell hook-ups, typical service panel circuitry and much more. A glossary of terms is also included.

CONSTRUCTION
The Blueprint Package contains information an experienced builder needs to construct a particular house. However, it doesn't show all the ways that houses can be built, nor does it explain alternate construction methods. To help you understand how your house will be built—and offer additional techniques—this set of Construction Details depicts the materials and methods used to build foundations, fireplaces, walls, floors and roofs. Where appro-priate, the drawings show acceptable alternatives.

MECHANICAL
These Mechanical Details contain fundamental principles and useful data that will help you make informed decisions and com-municate with subcontractors about heating and cooling systems. Drawings contain instructions and samples that allow you to make simple load calculations, and preliminary sizing and costing analysis. Covered are the most commonly used systems from heat pumps to solar fuel systems. The package is filled with illustra-tions and diagrams to help you visualize components and how they relate to one another.

PLAN-A-HOME®

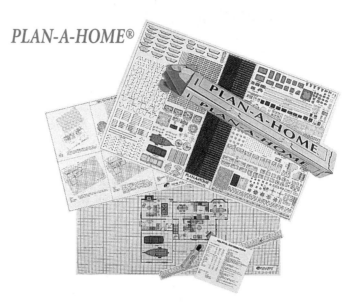

PLAN-A-HOME® is an easy-to-use tool that helps you design a new home, arrange furniture in a new or existing home, or plan a remodeling project. Each package contains:

✓ **More than 700 reusable peel-off planning symbols** on a self-stick vinyl sheet, including walls, windows, doors, all types of furniture, kitchen components, bath fixtures and many more.

✓ **A reusable, transparent, ¼" scale planning grid** that matches the scale of actual working drawings (¼" equals one foot). This grid provides the basis for house layouts of up to 140' x 92'.

✓ **Tracing paper** and a protective sheet for copying or transferring your completed plan.

✓ **A felt-tip pen**, with water-soluble ink that wipes away quickly.

PLAN-A-HOME® lets you lay out areas as large as a 7,500 square foot, six-bedroom, seven-bath house.

To Order, Call Toll Free
1-800-521-6797

After you've looked over our Blueprint Package and Important Extras on these pages, call toll free on our Blueprint Hotline: 1-800-521-6797 for current pricing and availability prior to mailing the order form on page 221. We're ready and eager to serve you. For customer service, call toll free 1-888-690-1116.

THE FINISHING TOUCHES...

THE DECK BLUEPRINT PACKAGE

Many of the homes in this book can be enhanced with a professionally designed Home Planners Deck Plan. Those home plans highlighted with a **D** have a matching Deck Plan, sold separately, which includes a Deck Plan Frontal Sheet, Deck Framing and Floor Plans, Deck Elevations and a Deck Materials List. A Standard Deck Details Package, also available, provides all the how-to information necessary for building *any* deck. Our Complete Deck Building Package contains one set of Custom Deck Plans of your choice, plus one set of Standard Deck Building Details, all for one low price. Our plans and details are carefully prepared in an easy-to-understand format that will guide you through every stage of your deck-building project. This page shows a sample Deck layout to match your favorite house. See page 217 for prices and ordering information.

THE LANDSCAPE BLUEPRINT PACKAGE

For the homes marked with an **L** in this book, Home Planners has created a front-yard Landscape Plan that matches or is complementary in design to the house plan. These comprehensive blueprint packages include a Frontal Sheet, Plan View, Regionalized Plant & Materials List, a sheet on Planting and Maintaining Your Landscape, Zone Maps and Plant Size and Description Guide. These plans will help you achieve professional results, adding value and enjoyment to your property for years to come. Each set of blueprints is a full 18" x 24" in size with clear, complete instructions and easy-to-read type. A sample Landscape Plan is shown below.

CONTEMPORARY LEISURE DECK
Deck ODA021

CAPE COD COTTAGE
Landscape OLA003

Regional Order Map

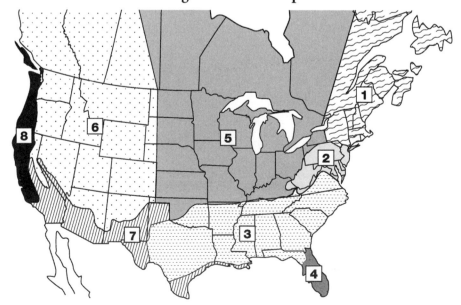

Most Landscape Plans are available with a Plant & Materials List adapted by horticultural experts to 8 different regions of the country. Please specify the Geographic Region when ordering your plan. See pages 217–219 for prices, ordering information and regional availability.

Region	1	Northeast
Region	2	Mid-Atlantic
Region	3	Deep South
Region	4	Florida & Gulf Coast
Region	5	Midwest
Region	6	Rocky Mountains
Region	7	Southern California & Desert Southwest
Region	8	Northern California & Pacific Northwest

HOUSE BLUEPRINT PRICE SCHEDULE

Prices guaranteed through December 31, 2002

TIERS	1-SET STUDY PACKAGE	4-SET BUILDING PACKAGE	8-SET BUILDING PACKAGE	1-SET REPRODUCIBLE
P1	$20	$50	$90	$140
P2	$40	$70	$110	$160
P3	$70	$100	$140	$190
P4	$100	$130	$170	$220
P5	$140	$170	$210	$270
P6	$180	$210	$250	$310
A1	$440	$480	$520	$660
A2	$480	$520	$560	$720
A3	$520	$560	$600	$780
A4	$565	$605	$645	$850
C1	$610	$655	$700	$915
C2	$655	$700	$745	$980
C3	$700	$745	$790	$1050
C4	$750	$795	$840	$1125
L1	$825	$875	$925	$1240
L2	$900	$950	$1000	$1350
L3	$1000	$1095	$1100	$1500
L4	$1100	$1150	$1200	$1650

OPTIONS FOR PLANS IN TIERS A1–L4

Additional Identical Blueprints
in same order for "A1–L4" price plans...$50 per set
Reverse Blueprints (mirror image)
with 4- or 8-set order for "A1–L4" plans.......................................$50 fee per order
Specification Outlines...$10 each
Materials Lists for "A1–C3" plans ....$60 each
Materials Lists for "C4–L4" plans...$70 each

OPTIONS FOR PLANS IN TIERS P1–P6

Additional Identical Blueprints
in same order for "P1–P6" price plans...$10 per set
Reverse Blueprints (mirror image) for "P1–P6" price plans ....$10 per set
1 Set of Deck Construction Details ....$14.95 each
Deck Construction Package ....add $10 to Building Package price
(includes 1 set of "P1–P6" plans, plus 1 set Standard Deck Construction Details)
1 Set of Gazebo Construction Details ....$14.95 each
Gazebo Construction Package ....add $10 to Building Package price
(includes 1 set of "P1–P6" plans, plus 1 set Standard Gazebo Construction Details)

IMPORTANT NOTES

- The 1-set study package is marked "not for construction."
- Prices for 4- or 8-set Building Packages honored only at time of original order.
- Some foundations carry a $225 surcharge.
- Right-reading reverse blueprints, if available, will incur a $165 surcharge.
- Additional identical blueprints may be purchased within 60 days of original order.

TO USE THE INDEX, refer to the design number listed in numerical order (a helpful page reference is also given). Note the price tier and refer to the House Blueprint Price Schedule above for the cost of one, four or eight sets of blueprints or the cost of a reproducible drawing. Additional prices are shown for identical and reverse blueprint sets, as well as a very useful Materials List for some of the plans. Also note in the Plan Index those plans that have Deck Plans or Landscape Plans. Refer to the schedules above for prices of these plans. The letter "Y" identifies plans that are part of our Quote One® estimating service and those that offer Materials Lists. See page 214 for more information.

TO ORDER, Call toll free 1-800-521-6797 or 520-297-8200 for current pricing and availability prior to mailing the order form on page 221. FAX: 1-800-224-6699 or 520-544-3086.

PLAN INDEX

DESIGN	PRICE	PAGE	MATERIALS LIST	QUOTE ONE®	DECK	DECK PRICE	LANDSCAPE	LANDSCAPE PRICE	REGIONS
HPT250001	A3	14							
HPT250002	C3	10	Y				OLA008	P4	1234568
HPT250003	L1	18							
HPT250004	C4	20					OLA004	P3	123568
HPT250005	C2	17							
HPT250006	A4	9							
HPT250007	A4	29	Y	Y					
HPT250008	C3	26	Y						
HPT250009	L3	22							
HPT250010	A4	28	Y	Y	ODA003	P2			
HPT250011	C3	24							
HPT250012	C4	13							
HPT250014	C4	32	Y	Y	ODA005	P3	OLA013	P4	12345678
HPT250015	C1	27							
HPT250016	A4	31							
HPT250017	L1	25	Y						
HPT250018	C4	30	Y						
HPT250019	C2	34							
HPT250020	A4	35							
HPT250021	A4	36	Y						
HPT250022	C1	37	Y						
HPT250023	C1	38	Y						
HPT250024	C4	39							
HPT250025	L2	40							
HPT250026	C3	41							
HPT250027	C4	42							
HPT250028	C3	43							
HPT250029	C4	44							
HPT250030	C2	45							
HPT250031	C2	46	Y	Y					
HPT250032	L2	47							
HPT250033	C2	48	Y						
HPT250034	C1	49							
HPT250035	L2	50							
HPT250036	C4	51							
HPT250037	A3	52							
HPT250038	C1	53							
HPT250039	A4	54							

BEFORE YOU ORDER...

BEFORE FILLING OUT THE ORDER FORM, PLEASE CALL US ON OUR TOLL-FREE BLUEPRINT HOTLINE. YOU MAY WANT TO LEARN MORE ABOUT OUR SERVICES AND PRODUCTS. HERE'S SOME INFORMATION YOU WILL FIND HELPFUL.

OUR EXCHANGE POLICY
With the exception of reproducible plan orders, we will exchange your entire first order for an equal or greater number of blueprints within our plan collection within 90 days of the original order. The entire content of your original order must be returned before an exchange will be processed. Please call our customer service department for your return authorization number and shipping instructions. If the returned blueprints look used, redlined or copied, we will not honor your exchange. Fees for exchanging your blueprints are as follows: 20% of the amount of the original order...plus the difference in cost if exchanging for a design in a higher price bracket or less the difference in cost if exchanging for a design in a lower price bracket. **(Reproducible blueprints are not exchangeable or refundable.)** Please call for current postage and handling prices. Shipping and handling charges are not refundable.

ABOUT REVERSE BLUEPRINTS
Although lettering and dimensions will appear backward, reverses will be a useful aid if you decide to flop the plan. See Price Schedule and Plans Index for pricing.

REVISING, MODIFYING AND CUSTOMIZING PLANS
Like many homeowners who buy these plans, you and your builder, architect or engineer may want to make changes to them. We recommend purchase of a reproducible plan for any changes made by your builder, licensed architect or engineer. As set forth below, we cannot assume any responsibility for blueprints which have been changed, whether by you, your builder or by professionals selected by you or referred to you by us, because such individuals are outside our supervision and control.

ARCHITECTURAL AND ENGINEERING SEALS
Some cities and states are now requiring that a licensed architect or engineer review and "seal" a blueprint, or officially approve it, prior to construction due to concerns over energy costs, safety and other factors. Prior to application for a building permit or the start of actual construction, we strongly advise that you consult your local building official who can tell you if such a review is required.

ABOUT THE DESIGNS
The architects and designers whose work appears in this publication are among America's leading residential designers. Each plan was designed to meet the requirements of a nationally recognized model building code in effect at the time and place the plan was drawn. Because national building codes change from time to time, plans may not comply with any such code at the time they are sold to a customer. In addition, building officials may not accept these plans as final construction documents of record as the plans may need to be modified and additional drawings and details added to suit local conditions and requirements. We strongly advise that purchasers consult a licensed architect or engineer, and their local building official, before starting any construction related to these plans.

LOCAL BUILDING CODES AND ZONING REQUIREMENTS
At the time of creation, our plans are drawn to specifications published by the Building Officials and Code Administrators (BOCA) International, Inc.; the Southern Building Code Congress (SBCCI) International, Inc.; the International Conference of Building Officials (ICBO); or the Council of American Building Officials (CABO). Our plans are designed to meet or exceed national building standards. Because of the great differences in geography and climate throughout the United States and Canada, each state, county and municipality has its own building codes, zone requirements, ordinances and building regulations. Your plan may need to be modified to comply with local requirements regarding snow loads, energy codes, soil and seismic conditions and a wide range of other matters. In addition, you may need to obtain permits or inspections from local governments before and in the course of construction. Prior to using blueprints ordered from us, we strongly advise that you consult a licensed architect or engineer—and speak with your local building official—before applying for any permit or beginning construction. We authorize the use of our blueprints on the express condition that you strictly comply with all local building codes, zoning requirements and other applicable laws, regulations, ordinances and requirements. Notice: Plans for homes to be built in Nevada must be re-drawn by a Nevada-registered professional. Consult your building official for more information on this subject.

Have You Seen Our Newest Designs?

At least 50 of our latest creations are featured in each edition of our New Design Portfolio. You may have received a copy with your latest purchase by mail. If not, or if you purchased this book from a local retailer, just return the coupon below for your FREE copy. Make sure you consider the very latest of what Home Planners has to offer.

Yes! Please send my FREE copy of your latest New Design Portfolio.

Offer good to U.S. shipping address only.

Name _____

Address_____

City _____ State _____ Zip _____

HOME PLANNERS, LLC
Wholly owned by Hanley-Wood, LLC
3275 WEST INA ROAD, SUITE 110 • TUCSON, ARIZONA 85741

Order Form Key

| HPT25 |

DISCLAIMER

The designers we work with have put substantial care and effort into the creation of their blueprints. However, because they cannot provide on-site consultation, supervision and control over actual construction, and because of the great variance in local building requirements, building practices and soil, seismic, weather and other conditions, WE CANNOT MAKE ANY WARRANTY, EXPRESS OR IMPLIED, WITH RESPECT TO THE CONTENT OR USE OF THE BLUEPRINTS, INCLUDING BUT NOT LIMITED TO ANY WARRANTY OF MERCHANTABILITY OR OF FITNESS FOR A PARTICULAR PURPOSE. **ITEMS, PRICES, TERMS AND CONDITIONS ARE SUBJECT TO CHANGE WITHOUT NOTICE. REPRODUCIBLE PLAN ORDERS MAY REQUIRE A CUSTOMER'S SIGNED RELEASE BEFORE SHIPPING.**

TERMS AND CONDITIONS

These designs are protected under the terms of United States Copyright Law and may not be copied or reproduced in any way, by any means, unless you have purchased Reproducibles which clearly indicate your right to copy or reproduce. We authorize the use of your chosen design as an aid in the construction of one single family home only. You may not use this design to build a second or multiple dwellings without purchasing another blueprint or blueprints or paying additional design fees.

HOW MANY BLUEPRINTS DO YOU NEED?

Although a standard building package may satisfy many states, cities and counties, some plans may require certain changes. For your convenience, we have developed a Reproducible plan which allows a local professional to modify and make up to 10 copies of your revised plan. As our plans are all copyright protected, with your purchase of the Reproducible, we will supply you with a Copyright release letter. The number of copies you may need: 1 for owner; 3 for builder; 2 for local building department and 1-3 sets for your mortgage lender.

ORDER TOLL FREE!
FOR INFORMATION ABOUT ANY OF OUR SERVICES OR TO ORDER CALL

1-800-521-6797
OR **520-297-8200**
Browse our website:
www.eplans.com

BLUEPRINTS ARE NOT REFUNDABLE EXCHANGES ONLY

FOR CUSTOMER SERVICE, CALL TOLL FREE **1-888-690-1116.**

HOME PLANNERS, LLC wholly owned by Hanley-Wood, LLC
3275 WEST INA ROAD, SUITE 110 • TUCSON, ARIZONA • 85741

THE BASIC BLUEPRINT PACKAGE
Rush me the following (please refer to the Plans Index and Price Schedule in this section):
___Set(s) of blueprints, plan number(s) _____ indicate foundation type _____ $_____
___Set(s) of reproducibles, plan number(s) _____ indicate foundation type _____ $_____
___Additional identical blueprints (standard or reverse) in same order @ $50 per set $_____
___Reverse blueprints @ $50 fee per order. Right-reading reverse @ $165 surcharge $_____

IMPORTANT EXTRAS
Rush me the following:
___Materials List: $60 (Must be purchased with Blueprint set.) Add $10 for Schedule C4–L4 plans $_____
___**Quote One®** Summary Cost Report @ $29.95 for one, $14.95 for each additional,
   for plans _____ $_____
   Building location: City _____ Zip Code _____
___**Quote One®** Materials Cost Report @ $120 Schedules P1–C3; $130 Schedules C4–L4,
   for plan_____(Must be purchased with Blueprints set.) $_____
   Building location: City _____ Zip Code _____
___Specification Outlines @ $10 each $_____
___Detail Sets @ $14.95 each; any two $22.95; any three $29.95; all four for $39.95 (save $19.85) $_____
   ❑ Plumbing ❑ Electrical ❑ Construction ❑ Mechanical
___Plan-A-Home® @ $29.95 each $_____

DECK BLUEPRINTS
(Please refer to the Plans Index and Price Schedule in this section)
___Set(s) of Deck Plan _____. $_____
___Additional identical blueprints in same order @ $10 per set. $_____
___Reverse blueprints @ $10 fee per order. $_____
___Set of Standard Deck Details @ $14.95 per set. $_____
___Set of Complete Deck Construction Package (Best Buy!) Add $10 to Building Package.
   Includes Custom Deck Plan _____ Plus Standard Deck Details

LANDSCAPE BLUEPRINTS
(Please refer to the Plans Index and Price Schedule in this section.)
___Set(s) of Landscape Plan _____ $_____
___Additional identical blueprints in same order @ $10 per set $_____
___Reverse blueprints @ $10 fee per order $_____
Please indicate the appropriate region of the country for Plant & Material List.
(See map on page 216): Region _____

POSTAGE AND HANDLING	1–3 sets	4+ sets
Signature is required for all deliveries. **DELIVERY** No CODs (Requires street address—No P.O. Boxes)		
•Regular Service (Allow 7–10 business days delivery)	❑ $20.00	❑ $25.00
•Priority (Allow 4–5 business days delivery)	❑ $25.00	❑ $35.00
•Express (Allow 3 business days delivery)	❑ $35.00	❑ $45.00
OVERSEAS DELIVERY	fax, phone or mail for quote	

Note: All delivery times are from date Blueprint Package is shipped.

POSTAGE (From box above) $_____
SUBTOTAL $_____
SALES TAX (AZ & MI residents, please add appropriate state and local sales tax.) $_____
TOTAL (Subtotal and tax) $_____

YOUR ADDRESS (please print legibly)

Name _____

Street_____

City _____State_____Zip _____

Daytime telephone number (required) (_____) _____

FOR CREDIT CARD ORDERS ONLY

Credit card number _____ Exp. Date: (M/Y) _____
Check one ❑ Visa ❑ MasterCard ❑ Discover Card ❑ American Express

Order Form Key

HPT25

Signature (required) _____

Please check appropriate box: ❑ Licensed Builder-Contractor ❑ Homeowner

☎ ORDER TOLL FREE!
1-800-521-6797 or 520-297-8200

BY FAX: Copy the order form above and send it on our FAXLINE: 1-800-224-6699 OR 520-544-3086

HOME PLANNERS WANTS YOUR BUILDING EXPERIENCE TO BE AS PLEASANT AND TROUBLE-FREE AS POSSIBLE.

That's why we've expanded our library of do-it-yourself titles to help you along. In addition to our beautiful plans books, we've added books to guide you through specific projects as well as the construction process. In fact, these are titles that will be as useful after your dream home is built as they are right now.

BIGGEST & BEST

1001 of our best-selling plans in one volume. 1,074 to 7,275 square feet. 704 pgs $12.95 1K1

ONE-STORY

450 designs for all lifestyles. 800 to 4,900 square feet. 384 pgs $9.95 OS

MORE ONE-STORY

475 superb one-level plans from 800 to 5,000 square feet. 448 pgs $9.95 MOS

TWO-STORY

443 designs for one-and-a-half and two stories. 1,500 to 6,000 square feet. 448 pgs $9.95 TS

VACATION

465 designs for recreation, retirement and leisure. 448 pgs $9.95 VSH

HILLSIDE

208 designs for split-levels, bi-levels, multi-levels and walkouts. 224 pgs $9.95 HH

FARMHOUSE

200 country designs from classic to contemporary by 7 winning designers. 224 pgs $8.95 FH

COUNTRY HOUSES

208 unique home plans that combine traditional style and modern livability. 224 pgs $9.95 CN

BUDGET-SMART

200 efficient plans from 7 top designers, that you can really afford to build! 224 pgs $8.95 BS

BARRIER FREE

Over 1,700 products and 51 plans for accessible living. 128 pgs $15.95 UH

ENCYCLOPEDIA

500 exceptional plans for all styles and budgets—the best book of its kind! 528 pgs $9.95 ENC

ENCYCLOPEDIA II

500 completely new plans. Spacious and stylish designs for every budget and taste. 352 pgs $9.95 E2

AFFORDABLE

Completely revised and updated, featuring 300 designs for modest budgets. 256 pgs $9.95 AF

VICTORIAN

NEW! 210 striking Victorian and Farmhouse designs from today's top designers. 224 pgs $15.95 VDH2

ESTATE

Dream big! Twenty-one designers showcase their biggest and best plans. 208 pgs $15.95 EDH

LUXURY

170 lavish designs, over 50% brand-new plans added to a most elegant collection. 192 pgs $14.95 LD2

EUROPEAN STYLES

200 homes with a unique flair of the Old World. 224 pgs $15.95 EURO

COUNTRY CLASSICS

Donald Gardner's 101 best Country and Traditional home plans. 192 pgs $17.95 DAG

WILLIAM POOLE

70 romantic house plans that capture the classic tradition of home design. 160 pgs $17.95 WEP

TRADITIONAL

85 timeless designs from the Design Traditions Library. 160 pgs $17.95 TRA

COTTAGES

25 fresh new designs that are as warm as a tropical breeze. A blend of the best aspects of many coastal styles. 64 pgs. $19.95 CTG

CLASSIC

Timeless, elegant designs that always feel like home. Gorgeous plans that are as flexible and up-to-date as their occupants. 240 pgs. $9.95 CS

CONTEMPORARY

The most complete and imaginative collection of contemporary designs available anywhere. 240 pgs. $9.95 CM

EASY-LIVING

200 efficient and sophisticated plans that are small in size, but big on livability. 224 pgs $8.95 EL

SOUTHERN

207 homes rich in Southern styling and comfort. 240 pgs $8.95 SH

SOUTHWESTERN

138 designs that capture the spirit of the Southwest. 144 pgs $10.95 SW

WESTERN

215 designs that capture the spirit and diversity of the Western lifestyle. 208 pgs $9.95 WH

NEIGHBORHOOD

170 designs with the feel of main street America. 192 pgs $12.95 TND

CRAFTSMAN

170 Home plans in the Craftsman and Bungalow style. 192 pgs $12.95 CC

COLONIAL HOUSES

181 Classic early American designs. 208 pgs $9.95 COL

DUPLEX & TOWNHOMES

Over 50 designs for multi-family living. 64 pgs $9.95 DTP

WATERFRONT

200 designs perfect for your waterside wonderland. 208 pgs $10.95 WF

PROJECT GUIDES

WINDOWS	STREET OF DREAMS	MOVE-UP	OUTDOOR	GARAGES	DECKS	HOME BUILDING	BOOK & CD-ROM

33 Discover the power of windows with over 160 designs featuring Pella's best. 192 pgs $9.95 WIN

34 Over 300 photos showcase 54 prestigious homes. 256 pgs $19.95 SOD

35 200 stylish designs for today's growing families from 9 hot designers. 224 pgs $8.95 MU

36 74 easy-to-build designs, lets you create and build your own backyard oasis. 128 pgs $7.95 YG

37 101 multi-use garages and outdoor structures to enhance any home. 96 pgs $7.95 GG

38 25 outstanding single-, double- and multi-level decks you can build. 112 pgs $7.95 DP

39 Everything you need to know to work with contractors and subcontractors. 212 pgs $14.95 HBP

40 Both the Home Planners Gold book and matching Windows™ CD-ROM with 3D floor-plans. $24.95 HPGC Book only $12.95 HPG

LANDSCAPE DESIGNS

SOFTWARE	EASY-CARE	FRONT & BACK	BACKYARDS	BUYER'S GUIDE	FRAMING	BASIC WIRING	TILE

41 Home design made easy! View designs in 3D, take a virtual reality tour, add decorating details and more. $59.95 PLANSUITE

42 41 special landscapes designed for beauty and low maintenance. 160 pgs $14.95 ECL

43 The first book of do-it-yourself landscapes. 40 front, 15 backyards. 208 pgs $14.95 HL

44 40 designs focused solely on creating your own specially themed backyard oasis. 160 pgs $14.95 BYL

45 A comprehensive look at 2700 products for all aspects of landscaping & gardening. 128 pgs $19.95 LPBG

46 For those who want to take a more hands-on approach to their dream. 319 pgs $21.95 SRF

47 A straightforward guide to one of the most misunderstood systems in the home. 160 pgs $12.95 CBW

48 Every kind of tile for every kind of application. Includes tips on use, installation and repair. 176 pgs $12.95 CWT

BATHROOMS	KITCHENS	HOUSE CONTRACTING	VISUAL HANDBOOK	ROOFING	WINDOWS & DOORS	PATIOS & WALKS	TRIM & MOLDING

       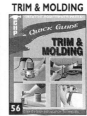

49 An innovative guide to organizing, remodeling and decorating your bathroom. 96 pgs $10.95 CDB

50 An imaginative guide to designing the perfect kitchen. Chock full of bright ideas to make your job easier. 176 pgs $16.95 CKI

51 Everything you need to know to act as your own general contractor, and save up to 25% off building costs. 134 pgs $14.95 SBC

52 A plain-talk guide to the construction process; financing to final walk-through, this book covers it all. 498 pgs $19.95 RVH

53 Information on the latest tools, materials and techniques for roof installation or repair. 80 pgs $7.95 CGR

54 Installation techniques and tips that make your project easier and more professional looking. 80 pgs $7.95 CGD

55 Clear step-by-step instructions take you from the basic design stages to the finished project. 80 pgs $7.95 CGW

56 Step-by-step instructions for installing baseboards, window and door casings and more. 80 pgs $7.95 CGT

Additional Books Order Form

To order your books, just check the box of the book numbered below and complete the coupon. We will process your order and ship it from our office within two business days. Send coupon and check (in U.S. funds).

YES!
Please send me the books I've indicated:

☐ 1:IKI $12.95	☐ 20:TRA $17.95	☐ 39:HBP $14.95
☐ 2:OS $9.95	☐ 21:CTG $19.95	☐ 40:HPG $12.95
☐ 3:MOS $9.95	☐ 22:CS $9.95	☐ 40:HPGC $24.95
☐ 4:TS $9.95	☐ 23:CM $9.95	☐ 41:PLANSUITE ..$59.95
☐ 5:VSH $9.95	☐ 24:EL $8.95	☐ 42:ECL $14.95
☐ 6:HH $9.95	☐ 25:SH $8.95	☐ 43:HL $14.95
☐ 7:FH $8.95	☐ 26:SW $10.95	☐ 44:BYL $14.95
☐ 8:CN $9.95	☐ 27:WH $9.95	☐ 45:LPBG $19.95
☐ 9:BS $8.95	☐ 28:TND $12.95	☐ 46:SRF $21.95
☐ 10:UH $15.95	☐ 29:CC $12.95	☐ 47:CBW $12.95
☐ 11:ENC $9.95	☐ 30:COL $9.95	☐ 48:CWT $12.95
☐ 12:E2 ....$9.95	☐ 31:DTP $9.95	☐ 49:CDB $10.95
☐ 13:AF $9.95	☐ 32:WF $10.95	☐ 50:CKI $16.95
☐ 14:VDH2 ....$15.95	☐ 33:WIN $9.95	☐ 51:SBC $14.95
☐ 15:EDH $15.95	☐ 34:SOD $19.95	☐ 52:RVH $19.95
☐ 16:LD2 ....$14.95	☐ 35:MU $8.95	☐ 53:CGR $7.95
☐ 17:EURO $15.95	☐ 36:YG $7.95	☐ 54:CGD $7.95
☐ 18:DAG $17.95	☐ 37:GG $7.95	☐ 55:CGW $7.95
☐ 19:WEP $17.95	☐ 38:DP $7.95	☐ 56:CGT $7.95

Additional Books Subtotal (Please print) $_____
ADD Postage and Handling (allow 4–6 weeks for delivery) $ 4.00
Sales Tax: (AZ & MI residents, add state and local sales tax.) $_____
YOUR TOTAL (Subtotal, Postage/Handling, Tax) $_____

YOUR ADDRESS (PLEASE PRINT)

Name _____

Street _____

City _____ State _____ Zip _____

Phone (_____) _____—_____

YOUR PAYMENT

Check one: ☐ Check ☐ Visa ☐ MasterCard ☐ Discover ☐ American Express
Required credit card information:

Credit Card Number _____

Expiration Date (Month/Year) _____ / _____

Signature Required _____

Canadian Customers Order Toll Free 1-877-223-6389

Home Planners, LLC
Wholly owned by Hanley-Wood, LLC
® 3275 W. Ina Road, Suite 110, Dept. BK, Tucson, AZ 85741

HPT25

223

Notes